VIRGINIA WOOLF, THE INTELLECTUAL, AND THE PUBLIC SPHERE

Virginia Woolf, the Intellectual, and the Public Sphere relates Woolf's literary reviews and essays to early twentieth-century debates about the value of "highbrow" culture, the methods of instruction in universities and adult education, and the importance of an educated public for the realization of democratic goals. By focusing on Woolf's theories and practice of reading, Melba Cuddy-Keane refutes assumptions about Woolf's modernist elitism, revealing instead a writer who was pedagogically oriented, publicly engaged, and committed to the ideal of classless intellectuals working together in reciprocal exchange. Woolf emerges as a stimulating theorist of the unconscious, of dialogic reading, of historicist criticism, and of value judgments, while her theoretically informed but accessible prose challenges us to reflect on academic writing today. Combining a wealth of historical detail with a penetrating analysis of Woolf's essays, this study will alter our views of Woolf, of modernism, and of intellectual work.

MELBA CUDDY-KEANE is Associate Professor of English and a Northrop Frye Scholar at the University of Toronto. She has written widely on Virginia Woolf, literary criticism, and cultural history.

VIRGINIA WOOLF, THE INTELLECTUAL, AND THE PUBLIC SPHERE

MELBA CUDDY-KEANE

University of Toronto

PUBLISHED BY THE PRESS SYNDICATE OF THE UNIVERSITY OF CAMBRIDGE
The Pitt Building, Trumpington Street, Cambridge CB2 1RP, United Kingdom

CAMBRIDGE UNIVERSITY PRESS
The Edinburgh Building, Cambridge, CB2 2RU, UK
40 West 20th Street, New York, NY 10011–4211, USA
477 Williamstown Road, Port Melbourne, VIC 3207, Australia
Ruiz de Alarcón 13, 28014 Madrid, Spain
Dock House, The Waterfront, Cape Town 8001, South Africa

http://www.cambridge.org

First published 2003
Reprinted 2004

Printed in the United Kingdom at the University Press, Cambridge

Typeface Adobe Garamond 11/12.5 pt.　　*System* LATEX 2$_\varepsilon$　[TB]

A catalogue record for this book is available from the British Library

Library of Congress Cataloguing in Publication data

Virginia Woolf, the intellectual, and the public sphere/Melba Cuddy-Keane.
p.　cm.
Includes bibliographical references (p. 220).
ISBN 0 521 82867 8
1. Woolf, Virginia, 1882–1941 – Knowledge and learning.　2. Woolf, Virginia,
1882–1941 – Political and social views.　3. Books and reading – Great Britain – History – 20th
century.　4. Education – Great Britain – History – 20th century.　5. Great Britain – Intellectual
life – 20th century.　6. Modernism (Literature) – Great Britain.　I. Title.
PR6045.O72Z57885 2003
823'.912–dc21

ISBN 0 521 82867 8 hardback

Contents

v

Acknowledgments

In 1928, according to *A Room of One's Own*, a woman cursed a famous library. Happily, this book, which looks further into Woolf's thoughts on libraries, begins with its author's sincere thanks to many of them. I have been well treated by the librarians and staff at the E. J. Pratt Library at Victoria University, the Thomas Fisher Rare Book Room, and the Robarts Library (all three at the University of Toronto), the University of Sussex Library, the New York Public Library, the Metropolitan Toronto Public Library, the Leeds Public Library, the University of North London Library, the National Library of Scotland, and the BBC Written Archives Centre. I owe them all sincere thanks.

Then, to adapt other words of *A Room of One's Own*, even books that are *not* masterpieces are not single and solitary births. I have benefited greatly from the chance to present ideas for this book at conferences of the Association of Canadian College and University Teachers of English (ACCUTE), the Modernist Studies Association (MSA), and the Society for the Study of Narrative Literature (SSNL), as well as the MLA Conventions, the Annual Virginia Woolf Conferences, and the 1996 Conference of the Virginia Woolf Society of Japan. I also thank the Work-in-Progress group of the University of Toronto's Department of English, who workshopped the very first conference paper I gave on this topic. I have an inexpressible debt to numerous friends and colleagues who willingly contributed stimulating conversation, helpful encouragement and support, and often valuable information. Particular thanks go to Todd Avery, Christopher Beer, Ted Bishop, Pamela Caughie, Stuart Clarke, Michael Coyle, Beth Daugherty, Susan Friedman, Christine Froula, Sally Greene, Heather Jackson, Robin Jackson, Andrew McNeillie, David McWhirter, Kathy Mezei, Heather Murray, Nigel Nicolson, Raymond Norman, Ben Rich, Brian Richardson, Joanne Trautmann-Banks, Elizabeth Shih, Brenda Silver, Anna Snaith, Michael Tratner, Pierre-Eric Villeneuve, and Melvin Wiebe.

My gratitude for a different kind of crucial support goes to the Connaught Committee at the University of Toronto for a Fellowship that supported a half-year's leave and to the Social Science and Research Council of Canada for grants in support of travel and research. My thanks go as well to Mary Newberry (Toronto) for her expert copy-editing and indexing assistance, and to Ray Ryan, Rachel De Wachter, Alison Powell, Audrey Cotterell, and my two anonymous readers at Cambridge University Press for their help and support.

The following permissions are gratefully acknowledged: permission to quote from Virginia Woolf's unpublished versions of "Three Characters" from the Society of Authors as the Literary Representative of the Estate of Virginia Woolf; from Leonard and Virginia Woolf's unpublished BBC broadcast "Are Too Many Books Written and Published?" from the Society of Authors, and from the University of Sussex for the Estate of Leonard Woolf; permission to quote from the typescript of J. B. Priestley's BBC broadcast "To a High-Brow" from Peters, Fraser & Dunlop on behalf of the Literary Estate of J. B. Priestley; and permission to reproduce the photograph of Virginia Woolf by Man Ray from the Man Ray Trust, SODRAC (Montreal), and Fotofolio. Acknowledgments for permission to adapt work of my own that has appeared previously in print are as follows: from "The Rhetoric of Feminist Conversation: Virginia Woolf and the Trope of the Twist," *Ambiguous Discourse: Feminist Narratology and British Women Writers*, edited by Kathy Mezei, copyright © 1996 by the University of North Carolina Press, used by permission of the publisher; from "Virginia Woolf and the Varieties of Historicist Experience," *Virginia Woolf and the Essay*, copyright © Beth Carole Rosenberg and Jeanne Dubino, used with permission of Palgrave Macmillan; from "Brow-Beating, Wool-Gathering, and the Brain of the Common Reader," *Virginia Woolf Out of Bounds: Selected Papers from the Tenth Annual Conference on Virginia Woolf*, edited by Jessica Berman and Jane Goldman, and "'A Standard of One's Own': Virginia Woolf and the Question of Literary Value," *Virginia Woolf: Turning the Centuries: Selected Papers from the Ninth Annual Conference on Virginia Woolf*, edited by Ann Ardis and Bonnie Kime Scott, copyright granted by Pace University Press; from "Defining Cultural Democracy: Modernism and Universal Individualism," used with permission of *Key Words: A Journal of Cultural Materialism*.

This book is dedicated to the memory of two inspiring teachers and genuine democratic highbrows: Melba E. Cuddy (1905–2000) and Karlheinz Theil (1943–99). And my writing it has been made possible by the surrounding context of love, and belief in the prospects of humanity, provided by my husband, David Keane.

Abbreviations

BA	*Between the Acts*. London: Hogarth, 1941.
Berg	The Virginia Woolf Manuscripts. The Henry W. and Albert A. Berg Collection. The New York Public Library.
CE I–IV	*Collected Essays*. 4 vols. Ed. Leonard Woolf. London: Hogarth, 1966–67.
CR I	*The Common Reader: First Series*. 1925. Ed. Andrew McNeillie. London: Hogarth, 1984.
CR 2	*The Common Reader: Second Series*. 1932. Ed. Andrew McNeillie. London: Hogarth, 1986.
CSF	*The Complete Shorter Fiction of Virginia Woolf.* Ed. Susan Dick. Expanded and rev. edn. London: Hogarth, 1989.
D I–V	*The Diary of Virginia Woolf*. Ed. Anne Olivier Bell and Andrew McNeillie. 5 vols. London: Hogarth, 1977–1984.
E I–IV	*The Essays of Virginia Woolf*. Ed. Andrew McNeillie. 4 vols. to date. London: Hogarth, 1986–.
HL	*The Hogarth Letters*. Intro. Hermione Lee. 1933. Athens: University of Georgia Press, 1986.
L I–VI	*The Letters of Virginia Woolf*. Ed. Nigel Nicolson and Joanne Trautmann. 6 vols. London: Chatto and Windus, 1975–1980.
LS	*The London Scene*. New York: Random House, 1975.
MHP	Monk's House Papers. University of Sussex Library.
MD	*Mrs. Dalloway*. London: Hogarth, 1925.
N&D	*Night and Day*. London: Duckworth, 1919.
O	*Orlando*. London: Hogarth, 1928.
PA	*A Passionate Apprentice: The Early Journals, 1897–1909*. Ed. Mitchell Leaska. London: Hogarth, 1990.
R	*A Room of One's Own*. London: Hogarth, 1929.
RF	*Roger Fry: A Biography*. London: Hogarth, 1940.

RN	*Virginia Woolf's Reading Notebooks.* Ed. Brenda Silver. Princeton: Princeton University Press, 1983.
TG	*Three Guineas.* 1938. London: Hogarth, 1986.
TTL	*To the Lighthouse.* London: Hogarth, 1927.
W	*The Waves.* London: Hogarth, 1931.
WE	*A Woman's Essays: Selected Essays* I. Ed. Rachel Bowlby. London: Penguin, 1992.

Introduction: a wider sphere

Virginia Woolf was an intellectual writing at a time of public debate about
the role of intellectuals and the nature and value of literary education. Between 1904 and her death in 1941, she published over five hundred essays
and reviews in more than forty periodicals and two volumes of collected
essays. These writings offer a magnificent compendium of literary opinions
and judgments, but they go further to scrutinize the process of reading, to
locate reading in a context of historically and ideologically variable standards, and to outline a model for active, self-reflexive reading practices.
The overall impact is pedagogical and empowering: Woolf's penetrating
readings make a vast range of literature accessible, but they also offer the
tools for readers to gain that access for themselves.

Concerns about reading and cultural literacy have been widespread in
the West for at least a century and a half. Yet the complexities of our increasingly global and technological age are disturbingly accompanied by
the shrinking priorities given to intellectual education and the belief that
intellectual interests are not particularly relevant to the lives of the people
known as "the mass." In these circumstances, uniting the highbrow values
of intellectual life with a broad public base may seem a paradoxical goal.
Yet, in a similarly threatened environment, Virginia Woolf, the "high modernist," was an advocate for both democratic inclusiveness and intellectual
education. In bridging these two spheres, she forged a positive answer to one
of her culture's most pressing concerns. The achievement of universal franchise, the extension of adult education to the working class and to women,
and the rise of mass publishing all added urgency to the need to foster
accessible cultural education. At the same time, the institutionalization of
English studies within the universities augured an increasing gap between
professional study and the general reading public. The intellectual debates
of the time revolved around issues only too recognizable today: the gap between specialized theoretical discourse and the generalist reader; the fate of
critical reading and thinking in an age of increasing mass communication;

the need to assert value while maintaining an awareness of historical and cultural contingency; and the dependency of a free democracy on a broad base of intellectually trained minds.

In the midst of such upheaval, Woolf's endorsement of the "common reader" was a significant intervention in public debate. At a time of growing specialization and increasingly objective methodology in academic English studies, Woolf defended an amateur status and a wide-ranging and catholic reading practice. She promoted a dialogic rather than an authoritarian relation between writer and reader and opposed the increasing standardization or "massification" of the reading public implicit in the processes of mass production and distribution. Publishing through a private press and seeking a readership in part through the public library, Woolf developed an alternative pedagogy outside the educational institutions. Working in the genre of the informal essay, she promoted the ideal of a classless, democratic, but intellectual readership, recasting "highbrowism" as radical social practice.

The approach I have just outlined opposes both the older image of Woolf as elitist or "aloof" and more recent accusations that she was an aesthetic capitalist bent on acquiring cultural and economic power through self-commodification.[1] As radical perhaps as the first representations of a "feminist Woolf," my subject is a "pedagogical Woolf" concerned about making highbrow intellectual culture available to all. Her essays, I argue, have a social project: she wrote about literature to inculcate good reading practices, and she did so because she believed that an educated public is crucial to the success of democratic society. I argue as well that Woolf was, in the words of Andrew McNeillie, "a considerable theoretician in her own oblique fashion."[2] Her way of reviewing a book was frequently to pose a question whose theoretical implications she then explored in the process of discussing the work. Positing theories through questions rather than statements, through the applied test of specific works rather than abstract conceptualizations, and in accessible rather than abstruse language – this is what seems to me to be at the heart of Woolf's writing about literature and what seems now in our "post-theory" climate to have some potential for guiding scholars and readers today.

In our own time, such terms as "organic intellectual," "transformative intellectual," and "public intellectual" have sprung into our vocabulary, raising questions about the intellectual's role in relation to the "mass" or "commodity" culture that is regarded as the dominant force.[3] In the 1920s and 1930s, "highbrow," middlebrow," and "lowbrow" were the terms that focused debate. But whatever the language, at issue is the relation of the intellectual to the general literate public – that audience whom presumably the intellectual, as opposed to the scholar, seeks to include.[4] From the earliest reception of Woolf's work, the predominant view assumed a separation between her highbrow status and the public sphere – an assumption implicit in the textual criticism that elevated her writing for its complex but difficult formal qualities, and overtly claimed by politically oriented critics who attacked the supposed "unreality" of her work. The latter argument was then supported by generalizations about modernism's opposition to mass culture, forcefully articulated, for example, in Andreas Huyssen's *After The Great Divide*.[5] But Huyssen's "divide" puts the ordinary female reader (typed in Madame Bovary) on the same side as mass culture, gendering the binary in a way that is problematic for a feminist intellectual like Virginia Woolf. And the antithetical positioning of modernists and masses (even begging the question of the categorical definition of *all* modernists) is further muddied by slippages among the concepts of popular, ordinary, and mass. John Carey, for example, one of the more hostile of modernism's critics, fails to note the crucial distinction between massification as an approach and the large number, or mass in another sense, of ordinary readers. Carey's argument in *The Intellectuals and the Masses* is "that modernist literature and art can be seen as a hostile reaction to the unprecedentedly large reading public created by late nineteenth-century educational reforms."[6] While there may be support for his view in what I would call certain misanthropic writers, or certain misanthropic moments in otherwise affirmative writers, when Carey claims that "the purpose of modernist writing was to exclude these newly educated (or 'semi-educated') readers, and so to preserve the intellectual's seclusion from the 'mass,'" or that "denial of humanity to the masses became, in the early twentieth century, an important linguistic project among intellectuals," he falls prey to a common fallacy.[7] He confuses the massive number of ordinary readers with those discourses that inscribe ordinary readers as an undifferentiated mass. Virginia Woolf definitely objected to the second; but she did so precisely to preserve the humanity of the first.[8]

Unfortunately the kind of misperception we see in Carey is too often accepted without scrutiny or examination. Even such solidly researched work as Patrick Brantlinger's *The Reading Lesson*, for example, after asserting "the modernist reification of the antithesis between high and mass culture," slips into an unexamined conflation of popular with mass: "the claim of modernist fiction to high cultural status entails rejecting or demoting ordinary novels as commercial, mass-cultural detritus."[9] Now Woolf, to take one significant modernist, was not immune from the effects of class privilege, but she did not dismiss ordinary novels and mass culture in the same breath. My concern is not that such critiques have no basis but that they miss both the value of Woolf as a complex, intelligent individual and the complexity of the culture in which she worked.

Some of that complexity is addressed, from a different perspective, by Jonathan Rose in his mammoth study, *The Intellectual Life of the British Working Classes*, a work that is interestingly both complementary and contradictory to the present study. Rose's thorough documentation leaves no doubt that the working classes *had* an intellectual life, and that their intellectual activities included the avid reading of literary classics in addition to a broad range of other reading materials. By pursuing for the first time a detailed history of working-class readers, Rose effectively dismantles the restrictive linkage between "intellectual" and "upper-class" and demonstrates that, for many working-class people, "the expanding culture of print opened up opportunities to write and act in the public sphere."[10] There is a marked compatibility between the results of his research into the Workers' Educational Association (WEA) and the arguments I make later in this book. But unfortunately, although Rose justifiably attacks the blind spot in academics who assume that ordinary citizens are the manipulated tools of popular media and hegemonic discourse, when it comes to an assessment of modernist writers, he falls victim to a similar blind spot himself. His otherwise useful and illuminating text is accompanied by the increasingly angry and repetitive accusation that modernists not only disdained the lower classes but deliberately cultivated difficulty as a way of maintaining ascendancy over the rapidly encroaching populace and preserving their cultural prestige. This monolithic construction of modernists produces an unremittingly antagonistic construct of "two rival intelligentsias squared off against each other";[11] it also creates an unbridgeable impasse between highbrow and democratic concerns.

While it is well beyond my present scope to defend a counter-definition of modernism or to argue the diversity of its many practitioners, the thrust of my entire study suggests that, in constructing "Mrs. Woolf" as disdainful of the ordinary reader, Rose misconstrues her goals. The problems themselves that Rose identifies, I must emphasize, are matters on which we agree. I share Rose's concern that his upbeat story may have a downbeat ending. If he is correct that the long, promising trajectory of working-class intellectualism ultimately succumbs either to a disaffected and alienated youth culture or to a fad-driven Bohemian entrepreneurism, then the consequences for the whole of society are grave. And I think that most educators today, at least in England, Canada, and the United States, wish that intellectual work were more highly valued by society and that teaching students how to think were not such an uphill battle. But the reasons for our difficulties are numerous, not the least being that the scope of knowledge now available and the corresponding diversity of interpretation makes genuine thinking an extremely difficult task. It is naïve to place the blame for our difficulties on the modernist highbrows, especially when there is substantial evidence that many of them were concerned about precisely such problems, when, for Virginia Woolf at least, an intelligent readership was a goal on which she focused much of her work.

Rose's specific accusations meet a counter-testimony in various ways throughout this volume, so I will merely outline a few of the radical differences between his work and mine. The running trope he uses for the modernist disparagement of the lower class is E. M. Forster's aspiring clerk Leonard Bast. I could argue with Rose's detailed interpretations to point out, for example, that Margaret Schlegel's desire that Leonard "wash out his brain" is in fact precisely the opposite of the "brain-washing" that Rose imputes to the phrase,[12] and that Margaret is imagining a kind of cultural detoxification, enabling Leonard to reject the platitudinous attitudes that he has absorbed from his culture and to learn to think for himself. But it is not a phrase that is at issue here; it is the shift in the object of critique that a different reading of the phrase implies. My own discussion of Leonard Bast focuses on Woolf's and Forster's belief in adult and working-class education and their concern that the education being provided was not of the best kind. Their critique is not of Leonard Bast's brain but of the way that conventional education tried to stuff it. But, unfortunately, when Rose unquestioningly repeats assumptions about "Mrs. Woolf's serene confidence that literary genius could not arise from the working classes,"[13] he precludes any real scrutiny of what she wrote. In *A Room of One's Own*, Woolf does state that it is "unthinkable that any woman in Shakespeare's day should have had Shakespeare's genius," and that genius is "not born" in her own day among the working class (*R* 73). But her words must be read in their context. Woolf's argument here is that "[i]ntellectual freedom depends upon material things" (*R* 162–63), and her point about genius is that scope and nourishment (both physical and intellectual) are needed to bring great ideas to birth. In context, that genius is "not born" offers a deliberate challenge to patriarchal assumptions about innate abilities, turning the phrase into a feminist and socialist indictment of unequal social conditions.

As for the theory that modernists cultivated difficulty to baffle those lacking privileged educations, my argument in this book is that Woolf tried to instill a love for reading by writing about non-modernist works, teaching at the same time the kinds of thinking practices that would make it easier to read modernist texts. Finally, Rose's discussion of the "brows" reinforces an antagonism that I work hard to undo: he entrenches intellectual culture in class war; I pursue a model in which intellectual interests, in multiple strata, are deployed across class, and in which the ordinary reader is not a working-class reader but anyone who reads for intellectual pleasure and goals. To Rose's assertion that "[t]he founders of the Labour Party and other self-educated radicals realized that no disenfranchised people could be emancipated unless they created an autonomous intellectual life,"[14] I respond that it is precisely Woolf's similar vision that I am examining in this book and that, in promoting the ideal of the *classless* intellectual, she pursued the emancipation of all. Immense differences, of course, separated the way Rose's working-class readers pursued their intellectual life and the way Woolf pursued hers and, in numerous instances, those differences produced a sense of distance and hostility on both sides. But the lines of division are not absolute, and there is more cause for hopefulness than for despair in the numerous parallels that I have sought to trace.

We must therefore turn from Rose to the other side of the critical spectrum, to engage with the historical work that examines Woolf's relation to her readers and her involvement with the public sphere. Our view of Woolf is changing as we learn more about her early teaching experiences in a working-class college, the "fan-mail" she received from previously unknown readers, her contributions to public organizations and projects, and her commitment to diverse audiences. The work that began as feminist investigation into the political dimensions of Woolf's writing has broadened to a growing appreciation of her activist role in promoting intellectual causes. Anna Snaith has written extensively on Woolf's supportive contributions to the Women's Service Library, founded in 1926 to assist the study of women's lives and women's history, and which now, as The Women's Library, houses the most extensive collection of women's history in Britain. As Snaith indicates, "[Woolf's] name was on much of the campaign publicity, she signed (in bright green ink) letters to nineteen friends and acquaintances asking them to donate books and/or money, she herself donated money and each month until her death she bought a list of books which the library requested from her."[15] Beth Rigel Daugherty has argued that Woolf's experience as a teacher was a formative influence on her essayistic style, an influence that Daugherty demonstrates through her analysis of Woolf's preparation for her classes at Morley College and the various versions and revisions she produced as she transformed a talk she gave to sixty young students at Hayes Court School for girls in Kent into the essay "How Should One Read a Book?"[16] Ann Banfield, in her profoundly argued study of the connections between Woolf, Bertrand Russell, and Roger Fry, relates the genre of "table talk" to the extensive evidence of Bloomsbury's commitment to a broad educational project: "The implicit *raison d'être* of Bloomsbury discussions was the extension of knowledge beyond the confines of the university elite."[17] And both Snaith and Daugherty share with me an interest in tracing Woolf's unknown readers – Snaith, introducing and editing the wide-ranging and fascinating letters to Woolf by readers of *Three Guineas*,[18] and Daugherty, like me, investigating related fan-mail housed in the archives of the University of Sussex.[19] While inevitably random and spotty, the letters that have survived provide ample evidence of the impact Woolf could have on people's lives. A woman writes from America to describe the way she and a friend are reading Woolf's essays out loud to each other and debating the ideas; a young man, nineteen years of age, writes from a small town in Missouri, to say, among other things, that *The Common Reader* has set him to reading Hazlitt and Donne. Readers say, too, how profoundly they have been moved by Woolf's novels, including the more challenging later works *The Waves* and *Between the Acts*.[20] That Woolf was an eccentric personality is not disputed, but that her eccentricity, or her indisputable intellectual superiority, inevitably removed her from the ordinary reader certainly is.

Our knowledge of the multiple dimensions of Woolf's life, however, is relatively new, so that what is surprising is not the lingering notion of Woolf's ivory-tower highbrowism but the vehemence with which this view is often upheld. As Brenda Silver's extensive survey in *Virginia Woolf Icon* demonstrates, representations of Woolf are particularly subject to "the ire and/or condescension of those who insist on a Virginia Woolf made only in their image, an 'authentic,' legitimate Virginia Woolf to whom, they assert, they have a direct line."[21] In this way, Silver argues, Virginia Woolf as icon becomes "symptomatic of embedded layers of cultural anxiety" – an anxiety perhaps fundamentally about the eroding of stable categorizations themselves. Such anxieties are understandably triggered by "boundary-dwelling, border-disrupting figures" of whom the intellectual woman can be a markedly threatening form. For Silver, it is "Virginia Woolf's uncanny ability to cross borders and reveal their arbitrary nature" that makes her cultural meaning so very difficult to limit and contain.[22]

My interest in this study, then, is to take Woolf outside the borders that would limit her sphere to Bloomsbury, or to high modernism, or to feminism, and to locate both the person and her ideas in a different context – one that involves public debates about books, reading, and education and, by extension, the changing construction of audiences and reading practices during her time. I offer this wider sphere as a valid historical context in which to investigate cultural and intellectual values in Virginia Woolf's essays, without any claims for its completeness or definitiveness in determining the meaning of "Virginia Woolf." I hope to show that Woolf circulated, both in her reading and in her personal contacts, in an environment rife with controversy about the dissemination and transmission of intellectual culture and that her essays in particular derive their meaning, at least in part, from their negotiations with on-going pedagogical debate. By pursuing the pedagogical outside institutional boundaries, Woolf took the intellectual into the border zone where professional and common reader/writer meet. None of this is to deny other public or private forums in which Woolf plays a role, nor the way, as Anna Snaith demonstrates, the public/private nexus itself is a border-crossing zone.[23] It is simply to propose that the context of historical debate about readers and reading is crucial to understanding the "intellectual Woolf."

Because my subject crosses the border between historical materials and textual analysis, this book has two main parts: Cultural contexts and Critical practice. Part I sets the essays in the historical context of concerns about reading: the institutionalization of English studies within the university, the activities of the Workers' Educational Association, and the developments in adult education after the First World War. It begins with a discussion of the words "highbrow" and "democratic" as cultural "keywords," in Raymond Williams's sense of this term. Part II examines Woolf's theories of reading and her rhetorical strategies for instilling good reading practices. Of course, because Woolf's critical practice derives much of its meaning from its relation to the cultural and critical debates of the time, Parts I and II necessarily intersect. Part I integrates discussion of Woolf's ideas with discussions of historical materials and examines a few specific essays at length. Detailed textual analysis is often crucial for understanding the complex thinking in which Woolf engages her reader and for avoiding the misinterpretation, or slanting of evidence, that can so easily occur when we quote isolated sentences out of context. What Woolf says cannot be considered apart from the process of thought in which an idea is embedded and the function of articulating it in a particular time and place. Part II turns to a more intensive analysis of her essays, but still with a constant eye on their pedagogical intent. For if my first question is, What does it mean that she said what she said when she said it? my second is, How was she getting her reader to think by the way she said what she said?

In bringing together historical and textual analyses, I seek a holistic approach not unlike Roman Jakobson's communicative model in which the "message" passing from addresser to addressee is informed by context, contact, and code.[24] And in my interweaving of the multiple voices of the modernist period, I attempt, in a modest way, to employ Marc Angenot's concept of social discourse: not an era's belief, but the subjects it considered important enough to debate and the terms in which its problems were thinkable.[25] My approach also has features in common with pluralistic pragmatism in terms of the breadth of methodological field. In *Democracy's Children: Intellectuals and the Rise of Cultural Politics*, John McGowan claims that "[p]ragmatism identifies four elements (agent, other people, material things, social meanings and arrangements) in any situation and insists that none of these elements is determinant."[26] One advantage of this approach, McGowan points out, is that it negotiates between the extremes of determinism and agency, resisting the purely regulatory models derived from Foucault and Bourdieu, on the one hand, and the earlier Nietzschean models of a radical free self, on the other. The model seems extremely appropriate to discussions of Woolf, who both exposed the way social and economic conditions determine intellectual possibilities and yet consistently stressed her readers' abilities to respond in active, autonomous ways. And Woolf's commitment to independent, critical thinking – and its attendant diversity – was the foundation for the model of social equality that she upheld. As McGowan continues,

Thus, pluralism suggests that intellectuals will find their work in the rhetorical effort to get people to change the names that they apply to situations. But it also suggests, in ways not fully compatible with that first task, that intellectuals, like teachers, will also direct their rhetorical efforts toward encouraging others to develop their own capacities as judges and to adopt a reflexive attitude toward their judgments after their production. Insofar as intellectuals can embrace this second task and cherish the rather chaotic and messy diversity of orientations and values that follow from it, they are aiding the cause of democracy.[27]

These words could easily describe the work of Woolf's essays, and the goal is one I can readily accept as my own.

This study of democratic highbrowism therefore seeks a broadly diversified readership. The core of my readers, I expect, will be students and teachers interested in Woolf's ideas about literature and their relation to intellectual and cultural history, and researchers in various disciplines who are themselves reassessing modernism and Woolf. I hope also to interest those working on the history of the book, on reception theory and history, on pedagogy and reading, on theories of historicism, and on value theory (an upcoming field). It is also my hope that this book will be read by the general intelligent reader who cares about the *fate* of the general intelligent reader. Woolf did, I argue, and, despite our differences of background and culture, we all have something to gain from her concern.

PART ONE

Cultural contexts

CHAPTER I

Democratic highbrow: Woolf and the classless intellectual

"When *I* use a word," Humpty Dumpty said, in rather a scornful tone, "it means just what I choose it to mean – neither more nor less."
"The question is," said Alice, "whether you *can* make words mean so many different things."
"The question is," said Humpty Dumpty, "which is to be master – that's all."

Lewis Carroll, Alice in Wonderland

It is also that the variations and confusions of meaning are not just faults in a system, or errors of feedback, or deficiencies of education. They are in many cases, in my terms, historical and contemporary substance. Indeed they have often, as variations, to be insisted upon, just because they embody different experiences and readings of experience, and this will continue to be true, in active relationships and conflicts, over and above the clarifying exercises of scholars or committees. What can really be contributed is not resolution but perhaps, at times, just that extra edge of consciousness.

Raymond Williams, Keywords[1]

CULTURAL KEYWORDS

To write about Virginia Woolf as a democratic highbrow is to invoke controversy. My approach challenges the notion of the modernist writer as aloof from the public and the idea of intellectuals as an elite; it resists identifications of the popular exclusively with the world of commodities and entertainment; it rejects the notion that declining standards must inevitably follow from "the mass." And, as I state in my introduction, my approach contests a number of prevailing constructions of "Virginia Woolf." Much depends, however, on what we take "democratic highbrow" to mean, or what we understand to be the ideological inflections of these terms. Words derive their meanings from their location within cultural and textual systems, and the approach of this chapter is to pursue, in a way that is guided by Raymond Williams's analysis of the "keywords" of culture and society, Virginia Woolf's words in relation to the systems of meaning being formed and contested in the interwar years. Inevitably, as my epigraphs imply, all words are subject to differing reception, depending on the ideological systems in which they are read. In the following discussion, I will try, like Humpty Dumpty, to make words fit my meaning; but my goal is also to show, like Williams, how certain terms in our vocabulary become, from time to time, sites of "different experiences and readings of experience" and how, in this very contestation over meaning, the crucial problems confronting a culture are revealed.

"Democratic" and "highbrow" are more revelatory here than Woolf's related words "common reader" precisely because the former are conspicuous sites of ideological debate. Their contested uses in the first part of the twentieth century highlight the formative processes of cultural definition; the words as they appear in Woolf's writing indicate how she herself understood the on-going controversies and confronted the issues that were being raised. The tensions surrounding "highbrow" and "democratic" furthermore extend to the complicated relations among "democratic," "popular," and "mass." The latter two words are often used interchangeably, with the result that modernism's opposition to mass culture is taken necessarily to mean hostility to popular literature and ordinary readers, leaving little possibility to consider modernist highbrowism as a democratic form. But much depends on how we use words and how we define our terms.

"Mass" and "popular" are most helpful when they signify different economies, as Michael Kammen argues in his analysis of American tastes. Quoting Richard Slotkin, Kammen draws attention to the distinction between works created for the purposes of *mass* consumption and the multiplicity of popular forms that are "produced by and for specific cultural communities like the ethnic group, the family-clan, a town, a neighborhood, or region, the workplace, or the street corner."[2] In similar fashion, W. Russell Neuman, focusing on the audience for contemporary mass media, distinguishes between homogenous mass audiences and complex communicative networks comprising many partially overlapping sub-groups of the whole people.[3] Resisting the technological determinism that assumes mass media necessarily produce a uniform audience, Neuman points to the way the Internet has fostered the development of special-interest "narrowcasting" and the emergence of diversified "issue publics." Non-geographical communities of varying sizes form because like-minded people find each other by utilizing a format accessible to mass participation. An opposition to *mass culture* does not then automatically imply an opposition to *mass communication* or to *popular forms*.[4]

Whether highbrowism can be regarded as one of many popular "issue publics" depends on our understanding of "popular." As Williams points out, from the sixteenth to the eighteenth century, "popular" signified large numbers – first referring to a political system that involved "the whole people" and later coming to mean anything that was "widely favoured" or "well-liked."[5] Subsequently, however, "popular" began to imply interests or activities that originate from the people, in the sense of grass-roots movements as opposed to culture or politics emanating from above. In this latter sense, "popular" moves away from an emphasis on large numbers to include forms that, while they may not appeal to the majority, are open to self-selected participation and generated from below. In relation to the law, for example, the *OED* defines "popular" as "affecting, concerning, or open to all or any of the people."[6] Highbrow, intellectual culture may never be popular in the sense of "widely favoured"; it requires, for one thing, a substantial commitment of time and energy. But intellectual culture might well be popular in the sense of being open to and generated by sub-groups of the whole – a focused interest shared by a mixed group of professional and non-professional people, rather like baseball, or fiddle music, or Tai Chi.

The meaning of "popular" relates in turn to the larger question of what it means to be democratic – whether we mean the participation of all the people or the potential for any self-selecting individual to participate. The question is not just "academic" (another interesting word) but a fundamental question about the place of the intellectual, or intellectual interests, in our society today. Can highbrow culture be a border-crossing zone where "common" and "professional" intellectuals meet? Can "highbrow culture" be both consumed and produced in ways that cut across divisions of education, class, wealth, and occupation? Can highbrowism be considered democratic, even if it is not popular in the sense of attracting large numbers, as long as it is open and available to any self-identified individual? Is a democratic highbrowism conceptually possible, as a matter of belief even if not of achievement, and what would its achievement mean?

These are the broad questions underlying this study, and they are as crucial to face in our current social formations as they are in understanding the place and role of the intellectual Virginia Woolf. To engage the historical in this instance is also to explore questions about reading and culture still unresolved today. As Thomas Bender has argued, "historians turn to the study of intellectuals, ideas, and culture in periods defined by uncertainty about the role and power of ideas, about the agency of human thinkers."[7] If the twenty-first century is such a time of uncertainty, marked by an intense social scrutiny of our educational systems and a questioning of the role of intellectuals, so too was the time of Virginia Woolf. Our starting place, then, is the cultural history of this chapter's two keywords.

THE "BROWS" IN THE 1920S AND 1930S

Virginia Woolf was a highbrow. Despite its frequently pejorative implications, it is a term that she once claimed, or perhaps reclaimed, for herself. Woolf knew only too well that language is never innocent or transparent and so, when calling herself a highbrow, she characteristically turned the word prismatically about to expose the cultural values encoded in its use. Literally, the word refers to the space between eyebrow and hairline, the height of the forehead, the signaling in physiognomy of the brain; metonymically, the high forehead signifies an intellectual – "a person of superior intellectual attainments or interests."[8] But although "highbrow" can substitute for "intellectual," the former word is more emotionally fraught. "Highbrow" usually assumes an attitude held by intellectuals toward non-intellectuals and, used with this connotation, it generally betrays an attitude *toward* intellectuals on the part of the user. If highbrows are intellectually superior, the reasoning goes, they must assume they are superior people; if they think they are superior people, then others resent such assumed superiority. As a charged term, "highbrow" is less about attributes than attitudes.

It was indeed to answer such "charges" against highbrows that Woolf appropriated the term in a letter she wrote, but never sent, to the editor of the *New Statesman and Nation* in 1932. The specific occasion of Woolf's letter was a clash between J. B. Priestley and Harold Nicolson in a series of talks on the BBC under the general title, "To an Unnamed Listener": Priestley unwittingly launched the exchange with a talk "To a High-Brow," and Nicolson responded, in rebuttal, with "To a Low-Brow" the following week.[9] The larger issue that Woolf addressed, however, was the growing cultural tension around the position of the intellectual in society – a tension she saw *both* Priestley and Nicolson exacerbating. The meaning of "Middlebrow" – both the word and the essay under which title her letter was posthumously published – is inseparable from its nature as a response to a heated public discussion taking place not only on the BBC, but in numerous newspapers, periodicals, and books. But to understand the furore, we need to know the history of the terms in which the controversy was being constructed at the time.

High, middle, and lowbrow are not included in Raymond Williams's 1976 list of keywords of British culture, since his study concerns words identifiably significant before the twentieth century begins. But two of his keywords, "elite" and "masses," are important forerunners of twentieth-century terminology, and significantly influence the meaning of the "brows." As Williams shows, in the nineteenth century the word "elite" shifts from its earlier theological signification of God's chosen, or "the elect," to the politically inflected definition of those best fit to govern. Now entangled with the redistribution of governmental power, it acquires associations of "*class* or *ruling class*" (emphasis in original) and of hierarchical privilege in the political state.[10] In a related definitional morphing, the word "masses," which originally combined the attribute of low status with the idea of a multitude (the lowest being also the largest class), became entangled with a second meaning signifying a rudimentary lump of raw material or a body of physical objects grouped together for common properties. The conflation of the two meanings came to signify an aggregate of persons viewed as individually indistinguishable. Both conservative and revolutionary groups tended to construct the lower or working class as uniform and homogeneous, although with the antithetical implications of unthinking "mob" versus united "solidarity."[11] This ideological inflection then colored modes of action: manipulation of the masses for the ends of electoral control or marketing consumerism, on the one hand, and for the purpose of organized collective action, on the other.

In the early decades of the twentieth century, the terms "high" and "lowbrow" came into use, carrying over much of the baggage of the older constructions of "elites" and "masses." Various assumptions – *not of necessity attached to the existence of different kinds of culture* – were imported into cultural debate. In the nineteenth century, the perceived division between elites and masses revolved around reformations in the distribution of governmental power, extending to questions of economic control. In the twentieth century, the clash over brows arose largely from changes in communication technology – in particular, the advent of broadcasting and the ever-increasing capabilities for cheap mass publication – and the attendant creation of new listening and reading audiences. But the new audiences generated by the new media became inflected with the inherited paradigms governing the distinctions between elites and masses. High became inseparable from upper and popular became synonymous with low, with the attendant respective assumptions of hierarchical privilege versus homogeneous mass.

The hostilities surrounding the debates about brows were thus derived in large part from the way traditional political and economic inequalities bled into and limited the possibilities for thinking about new cultural formations. The established oppositional relation between elites and masses imported essentialist notions about cultural division into the realm of aesthetic and informational systems. It was widely assumed that intellectual culture was upper class and popular culture, low class; that these cultures were inevitably oppositional and would, with differing reasons, claim superiority over each other; and that intellectual culture would necessarily be a small group as opposed to the large group of popular culture, an assumption enabled by the categorization of all popular culture as one undifferentiated whole. I do not claim that Virginia Woolf was herself totally free of the entrenched constructions; I will try to demonstrate, however, that she was able to envision possibilities for moving beyond them in a way that most others involved in the cultural debates could not.

The "brow" words come into currency at the beginning of the twentieth century, moving quickly from innocent description to emotionally charged slogans of battle. In the mid-nineteenth century, the adjective "high-browed" could be used as a straightforward compliment, as in George Eliot's description of "gentle maidens and high-browed brave men."[12] However gendered her epithets, "high-browed" carries no implication of conflicts or opposition between intellectual and physical strengths. When "highbrow" appears just before the turn of the century and "lowbrow" shortly after, the polarities begin to form. The *OED*'s first recorded use of "highbrow," in 1884, distinguishes the pleasures of the mind from those of the body, with a lightly humorous inflection about which might be more fun: "Mr. Hope had suggested that we would be at some highbrow part of the Exhibition – looking at pictures I think, but Jo had said firmly, 'If I know the Troubridges they will be at the Chocolate Stall,' and we were."[13] By the time we reach the pre-war fiction of H. G. Wells and Sinclair Lewis, "highbrow" and "highbrowed" have acquired the negative associations of asceticism, repression of the physical, and a pretentious, high moral stance.[14]

By the mid-1920s, the oppositional relation of the brows was established enough for the hostilities to become a target of fun in *Punch*. In 1922, the inauguration of the BBC helped to escalate the tensions, creating the airwaves as contested space; highbrow pleasures came to be protested as the imposition of the interests of a dominant minority upon the general public. In the pages of *Punch*, a fictional husband writes to an appropriately named lowbrow paper, *The Daily Scoop*, to complain, "The programmes are too highbrow...They are hopelessly beyond the intelligence of the mass, at any rate."[15] And the BBC was apparently the occasion for the facetious creation of a third term, descriptive of the new audience that the highbrow programmes were reputed to produce: "The B.B.C. claim[s] to have discovered a new type, the 'middlebrow'. It consists of people who are hoping that some day they will get used to the stuff they ought to like."[16]

Whereas *Punch* maintains its tone of light satirical banter, no such detachment is shown by most of the writers and journalists who take these issues up. By the 1930s, the terms have clearly become sites of cultural anxiety and, in the hands of the journalists, they become implements of war. For the most part, the viciously phrased attacks are aimed at the highbrow, although some self-identified highbrows return fire by constructing a despicable "lowbrowism" with equal zeal. Frank Swinnerton, writing as "Simon Pure" in the New York *Bookman*, condemns Woolf as a member of the small neo-Georgian "caste" of aesthetic "highbrows" who, in their rarefied self-enclosure, pose "a small menace to creative writing."[17] In a 1928 review, Arnold Bennett labels *Orlando* a "high-brow lark," by which he means, however, not that it is full of witty fun, but that it is a mere collection of "oddities," so "tedious in their romp of fancy," that the book amounts to "[f]anciful embroidery, wordy, and naught else!"[18] The next year, reviewing *A Room of One's Own*, Bennett calls Woolf the "queen of the high-brows," while positioning himself firmly as a "low-brow"; although suggesting the world needs a mixture of both, he nevertheless again declares her "the victim of her extraordinary gift of fancy" and disparagingly implies the irrelevancy and inconsequentiality of her work.[19] By the early 1930s, Aldous Huxley, on the other side of the fence, was attacking the complacent superiority of those who adopted an exaggerated, self-satisfied lowbrowism as a deliberate anti-intellectual pose: "It is not at all uncommon now," he claims in "Foreheads Villainous Low," "to find intelligent and cultured people doing their best to feign stupidity and to conceal the fact that they have received an education." Somewhat facetiously, Huxley goes on to attribute this reverse snobbism to the ascendancy of "a society that measures success in economic terms"; in this ideology, "[h]appiness is a product of noise, company, motion, and the possession of objects" and, correspondingly, "highbrows, being poor consumers, are bad citizens."[20] Huxley's essay won supportive comments from Desmond MacCarthy, whose essay "Highbrows" similarly takes issue with "the new stupidity-snobbery and ignorance-snobbery." MacCarthy, however, also argues the need to counter the exclusionary tendencies of the highbrow; the highbrow journalist, he suggests, could usefully expose highbrow "shibboleths" with the reminder that "the [only] qualification for becoming a highbrow is to care for the things of the mind."[21] But even MacCarthy's proposed border-raid reveals how the cultural debate had hardened into the form of antithetical camps, each "brow" convinced of the superiority of the self and the narrowness and limitation of the others.

There were other more reasoned arguments, although they too make us wonder what more was invested in these issues than simple divergence of taste. The title of Leonard Woolf's pamphlet *Hunting the Highbrow* suggests the violence of aggressive attack, implying that a great many were victimizing a few. Leonard's defense is to be supremely logical, trying to cut through misconceptions and misperceptions by breaking down highbrows into sub-species of legitimate and pseudo forms. Against the "real" forms of rational and aesthetic highbrows, Leonard opposes *Pseudaltifrons intellectualis* and *Pseudaltifrons aestheticus*, the first who likes "what nobody else can understand" and the second, "the thing which the majority dislikes."[22] More interesting than these satiric categories, however, is Leonard's attempt to undercut the supposed oppositions between *real* highbrows and the general public, and between classics and best-sellers. The highbrow, he states, recognizes great works before the general public does but the public later recognizes them too. Shakespeare, as a writer, is both popular and highbrow, though these are different elements in his work. Quality and popularity need to be disentangled: highbrow work will by definition appeal to only a small percentage of people but this is different from saying that popular work cannot have artistic merit. In many ways, Leonard attempts to defuse the hostilities and break down barriers, yet his pessimism backs the highbrow into an oppositional corner. Intellect and reason, he concludes, have little chance against passion and prejudice, and the latter hold current sway. Although Leonard's approach to highbrow and popular is definitely a border-crossing one, he seems defeated by the growing irrationality of the mass. And the underlying anxiety is not about differences in interests but about differences in power.

For Leonard, the endangered highbrow stands for the threatened loss of intellectual influence, given his contemporary society's pervasive unresponsiveness to intellectual work. Beneath the literary discussion of tastes and the question of what characterizes highbrowism lies a deeper ground of investment – the contest for readership, for being read. For, as I discuss in the next chapter, the particular conjunction of cultural and economic pressures during this period caused long-standing concerns about audience to emerge as a source of anxiety for the highbrow press. The explosive rise of mass media and mass communication, coupled with the rapidly growing diversity in the reading and listening audiences, intensified concerns about capturing the reader's attention and raised questions about which kinds of publication were going to survive. These were the questions, too, at the heart of a ground-breaking study entitled *Fiction and the Reading*

Public – the Cambridge thesis written by Q. D. Leavis under the direction of I. A. Richards, and published in the spring of 1932.

Although it is customary now to place the Leavises in opposition to "Bloomsbury," the fundamental ideas in *Fiction and the Reading Public* have a great deal in common with Leonard Woolf's. Q. D. Leavis's study is probably the first to undertake a serious categorization of brow levels but the more significant similarity to *Hunting the Highbrow* is the expressed fear about the survival of intellectual culture. Rather than the earlier nineteenth-century view of bridges between one reading level and another, Leavis posits an impassable gap – one so large that all Western intellectual culture could fall into it and disappear. The crucial problem, as Leavis presents it, is the damaging effect of new lowbrow entertainments on highbrow reading practices. And here, while Leonard attempts to separate mass psychology from popular culture, Leavis conflates the two by directing her critique at the debasement of language, the sentimentalization of feeling, the erosion of the powers of concentration, reconstruction, and self-examination – all occasioned by the lowbrow forms of radio, cinema, magazines, and best-sellers. Aside from her claim that best-sellers unfit the reader to think, Leavis argues that they rely for their appeal on reflecting what the reader is already predisposed to believe, further entrenching "social, national, and herd prejudices"; then, since one of the prejudices of the age is "a persistent hostility to the world of letters," the best-sellers actually instill an attitude of disdain toward serious modern literature.[23] Leavis quotes a typical attitude, for example, from a novel by the popular Warren Deeping: "Well, a good novel is real, far more significant than most of the highbrow stuff – so called."[24]

The hostilities that arose when people wrote and talked about the brows were thus fueled by perceived or feared injustices in the distribution of power. For the defenders of "high culture," the issue was the threatened loss of economic and communicative resources, since they were concerned that small volume publication was becoming less financially viable and that intellectual influence on general culture was rapidly diminishing in its effect. For those engaged in "middle or low culture," the compelling issue was exclusion from cultural prestige – or cultural capital – especially since threatened highbrows frequently responded by disparaging the quality of non-highbrow work. People were arguing but not quite for the same thing: a fight for readership, on one side, and a fight for respect and le-gitimization, on the other. These problems were then compounded by the inherited opposition between elites and masses that I have discussed. The nineteenth-century political construct, imported into twentieth-century cultural debates, imposed a binary model that took a complex interlocking network of numerous sub-groups and reduced them to two categories. A resulting misconception – one that we have seen that Leonard Woolf tried to dispel – was that if highbrow was quality, and highbrow was not popular, then popular could not be quality. But perhaps a more serious, because more hidden, misconception was that if intellectual was not popular, then intellectual was necessarily elite.

Again, some of the problems derive from the conflation of different terms, from the homogenization of common, popular, and mass. These terms, which may have had the same referent in nineteenth-century social groupings, become, as I have already suggested, problematic when applied to twentieth-century readerships. Once we open ourselves to possibilities for new configurations, various questions occur. Are intellectual readers necessarily elite readers if the required knowledge and skills can be made available to all? Is there any reason why intellectual reading cannot be popular, in the sense of arising from a grass-roots, common readers' need? Why should reading for entertainment and relaxation – the currently prevailing sense of popular – not be seen as complementary to reading for mental stimulation, allowing diverse kinds of reading practice peacefully to co-exist? What is at stake in the confrontations over these issues, and in what terms do these confrontations proceed? Questions such as these underlie Virginia Woolf's essay, "Middlebrow" and, as Woolf attempts to reconfigure the debate, another kind of reformulation takes place. Rather than mounting assertive arguments in defense of the highbrow writer, Woolf writes a multi-faceted, intertextual prose that in itself makes her most important point: highbrow writing, instead of subjecting the reader to a harangue, invites the reader to think.

"Middlebrow" (1932) and its cultural intertexts

In February 1932, after sounding off to Hugh Walpole about the pretentiousness of certain popular novels, Woolf then both admitted and parodied her own vulnerability to attack: "Anyhow, dont dismiss me as an etoliated, decadent, enervated, emasculated, priggish, blood-waterish, 'ighbrow: as Arnold Bennett used to say" (*L* v:25).[25] In August of the same year, Woolf complained to Ethel Smyth, "I get so much heckled by journalists for Bloomsbury Highbrowism" (*L* v:89). A few months later, in October, Woolf wrote her letter to the *New Statesman and Nation*, which was later posthumously published as the essay "Middlebrow."[26] And that same month, she brought out her second collection of essays entitled *The Common Reader*. The title, as critics have noted, presents its author as writing both *for* the common reader and *as* a common reader, yet Woolf identifies herself, in her letter on middlebrows, as a "highbrow." The conjunction of highbrow and common reading was no accident, however, as the full situation makes clear. The role of intellectuals was being hotly debated both on the radio and in print and these confrontations are embedded in the dense inter-textuality of Woolf's letter. Uncovering this public dimension helps us to see just why it was so important to Woolf to cross the highbrow/common divide.[27]

October 1932 was, for Woolf, a particularly intense time. She herself recorded how, during this month, she became so "fire[d] up about Priestley and his priestliness" that she dashed off an "essay," only to suffer a subsequent collapse with rapid heart-rate problems on October 31 (*D* IV: 129). The immediate stimulus for her anger was the BBC: J. B. Priestley's talk "To a High-Brow," on October 17, and Harold Nicolson's rebuttal, "To a Low-Brow," on October 24.[28] Since these broadcasts became a subject for subsequent comment in the *New Statesman and Nation* on October 29, and since Woolf cast her views as a letter "To the Editor of the *New Statesman*," we can reasonably surmise that her letter was written sometime between the 29th and the 31st. And the month had been extremely busy. At the beginning of October, she traveled with Leonard to the Annual Conference of the Labour Party in Leicester, after which she returned to work on the final chapter of *Flush*. On the eleventh, she broke off to begin writing, at phenomenal speed, the essay-novel that she planned to call *The Pargiters*. October 13 saw the publication of *The Common Reader: Second Series* and, shortly after, the first reviews of it and of Winifred Holtby's *Virginia Woolf* began to appear. Woolf was writing, according to her own description, in a state of "incandescence." My argument here is that, in these intense and "incandescent" days, the BBC talks became a lightning rod for Woolf's broader cultural concerns. Innumerable things coalesced in her mind: the critical reception of her work, the social regulation of women's lives, cultural valuations of the intellectual, the prevailing controls and restrictions governing such public institutions as education and broadcasting – more precisely, the whole operation of public discourse in her time.

Such an amazing coalescence of concerns may help to explain why Woolf felt so compelled to respond to "Priestley and his priestliness" – to the extent of breaking off her writing of *The Pargiters* – when not only had Nicolson already done so but the *New Statesman* had celebrated Nicolson's victory. Mr. Nicolson, the review states, "took up the cudgels against Mr. Priestley and gave the low-brow a tremendous doing-down," showing "apparent enjoyment in trouncing his victim."[29] But this language also suggests the source of disturbance: the *New Statesman* picks up and recirculates the discourse of battle with its vocabulary of "cudgels," "doing-down," and "trouncing." Addressing *both* talks, it appears, Woolf stated, "the Battle of the Brows troubles, I am told, the evening air" (*CE* 11:196). The Battle of the Brows, her phrase implies, is one conducted by brow-beating.

Priestley's script survives in the BBC archives. The style of his talk can be described as informal, matey, and pugilistic; the unnamed listener, addressed as "my dear fellow," is constructed as male; and the gist of the message is to fight off the dangerous temptation to be a highbrow and join the speaker in going out for a drink. All the familiar clichés about highbrowism are rehearsed: that it sneers at popularity and can only admire what is liked by a small group; that it is divorced from ordinary life and characterized by affectation; that it is a product, just as much as low-browism, of fashion and the desire to move in herds. Priestley's call to his listener is, "don't be either a highbrow or a low-brow. Be a man. Be a broad-brow."[30] It must have been particularly irksome for Woolf to hear Priestley reinforcing the stereotypes that Leonard had already demolished as pseudo-highbrow and citing MacCarthy and Huxley as perpetrators of highbrow "bunkum."[31] Another source of annoyance might have been the hint of personal insult. One breed of highbrow, Priestley asserted, consists of "authors entirely without feeling, who write about human life as an educated *wolf* might be expected to write about it" (emphasis added).[32] But the discourse betrays a still more objectionable facet. The implicit message is that nothing here is worth the trouble of thinking about; we should have a good laugh over the matter and take comfort in sensible views.

Nicolson's script has unfortunately been lost but his diary traces a fascinating history of its composition. Though his talk was initially written before he heard Priestley, Nicolson rewrote it immediately afterward in angry rebuttal, only to have second thoughts: "*Tuesday October 18.* Work all morning [*sic*] on my reply to Priestley. Abuse him bitterly. Take the talk off in my pocket to drop it at the B.B.C. but then think better of it. The wireless is not there for scoring off people one dislikes." Nicolson rewrote the talk entirely, "toning down the attack," but even the revised version did not suit the BBC: "*Thursday October 20* ... Joe Ackerley has telephoned to the effect that my talk will not do. I rewrite the whole thing." And still, the revised talk did not suit the listeners: "*Thursday, October 27* ... I get a batch of insulting letters over my last boradcast [*sic*]. Evidently I have hit the British public on the raw."[33]

The excerpts from Nicolson's talk that I *have* been able to locate suggest that all his rewriting did produce a more reasoned tone.[34] The *Yorkshire Post* devoted a long column to Nicolson's "lively wireless talk" on Anglo-Saxon anti-intellectualism, noting his question, "Has it ever struck you... that there is no equivalent for the words 'low-brow' or 'high-brow' in any language other than the English language?" and his inference that "The Anglo-Saxon race is the only race in the world which openly distrusts the intellectual." But although Nicolson speaks up for the neglected potentials of the Anglo-Saxon brain, he manages to imply its inactivity in his designated listener. Driven by "herd instinct" and marked by "intolerance," the lowbrow, Nicolson warns, "will end by producing a race which, like the wasps, have no ideas at all."[35] It would seem that Nicholson, too, adopted an oppositional, assertive style pleasing only to listeners who agreed with his views. What runs through the whole story is the polarization into sides.

In contrast and characteristically, Woolf enters the fray at the foundational level, interrogating the discourse of the argument itself. Instead of defending the highbrow, she challenges her reader to scrutinize conventional thinking, beginning with the assumption that high, middle, and lowbrow correspond to high, middle, and low class. "I love lowbrows; I study them," Woolf writes, "I always sit next the conductor in an omnibus and try to get him to tell me what it is like – being a conductor" (*CE* II:197). Momentarily allowing the reader to conflate lowbrow with working class, Woolf then reverses direction by invoking a miscellany of occupations that make any social categorization of lowbrow impossible: "In whatever company I am I always try to know what it is like – being a conductor, being a woman with ten children and thirty-five shillings a week, being a stockbroker, being an admiral, being a bank clerk, being a dressmaker, being a duchess, being a miner, being a cook, being a prostitute. All that lowbrows do is of surpassing interest and wonder to me" (197–98). Having broadened the category of lowbrows to include both duchess and prostitute, Woolf then resituates the duchess and destabilizes *any* relation between brow and social position: "I myself have known duchesses who were highbrows," she continues, "also charwomen" (199). Interests are one thing; economics, another. We are warned not to confuse them.

Secondly, whereas the BBC represented voices in neat binaries, Woolf undercuts such simplicity of opposition. Whereas Priestley lumps highbrows and lowbrows together as equally moving in herds, Woolf recasts them as riders on galloping horses, each intent on a different goal: the highbrow in pursuit of ideas, the lowbrow in pursuit of a living. The brain and the body, hierarchically disposed in Western cultural thought, are, in

Woolf's typology, placed on equal footing as riders equally committed to their course. But, having suggested a division, however complementary, between body and brain, Woolf undercuts the viability of classification when it comes to what people do. The lowbrows, after their busy day of work, go eagerly to the movies to see what the highbrows – whose work is reflection – can reveal about life. Uniting creators and audience, cinema is a crossroads where highbrows and lowbrows meet. Then, later in the essay, when she tells us that lowbrows write and are desirous of education, she acknowledges a lowbrow production as well as consumption of art. And although she first defines lowbrows as pursuing a living, she notes later that highbrows have livings to earn as well. One distinction she does assert is that "when we [the highbrows] have earned enough to live on, then we live. When the middlebrows, on the contrary, have earned enough to live on, they go on earning enough to buy" (201). Remembering Woolf's attendance at the Annual Conference of the Labour Party at the beginning of the month, we might note her distinction between having to live and living to have – the difference perhaps between socialist and capitalist approaches to money.

Like Priestley, Woolf invokes a third brow. But whereas Priestley simplifies his opposition by making "broad-brow" the only group with real values, Woolf develops a more complex model of difference. Addressing the arena of what is not highbrow, Woolf distinguishes between lowbrow and middlebrow in a way that discriminates between popular and mass. Lowbrows, although they may lack education, nevertheless write "beautifully" when they write "naturally" – that is, when they are not seduced by middlebrow models (*CE* II:200). Middlebrow, in contrast, produces merely conventional work that asks its audience not to think but to agree. Again Woolf avoids collapsing non-highbrow writing into a unified group: she separates lowbrow writing that does not *require* you to think from middlebrow writing that fails to deliver its *promise* of thinking. Middlebrow masks its own discourse: duplicitously pretending to engage in intellectual debate, this brow in effect sells readers prepackaged views. By distinguishing between the two groups that are not her own, Woolf achieves a more penetrating critique.

Highbrow writing, for its part, strives to get its readers to think and Woolf challenges her own reader by writing a layered text. Her letter has not just one Priestlian intertext but at least three.[36] Going back years before the BBC talk – which she would only have heard once on the wireless – Woolf takes issue with Priestley's "High, Low, Broad," another blatant entertainment for those who share his views. After a laughing admission of the self-satisfaction in being like-minded people, Priestley is blunt about his aggressive intent. Admitting that the "'brow' business" is too entrenched to escape, he asserts that the one thing to do is "to see that the terms are used properly, that the pleasantest of them is appropriated for the use of our own party, and that the others, loaded with the worst possible meanings, are fastened upon people known to disagree with us." Such outrageous humor might possibly be used to defuse hostilities; instead, Priestley indulges in a rather nasty form of fun. From their superior position as "Broadbrows," he unites with his reader in disparaging both highbrow and lowbrow as sheep moving in herds led by whatever fashion prevails: "Just as Low, you might say, is the fat sheep with the cigar from the City of Surbiton, so High is the thin sheep with the spectacles and the squeak from Oxford or Bloomsbury."[37] Broadbrow, he claims, is the only critical intelligence of the lot and the only one whose range of interest and experience takes in the whole of human life.

There are two hits in this passage that Woolf overturns: the identification of highbrows with sheep and the objectification of Bloomsbury as representative of "High." But instead of offering a counter-argument, Woolf writes a counter-discourse. Pugnacious prose that badgers the listener to agree is countered by an elastic, pluralistic prose that challenges the reader to think. Priestley's insult, and of course also his humor, depends upon cliché and stereotype; Woolf responds to the abuse with a series of nimble-footed turns upon language that imply the more devastating criticism that middlebrow discourse displays a limited and reductive understanding of words. Woolf takes Priestley's conventional metaphor – sheep are easily led and behave in the same way – and, through extended word play, turns it back against himself. First, countering Priestley's typing of "Bloomsbury" with sheep-like behavior, Woolf introduces literal sheep to subvert his categorizing geographical trope: "The hungry sheep," she writes, "did I remember to say that this part of the story takes place in the country?" (*CE* 11:200).[38] Next Woolf enacts a passage through the literal to re-turn the metaphorical, shifting the sheep from a fashion-following herd to an expectant but disappointed reading audience. As she tosses Middlebrow's book out the window and "over the hedge into the field," "the hungry sheep look up but are not fed" (200).

Woolf's reinvigorated metaphorical is complex and layered, now introducing the further intertext of Milton's "Lycidas." In Milton's poem this line occurs in a passage that suddenly digresses from the pastoral elegiac mode: the speaker's lament and his questioning of the meanings of fame and of fate are broken by a diatribe delivered by St. Peter against the false herdsman who fails to provide the necessary sustenance for his flock. In the political context of the poem, the digression, as Lawrence Lipking has shown, invokes a larger sense of religious purpose. St. Peter's words imply that the Irish – to whom the Lycidas of the poem, Edward King, was sailing when he drowned – are in need not simply of the consolation offered by poetry but of the salvationary promise of the Protestant faith.[39] As Lipking points out, such salvation might not be seen by the Irish as answering to their needs; nevertheless, in the context of the poem, the digression serves the function of conjoining the figure of the shepherd-poet with that of the herdsman-pastor, expanding and deepening the expectation that poet and poem must be judged according to the worth of the food provided for the flock.

The extraordinary layering of Woolf's allusion allows her text to be read at different levels. To begin, the sentence makes sense in its own context with no further explanation: Middlebrow's book does not feed its readers. But readers could also pick up the turn upon Priestley's use of sheep, or the countering of cliché with poetry, or the dislodgment of banter by ded-ication and serious purpose. The quotation from "Lycidas" was evidently a common expression in Woolf's time for an expectant but disappointed audience,[40] and the thoroughly literary might perceive that Priestley is be-ing cast as false herdsman, as false priest. The quotation adds incredible density to Woolf's text; at the same time, it could be read with varying degrees of previous knowledge.

A similar layering emerges in the next turn that Woolf performs upon sheep. Having shifted from cliché to poetic allusiveness, Woolf shifts to freer and deeper kinds of thought, describing herself as "lapsing into that stream which people call, so oddly, consciousness, and gathering wool from the sheep that have been mentioned above" (*CE* II:202). Woolf again em-ploys an expression in common use, and again with a defamiliarizing shock. Wool-gathering originally referred to a process of roaming a countryside and picking up the bits of sheep's wool caught on bushes and hedges; as early as the sixteenth century, however, it had become a metaphor for wan-dering fancies or idle speculation. Among its numerous pejorative uses is yet another possible intertext, an essay by Desmond MacCarthy the previous year, about which Woolf wrote, "Oh I was annoyed with Desmond's usual sneer at Mrs. Dalloway – woolgathering" (*D* IV:42).[41] In *Orlando*, Woolf had already had ironic fun with conventional notions of wool-gathering, parodying the biographer's horror when faced with the task of describing a woman's thinking: "this mere woolgathering; this sitting in a chair day in, day out, with a cigarette and a sheet of paper and a pen and an ink pot" (*O* 241). In "Middlebrow," Woolf similarly challenges conventional associations, repossessing the sheep, and their wool, in her own terms. In the image of "gathering wool from the sheep mentioned above," language wobbles on the literal–metaphorical axis, with the radical implication that writing – the action of the roaming, scavenging brain – might just be practical, real work.

There is yet one further Priestlian intertext in "Middlebrow" – his column in the *Evening Standard* on October 13, in which he reviewed Harold Nicolson's *Public Faces*, Vita Sackville-West's *Family History*, Virginia Woolf's *Common Reader*, and Winifred Holtby's *Virginia Woolf*. The review, while favorable to Sackville-West and damning to Nicolson, is either fairly balanced or underhandedly two-faced – whichever way we choose to view it – about Woolf. Admitting that she is "a very good critic indeed," and claiming *To the Lighthouse* as "one of the most moving and beautiful pieces of fiction of our time," Priestley nevertheless undercuts his praise with unkind and personal remarks about Woolf's "deeply feminine" mode. Repeating Arnold Bennett's epithet describing Woolf as the "high priestess of Bloomsbury," Priestley recasts Holtby's evocation of the poetic qualities in Woolf's writing into a patronizing slur on novels "written by ter-rifically sensitive, cultured, invalidish ladies with private means" – a phrase that Woolf quotes with heavily underscored irony in her letter.[42] Again inscribing the art/life binary, Priestley contrasts those novels, like hers, that "draw near to poetry" with those that "draw near to social history" and "cast a wider net."[43]

In "Middlebrow," Woolf undoes this last binary by combining allusive poetic prose with the bite of social critique. The "wider net" of Woolf's essay goes beyond Priestley's insult to challenge the middlebrow discourse of the BBC – renamed the "Betwixt and Between Company" for the way it packages and polarizes controversy instead of promoting genuine dialogue (*CE* II:202). Unlike the thoroughbred commitment of highbrows and low-brows, "middlebred" (199) middlebrow is a neutered, in-between creature, driven by neither bodily nor mental passions; "betwixt and between" (198) in another sense, it feeds on the rancor it stirs up between different groups in society, commodifying opposition for entertainment value and invest-ing in showmanship rather than dialogue. Despite Joe Ackerley's attempts to tone down Nicolson's language, Woolf's objections to the BBC format resemble those now leveled against mass culture: it constructs its product in order to sell and constructs its audience for an easy sale.

Woolf furthermore implicates a second public institution in middlebrow discourse, although she draws it into her net more subtly than the BBC. One of the several examples she offers of middlebrow are "people who call both Shakespeare and Wordsworth equally 'Bill'" (*CE* II:199). The implied lack of discrimination among writers and the chummy slap-on-your-back heartiness in themselves suggest a reductive approach to literature, but there is yet another specific intertext here. In 1926, when Woolf reviewed Professor Walter Raleigh's letters, she was irritated by his slangy talk about "Bill Blake or Bill Shakespeare or old Bill Wordsworth," in which she heard the defensiveness of a man ashamed of his sentiments about English literature (*E* IV:343; *L* III:242) coupled with a desire to shock.[44] Raleigh was a prominent figure in the introduction of English into the university curriculum but, despite his appointment in 1904 as the Merton Chair of English Language and Literature at Oxford, Woolf's quotation from his letters of the same year reveals his hostile denigration of literary criticism as a feminized soft option: "Bradley's book on Shakespeare is good," he wrote, but continued, "Even with it I can't help feeling that critical admiration for what another man has written is an emotion for spinsters."[45] And Woolf's review refers to an earlier letter, written to his fiancée, in which Raleigh is even more derogatory in his association of "culture" with intellectual women:

Culture is what they [two female visitors] are after and there is an element of barbarity in my instincts that makes me ill contented in such company... I really believe, not in refinement and scholarly elegance, those are only a game; but in blood feuds, and the chase of wild beasts and marriage by capture. In carrying this last savage habit into effect there would be an irresistible dramatic temptation to select the bluest lady of them all.[46]

Certainly Raleigh's letters reveal a good deal of posturing, as he seeks to portray himself as a down-to-earth, virile male. But Raleigh, Woolf suggests, typifies a general turn against intellectual interests, denigrated as effete and feminine, in favor of an aggressive, masculinized ethic. As I show in the next chapter, Woolf was further disturbed by the tie between Raleigh's code of virility and his increasing celebration of military patriotism. Behind Priestley's jocular "don't be a highbrow, be a man," Woolf implies, lies a gendered discourse intimately connected with war.

The dense intertextuality of this essay thus becomes a web of searching cultural critique, exposing the complicity of unquestioning patriotism, capitalist values, media control of public discourse, and anti-intellectual complacency. Furthermore, the intricate play of Woolf's language emerges as a rhetorical technique for shifting positionality, destabilizing ideology, and putting the reader into active relation to the text. Woolf's poetic discourse – her wool-gathering – is an elastic, allusive prose that draws upon and stimulates the reader's mental perceptivity. In contrast, middlebrow's discourse – which she likens to worms in the cabbages, tarnish on the moon, red-brick villas infecting the countryside – is the insidious perpetrator of reductionism and discord.

In its elasticity, Woolf's supposedly difficult "highbrow" discourse functions as an activist response to a pressing social need: the need to reject clichés, to shake off the nation's "priestliness," and to learn to think in flexible, relational, intelligent ways. The lines from her essay "Middlebrow" lead out into the public arenas of writing, broadcasting, and education, grounding her essay in public debate and demonstrating why, for her, common reader and highbrow were not oppositional terms. Although Priestley may be the immediate target of her satire, the proliferating allusions and slippages reveal her true antagonist to be not a person, or a group of people, but a whole discursive system. Middlebrow is a product of a mass – not popular – culture and of a masculinized institutional discourse that dogmatically interpellates the reader/listener into its own ideology. In contrast, the letter-essay "Middlebrow" shares with *The Common Reader* a respect for the reader's intelligence and the reader's intellectual needs. Ultimately, Woolf both "draws near to social history" and "casts a wider net" by demonstrating how an education in wool-gathering is of more use to the brain of the common reader than the brow-beating of the educational system and the BBC.

I have, as no doubt some of my readers will have noticed, spent an unconscionably long time discussing a "Letter to the Editor" that Woolf never sent. However, we should also remember that Woolf intended not to abandon this letter but to "re-write it as an essay" (*D* IV:129).[47] Why Leonard advised against sending it, we can only guess, but it is obvious that, in scope and complexity, her letter had far outgrown her initial intent. We can also surmise something about both Leonard's advice and her planned revisions from an exchange she had with Ethel Smyth some eight months later, in June 1933. In suggesting revisions to the manuscript of *Female Pipings in Eden*, Woolf urged Smyth to focus on the impediments other women had faced in the field of music and to delete personal anecdotes and autobiographical tales. Using nonetheless a personal anecdote to reinforce her point, Woolf offered what we can now see as a disguised reference to the Middlebrow letter:

I was wound to a pitch of fury the other day by a reviewers attacks upon a friend of mine to do a thing I have never yet done – to write to the papers a long letter. "Yes" said L. when I showed it to him; but itll do more harm than good; its all about yourself. When a fortnight later in cold blood I read it, there was "I" as large, and ugly as could be; thanks to God, I didn't send it . . . Well theyd have said; she has an axe to grind; and no one would have taken me seriously. (*L* v:194–95)

Warning Smyth about such hostile reading strategies most likely imitated her own warnings to herself. And her sensitivity to the issue was perhaps more keen because, reading Smyth's prolific narratives, Woolf was conscious both of sympathizing with the response, "Oh the womans got a grievance about herself; Shes unable to think of any one else," and of struggling with these voices herself: "how vain, how personal, so they will say, rubbing their hands with glee, women always are; I can hear them as I write" (*L* v:194; 195). And Woolf herself most likely recognized the irony that in challenging Middlebrow's feminizing of intellectual discourse, she had left herself open to the charge that, like all women, she was being merely personal rather than engaging in public debate.

Despite its posthumous publication, "Middlebrow" is a highly significant document for understanding Woolf's approach to the "brows." It is a document, furthermore, that helps to historicize the debate. Whereas current discussions of the "brows" tend to focus on "lifestyle" and taste, for Woolf – witnessing, as she did, the emergence of strategies aimed at the mobilization of "the masses," whether for war or for marketing – the key issue was the relation between writer and audience. This concern is definitively caught in one last context for the essay-letter "Middlebrow" in October 1932.

On October 17, Vita Sackville-West broadcast her review of Woolf's *The Common Reader*, only a few hours before Priestley's "To a High-brow" talk. Sackville-West gave a glowing recommendation to Woolf's essays, offering her own brand of defense against highbrow attacks. She asserted that there was no art/life dichotomy in *The Common Reader*, since Woolf's appreciations of literature were, at the same time, interpretations of life. Adopting the middlebrow usage of terms perhaps more than would have been to Woolf's liking, Sackville-West proclaimed Woolf's approach to be "not a bleak and so-called highbrow sort." But for all its praise of Woolf's essays, the talk gave even greater prominence to two books by D. H. Lawrence – *Etruscan Places* and the recently published *Letters*. After being told about Woolf's "remarkably human mind," listeners heard Lawrence exalted as a "truly great writer" with "a truly noble mind" of the type that "occurs once or twice in a century."[48] Woolf wrote her "dearest Creature" a letter of thanks the very next day – asking too, "Did you see Priestly on Harold you and me?" (*L* v:111).[49] But it was not until November 8 that Woolf rather more pungently wrote to Sackville-West, "I dont altogether agree with you (on the wireless) about Lawrence" (*L* v:121). What Woolf did not say was that she had been in the process herself of reading Lawrence's *Letters* to review in the *New Statesman* but had declined and returned the book to Kingsley Martin on November 4.[50]

Reading Lawrence's letters on October 2 – well before the brow battles that I have been discussing – Woolf recorded her intense frustration in her diary. While distressed by "the brutality of civilised society" against him, she was distressed even more by his repetitive philosophy, incessant explanations, and constant preaching (*D* IV:126). And again, her objection is to the narrow and confining place for the reader: "But in the Letters he cant listen beyond a point; must give advice; get you in to the system too. Hence his attraction for those who want to be fitted; which I dont" (126). "Art," she protests, "is being rid of all preaching: things in themselves; the sentence in itself is beautiful" (126). Of course, this is precisely the kind of statement that has brought accusations against Woolf of an "aestheticism" divorced from social issues, an aloof elitism removed from life. And the existence, even at that time, of such accusations was presumably what lay behind Vita's rousing testimony for Woolf on the basis that "literature *is* life."[51] But in the context of Woolf's comments on Lawrence, and in the larger context of October 1932, it is obvious that the value Woolf attached to "things in themselves" was grounded in social commitment; as an artist, her social and ethical responsibility was not to appropriate the reader's intelligence by forcing a system but to write in a way that empowered her reader's own eyes. "Its the preaching that rasps me," she wrote in her diary (126); and, in her letter to the *New Statesman*, abjuring Priestley and Lawrence and her supposed role as "high priestess," she wrote that Bloomsbury is "a place where lowbrows and highbrows live happily together on equal terms and priests are not, nor priestesses, and, to be quite frank, the adjective 'priestly' is neither often heard nor held in high esteem" (*CE* II:203).[52]

Protesting against Lawrence's egotistical impositions, Woolf longed for a greater inclusiveness: "Why all this criticism of other people?" she asked. "Why not some system that includes the good?[53] What a discovery that would be – a system that did not shut out" (*D* IV:127). In longing for "a system that did not shut out," Virginia Woolf was imagining a fully inclusive community that would incorporate, in the historical tradition, both the obscure and the prominent as well. After all, "Shakespeare's democracy," she noted in 1919, extended not just to the common man but also to

Lear, "who was probably a 'highbrow' and certainly a king" (*E* II:28). But communal inclusiveness in a modern democracy was, as the interwar period prophetically recognized, no simple goal to achieve.

If there is a common theme that runs through this book, it is that understanding language is a relational enterprise; the meaning of texts exists in relation to the time of their writing (and of their reading) and the meaning of words inheres in their relation to each other and to their pasts. If "highbrow" during Woolf's time was a site for anxieties about a lingering class privilege attached to intellectuals and a publishing and marketing economy that threatened to construct readers as an undifferentiated mass, the word "democratic" was an even stronger magnet for cultural concerns. Furthermore, just as "highbrow" was inflected with the inherited opposition of elites against masses, "democratic" had been delimited by the assumed binary that *all* attributes of the terms "aristocratic" and "democratic" are diametrically opposed. Certainly as systems of governance, an absolute monarchy is antithetical to a constitutional democracy, and various associated oppositions reasonably follow: hierarchy versus equality, hereditary privilege versus value accorded to accomplishment, and exclusionary versus openness to all. But when we shift from governance to general culture, the binaries break down. Limitation, narrowness, decadence, or childishness may have been marked features of aristocratic circles at various times in British history; these qualities unfortunately do not remain the aristocracy's preserve. By similar token, if aristocracy has also lent itself to education, freedom, ease, eccentricity, and high standards, there may be good arguments in favor of preserving those qualities *within* a democracy – especially if that culture, for reasons of vastly escalating scale, is threatened by standardization and mass conformity.

Loosening the binaries shifts our definitional thinking: rather than signifying populace as opposed to upper class, "democratic" embraces the full society. This principle has been affirmed in the vote, but perhaps not so well when it comes to culture. In the early twentieth century, however, it was precisely the meaning of democratic culture that drew the intellectuals' concern. Achieving the final stage of universal franchise shifted debate away from democracy as a form of governance to the democratic values that political forms were intended to obtain. The primary question became not "whether democracy" but "whither democracy." But the project was complicated by different meanings, applications, and understandings of democratic beliefs. Again, the debates circulated around the meaning of a cultural keyword.

"Democracy," as Raymond Williams demonstrates, has been a keyword of British culture since it entered the English language in the sixteenth century. Up to the late eighteenth century, Williams argues, the word was used primarily to refer to rule by the largest and, by implication the lowest, class. Implying the tyranny of the commoners as the obverse of the tyranny of the despot, "democracy" was employed in almost all instances as "a strongly unfavourable term."[54] During the eighteenth and nineteenth centuries, concepts of democracy shifted gradually toward positive, modern connotations, but practical applications of democratic principles bifurcated along two distinct political paths. In the liberal tradition, the focus is on "democratic rights" achieved through "the conditions of open argument" and "freedom of speech" whereas, in the socialist tradition, "to be democratic... is to be unconscious of class distinctions, or consciously to disregard or overcome them in every day behaviour," and to treat all people as equal. The two paths resulted not in differing but in antithetical meanings, so that "democratic" according to one usage actually implied "anti-democratic" in the other; nevertheless, within each tradition, the term had positive force. What is striking about Williams's discussion of its subsequent history is his conclusion that, during the twentieth century, the term became subject to such variation and distortion that the resulting confusion saw "nearly all political movements claiming to stand for democracy or real democracy."[55] Ultimately, "democratic" evolved into a rather meaningless gesture for what is good.[56]

Just a year before Woolf's letter about the "brows," the vagaries and imprecisions in the word "democracy" provided the starting place for a series of six talks Leonard Woolf gave on the BBC.[57] In his opening talk, Leonard asserted that around 1900 almost everyone was a self-styled democrat and almost everyone thought to be a democrat was good. By the 1930s, he argued, the pendulum had swung to the other side. The prevailing attitude was now general disillusionment and the sense that the democratic project had run its course. Leonard's own response to such waves of generalized emotion was to define clearly what he considered the precise implications of democracy to be, as a corrective to both sloppy usage and sloppy ideology.

For Leonard, the fundamental democratic principle was a belief in equality, not in a system of government; universal suffrage was merely a way of implementing equality. The paradigmatic change that ushered in democratic belief, he argued, was the new idea, brought about by the American and French Revolutions, that the happiness of ordinary people was as important as that of the military and aristocratic classes. Furthermore, valuing the happiness of all people logically implied a belief in the equality of all people. Democracy had therefore to be recognized as being in conflict with any notion of privilege – whether that meant the privileging of the upper classes endemic to fascism and imperialism or the potential privileging of manual laborers that he attributed to communism. Then, from the principle of equality, Leonard traced a chain of logical consequences from (1) equal rights to happiness, to (2) equal access to occupations, and (3) equal opportunities to acquire the best education so that (2) and then (1) could be achieved. A democrat, he argued, "would say that the happiness of a person depends enormously upon the kind of education which he received when a child or young person."[58] However, Leonard continued, R. H. Tawney, in his recently published *Equality*, had provided statistical data demonstrating that "unless you are the child of middle-class parents who send you to a public school, your chances in life are distinctly limited."[59] Privilege still prevented equal access to educational opportunities; a further enemy of democratic education was standardization. "Standardization," Leonard asserted, "seems to mean a kind of disease of democracy, for it destroys individuality and teaches people to follow one another like sheep instead of choosing for themselves."[60] Leonard's theme moved as well from the issue of social equality to the even more controversial topic of economic equality, where he argued that it was incompatible with democracy to "allow incomes to vary from a million in the case of one man to £78 a year in the case of another."[61]

The series ended by extrapolating from relations among individuals within a nation to global relations among "Citizens of the World." Looking to the past, Leonard praised the way the nineteenth-century democrat Giuseppe Mazzini applied the ideal of equal individuals to "relations between whole peoples of different nationalities"; turning to the present, however, Leonard saw Mazzini's vision of free and equal citizens replaced by an aggressive nationalism and imperialism that attacked democracy at its core. The prevailing notion of the homogeneous nation-state masked real diversity and, within many European states, minorities were denied equal rights and liberties and lived "in a condition of permanent political discontent." The same oppression by the majority characterized the international level as well. European states assumed the prerogative of self-government but regarded the inhabitants of Asia and Africa as incapable of managing their own affairs. It was a question, Leonard asserted, of "the kind of civilisation we desire," and democracy was doomed without a full commitment to the equal value and the equal importance of each and every individual.[62]

An interesting feature about the whole series is that, while Leonard Woolf is often constructed as political in contrast to Virginia Woolf's apoliticism, his focus here is not on matters such as votes, suffrage, or legislative powers but on the ordinary realm of everyday life and happiness. While he mentions the importance of social services and equalized incomes, his emphasis falls on the way individual freedom is intimately bound up with access to higher education and education of the best quality. His democratic vision is defined less through the rights of manual workers than through the rights of all to become intellectual workers, if they so desire. And the recurrent image of sheep will recall the various fears about herd behavior articulated by different sides in the ongoing debates. For Leonard, guaranteeing individual rights was inextricable from preserving individual thought. The other significant feature in Leonard's approach is that his defense of individualism was offered not in opposition to the demands of society but as the very foundation of social organization. In his view, the basis for both national and international community lies in a respect for the individual thoughts of others. He did not, however, gloss over the difficulties of achieving such a goal. The fundamental problem to be faced by a democracy, he admitted, was the difficulty of resolving "the claims of the whole community with the claims of the individual."[63]

As BBC talks, Leonard's series had high exposure in a public forum. From the few published letters in response, clearly some readers/listeners took exception to what he said, and his fourth talk began with the defensive argument that he was merely clarifying the logical corollaries of his fundamental democratic premise and not advocating any particular view.[64] But despite disagreements, Leonard's talks, and other articles in the *Listener* around this time, indicate that, in the social discourse of the time, debates about democracy were being conducted in economic and cultural, rather than parliamentary, terms.[65] The opposition between democracy and totalitarian rule was naturally a matter of increasingly central importance given the political developments in Spain, Italy, and Germany. With regard to the issue of *defining* democracy, however, the emphasis now fell not on systems of democratic rule but on the social consequences of democratic thought.[66]

In a manner closely connected to Leonard's approach, the tie between democracy and education came into international prominence through the work of John Dewey. In his influential *Democracy and Education*, Dewey argued for democratic education first on pragmatic lines: "a government resting upon popular suffrage cannot be successful unless those who elect and who obey their governors are educated." But for Dewey, the implications of democracy extended far beyond methods of government; democracy, he claimed, is "a mode of associated living," and his idea of associated living, like Leonard Woolf's, was inseparable from individual growth. According to Dewey, for true development "each [person] has to refer his own action to that of others, and to consider the action of others to give point and direction to his own"; in this way, the requirements for educating the individual also require "the breaking down of those barriers of class, race, and national territory which [keep] men from perceiving the full import of their activity."[67] Since the individual experiences the greatest expansion of identity by sharing in the "associated activity" of the widest possible community, individual freedom and the democratic community go hand in hand.[68]

In England, the connection between democracy and education was a vital component in arguments made both by and on behalf of the newly literate working class. An influential essay by R. H. Tawney, published in 1914, was entitled "An Experiment in Democratic Education." Arguing on behalf of the working class, Tawney claimed their right to study for the purposes of a "reasonable and humane conduct of life."[69] Similar arguments were brought forward by G. D. H. Cole, one of the formative figures, like Tawney, in the Workers' Educational Association (WEA). According to L. P. Carpenter, democracy for Cole, "was more than a political principle; it was a moral relationship among men";[70] it related not "to politics alone, but to every aspect of human life."[71] While bitingly critical of the reigning educational system, Cole built his arguments for reform upon the general belief that increased educational opportunity would lead to a new era of equality and social peace: "every working-class student who has found his way to Oxford or Cambridge has been acclaimed as a sign and portent of the coming educated democracy."[72] I return to Cole and the WEA in the next chapter; my point here is that interest in democratic education was inseparable from larger social concerns. And the issue was not only raised in public journalism; it became a topic *about* public journalism, due to the pedagogical aspirations of the BBC.

The role of broadcasting in democratic education was, again in 1932, the topic for a prolonged exchange of views involving the BBC. On October 5, an editorial in the *Listener* headed "Culture and Democracy" highlighted a recent talk at the British Institute of Adult Education given by Charles Siepmann, the Director of BBC Talks; the same issue then offered a summary of Siepmann's talk entitled "The Changing Audience." While recognizing the vital contribution of the universities' tutorial classes in adult education, both articles provocatively suggested that broadcasting might be the form of education most suitable for modern democracy. The implication was that the universities had simply adapted "the culture of the landed aristocracy of the eighteenth century," whereas radio had prompted "the first awakening of what might in time become a distinctive and articulate democratic culture."[73] What Siepmann had in mind was not only the broad listening audience for radio but more specifically the formation of "Wireless Discussion Groups." Such groups, most often informally organized under discussion leaders, ranged from listening groups in the prisons to a discussion group of teachers led by the Chief Inspector for Schools; the Executive Committee of the Central Council for Broadcast Education reported 174 of such groups meeting in the summer of 1932.[74]

Siepmann clearly overstepped the limits of most of his reading audience, and a series of letters, largely defending the superiority of the Tutorial Class over the wireless discussion group, enlivened the columns of the *Listener*, continuing up to November 23. But although positions differed, the nature, form, and delivery of democratic education were clearly common topics both in and on the air. Debate ranged from the extension of democratic education, to the most appropriate pedagogy for such education, to alternative venues for such education apart from the schools. This particular controversy in the *Listener*, we might note, ran concurrently with the clashes among Priestley, Nicolson, the *New Statesman*, and Virginia Woolf on the matter of the brows.

In the early twentieth century, cultural usage was thus extending the meaning of "democratic" from a system of government to the whole framework of cultural thinking and expression within a society. And it is the second sense that most engaged Virginia Woolf. We should not, of course, ignore her participation in various associations devoted to democratic aims in the first sense, most notably her work for adult suffrage and the Women's Co-operative Guild.[75] As a writer, however, her primary political involvement focused not on organized committees but on the social dynamics of a literate community and, in particular, on the empowerment of marginalized, repressed, or absent voices. For Woolf, moreover, democracy was no simple ideal and she was acutely aware of the problem that Leonard identified as endemic to all democratic formulations: the tension between individual and social interests that, as Raymond Williams shows, is firmly embedded *within* democratic beliefs in the differing emphasis of liberal and socialist systems. For Leonard, the conflict between individual freedom and social equality could be resolved by basing the model for communal relations – whether at the national or international level – on a respect for the individual rights of others. For Dewey, these tensions were best negotiated

through an interdependent model in which the individual's growth depends on an ethical consciousness of the effect of our actions on others,
a consciousness developed through co-operative sharing in the activity of
the widest possible community.[76]

Virginia Woolf's model of democratic community is less easily sum-
marized, in part because she resisted simple objective definitions, in part
because she believed that the identity of such a community could be determined only in collaboration with voices that had not yet been heard. As
we have seen in the essay "Middlebrow," Woolf did not consider definition
apart from the dynamic of how that definition proceeds. If "democratic"
was to refer to the whole people, she asked, how could a part define what
that whole would mean? For Woolf to give her primary attention to social
discourse rather than social structures was not an apolitical gesture but the
very foundation of her political thought. In her model of democratic community, the liberal conditions of open argument could only be achieved in a
socialist dialogue in which all voices were equal participants. Individual expression would be legitimized – allowed, that is, free reign to be individual –
only if writing were not authoritative but part of an open and equal conversation, operating without aggression, suppression, or domination. But
that, she constantly argued, was not the social discourse of her time.

Virginia Woolf and "democratic"

"Democratic" as an ideal condition differed, for Virginia Woolf, not only
from the prevailing political paradigm but even, it would seem, from constructions of "democratic" that were possible at that time to imagine. But
like Raymond Williams, Woolf exposes the contesting ideological possibilities through an examination of language. When she uses the word
"democratic," there are different inflections in her use of the term and
different times when certain inflections prevail. The very shifts in Woolf's
usage expose the word "democratic" as a site of twentieth-century anxiety
and reveal Woolf's own sense of it as a cultural keyword.

Fairly early in her career, for example, Woolf distinguishes "Democratic"
from "democratic." In *Night and Day*, when Mary Datchet writes on "Some
Aspects of the Democratic State" or plans with Mr. Basnett the formation
of the "Society for the Education of Democracy" (*N&D* 281, 376), her
work involves three straightforward formal democratic projects: votes for
women, provision of education for the working-class, and the overthrow of
capitalism. Mary's intense dedication testifies to the fervor and enthusiasm
of the young radicals, but precisely how Woolf regards their work is more

difficult to say. Certainly it is marked by intelligence and selflessness, but it is also touched with a certain naïveté and an endearing but slightly pitiable idealism. The narrative view is ambivalent: positive about Mary's achievement of an independent identity through her work, but cautious and skeptical about the likely accomplishment of her aims. Once we put "democratic" into the titles of papers and the names of societies, Woolf suggests, it becomes one of those big words, like "Women" and "Fiction," that are difficult to relate to daily life.

Conversely, "democracy" as a little, lower-case word connects to ordinary life in both its individual and communal aspects. In "Melodious Meditations," Woolf opposes small-d democracy to the pretentious, pompous style of writing that inflates its own importance by literally or metaphorically "spelling certain qualities with a capital letter" (*E* 11:80). Reviewing Henry Sedgwick's essays, Woolf does more than mock his attempt to elevate his prose by cultivating eighteenth-century abstractions; she discovers beneath his mild civility an insidious attempt "to refine and restrain the boisterous spirit of democracy" (81). For her part, Woolf decries any move to turn literature into a "special cult" of "geniuses" and "great men" who are treated with "special reverence" by "the masses," asking, "[w]as there ever a plan better calculated to freeze literature at the root than this one?" (81). Bitingly ironic about the diminution of "ordinary people" implied by the very word "masses," Woolf argues on behalf of an egalitarian democracy, asserting that "the best artistic work is done by people who mix easily with their fellows" (81).[77] Against Sedgwick, she upholds Walt Whitman's 1855 preface to *Leaves of Grass*, concluding with a stirring invocation of his prophetic vision: "As a piece of writing it rivals anything we have done for a hundred years, and as a statement of the American spirit no finer banner was ever unfurled for the young of a great country to march under" (81–82). She then concludes with Whitman's own words – which seem echoed indeed in her words about "priestly" in "Middlebrow": "There will soon be no more priests. Their work is done [...] A new order shall arise, and they shall be the priests of man, and every man shall be his own priest" (quoted by Woolf, *E* 11:82; ellipsis added by McNeillie).

Woolf and Whitman: this may be a surprising affinity to those for whom Woolf is marked by upper-middle-class or even upper-class Englishness. But Whitman, the self-styled poet of democracy, is, both here and elsewhere, a democratic touchstone for Woolf. Although she never wrote extensively about him, she was unreservedly sympathetic to his beliefs, both at the beginning and at the end of her career.[78] For Whitman is given, we might say, the second last word in *Three Guineas*. In the last note, just before quoting the words of George Sand on the solidarity that unites all individual human lives within the larger general life, Woolf turns to Whitman for the basis of a democratic vision: "Of Equality – as if it harm'd me, giving others the same chances and rights as myself – as if it were not indispensable to my own rights that others possess the same" (quoted by Woolf, *TG* 206; n. 49).[79] And in an essay on Whitman, Woolf comes closest to figuring the ideal bond of democratic solidarity that brings together, on a equal basis, common readers and common writer.

"Visits to Walt Whitman" (1918)

On the third of January 1918, Woolf published a review, in the *TLS*, of *Visits to Walt Whitman in 1890–1891*, written by "Two Lancashire Friends," J. Johnston and J. W. Wallace. A glance at Woolf's letters and diaries written during the preceding month shows her characteristically immersed in the activities of the Hogarth Press, her reviewing, and the lives of her friends; but her writing is also pervaded by the particular crisis of the time. At the beginning of December, Leonard's brother Cecil was killed and his brother Philip wounded at the front; on the 6th and the 18th, the Woolfs were forced to take shelter from the air raids, waiting them out in the kitchen passage and cellar of the house. On the 2nd they were both in Hampstead for Leonard's lecture to the UND (Union for Democratic Control) and on the 19th, they attended the first general meeting of the 1917 Club, a club Leonard had worked to establish, named in honor of the February Revolution in Russia and dedicated to promoting peace and democracy. Writing glowingly about Whitman's visitors seems almost, in this context, to be a nostalgic evocation of other, calmer, more peaceful days. But it is precisely this kind of juxtaposition that raises for Woolf's readers a challenging crux for interpretation. Does the Whitman review signal Woolf's ability to remove herself from current events? Or does it confront the war by invoking an alternative discourse – one, in her view, more in accord with the interests of democracy and peace?

The visits to Walt Whitman grew out of a reading and discussion group formed in the town of Bolton, Lancashire, around 1885. Ordinary, middle-class young men, with the occupations of "clergymen, manufacturers, artisans, and bank clerks" (*E* II:205), the members resemble the common readers Woolf later inscribes as the audience for her essays. In its composite nature, the group also intrigued Woolf as a model of community, for it combined individual difference with participatory togetherness, prefiguring the communal dynamics that she explored throughout her own writing, culminating in her last novel *Between the Acts*.[80] According to one of the members, J. W. Wallace – an assistant architect whose father was a millwright – the group was initiated shortly after his mother's death, when a number of intimate friends began to meet in his house every Monday evening to discuss, in addition to current events, "subjects of more permanent interest and value." Although the group grew to include many members, they never organized into a society, never attempted to designate a leader, but remained "a little company of men of widely different characteristics, ideas and training, who were united only in common friendship." Their strikingly "composite character," however, was informed by these differences. According to Wallace, "[i]t resulted in part from our very diversity and from the curious way in which our several personalities seemed to fit in with each other, the limitations and idiosyncrasies of each other being offset and harmonized by the complementary qualities of the rest." They were bound as well by a mystic sense of common identity: "And there were times when it led us, by imperceptible stages, to a deepened intimacy, in which the inmost quests and experiences of the soul were freely expressed, and each grew conscious of our essential unity, as of a larger self which included us all."[81] Representing unity in diversity, the group suggests one possible resolution to the tensions, addressed by John Dewey and Leonard Woolf, between individualism and society in a democratic state.

But what most united the group was their interest in "Cosmic Consciousness" – the title of a pamphlet that Wallace wrote after his mother's death and the title of a book extolling Walt Whitman, written by a North American visitor to the group, Dr. Richard Maurice Bucke.[82] For Whitman became the inspiring presence in the group; perhaps more strongly than anything else, they were united in their shared conviction of Whitman's preeminence as a writer and a thinker, claiming him to be "the greatest epochal figure in all literature."[83] Such an intellectual passion among men not in intellectual professions stirs Woolf's admiration and optimism much more than the "well tended and long established" fires burning at Oxford and Cambridge; when, she notes, "one stumbles by chance upon an isolated fire burning brightly without associations or encouragement to guard it, the flame of the spirit becomes a visible hearth where one may warm one's hands" (*E* II:205). Woolf's tone is one of absolute sincerity and respect; her only irony is that the historical fame of Bolton rests on its cotton market, not on these young men.

Woolf's admiration for these readers spills over to her admiration for Whitman when two of the Lancashire company finally cross the Atlantic to meet him. For Woolf celebrates in Whitman a "new type of hero"

(*E* 11:206), just as Whitman before her discovered a new heroic in "the average of the American people" (207). Surprising and slightly shocking his visitors at first with his simple, homely manner, his rough ways, his resemblance to a "retired farmer," Whitman ultimately impresses more profoundly with the message that "he had no relish for a worship founded upon the illusion that he was somehow better or other than the mass of human beings" (206). He is no less "wise," no less "free-thinking" for making his "common humanity" the dominant note. And the same easy commerce with his readers marks his relations with his "great" English contemporaries, Symonds, and Tennyson, and Carlyle: "Their names dropped into his talk as the names of equals" (206). Then, just as Woolf was later to quote, in *A Room of One's Own*, Sir Arthur Quiller-Couch's words "the poor poet has not...a dog's chance" (*R* 162) so, in her review, she singles out Whitman's reported words, "no man can become truly heroic who is really poor."[84] In the democratic vision, there is no elevation of priests; there is also no acceptance of poverty.[85]

In the context of the war, Woolf heard one kind of democratic talk in Beatrice Webb's monologues in which "every tenth word was 'committee'" (written by Leonard, *D* 1:74), in meetings where listeners "[didn't] pay much attention" and there were "no questions asked" (*D* 1:76), at lectures that started with "everyone agreeing of course beforehand" (83), and with late-arriving speakers who exhibited "more words than brain" (90).[86] Although she described the 1917 club as "a success" and a "lure" (99, 102) and could envy the range of Leonard's activities (82), she was unstintingly critical of political method. But in contrast to organized political work, in which she admired the goal but generally despaired of the process, there was everything about Whitman and his readers to like: openness, honesty, kindliness, equality. The Lancashire group "could broach the most intimate and controversial matters frankly and without fear of giving offence"; as for Whitman, "in his opinion it behoved him to 'give out or express what [he] really was, and if [he] felt like the devil, to say so!'" (*E* 11:205, 206). And Woolf emphasizes not only the readers' respect for the writer, but the writer's affection for his readers: "Whitman as he lay dying had the thought of 'those good Lancashire chaps' in his mind" (205). Not surprisingly, she ends her essay with the image of "an 'immense background or vista' and stars shining more brightly than in our climate" (207).

In place of a capital-D Democratic Society, Woolf found, in Whitman's extended circle, a democratic culture of equality in daily life and a truly democratic discourse. The aims of peace and democracy, so fervently sought by many formal organizations of her time, were realized in Whitman's democratic vision and his democratic relation to his common readers. Instead of a retreat from political issues, the Whitman review points the way to a political answer. The essay is somewhat uncharacteristic of Woolf in its non-ironized, straightforward manner, although the same could be said about her essay on Thoreau the previous year. Both Whitman and Thoreau struck a sympathetic chord with her, perhaps because of her Carlylean sympathies for a movement "that represented the effort of one or two remarkable people to shake off the old clothes which had become uncomfortable to them and fit themselves more closely to what now appeared to them to be the realities" (*E* 11:134). Yet, at the same time as she upheld Whitman as an ideal, she did not confuse *his* common readers with the common readers of her own time. Nor did she ignore the awkward, discomforting questions that a thorough extension of the democratic principle would entail. The modern crowd, the modern mass of people, was quite unlike the intimate group of Whitman and his "Lancashire chaps."

WOOLF AND MODERN CROWDS

Despite the commonalities linking Woolf to forms of nineteenth-century democratic thought, her concerns are differently articulated and inflected because the social and discursive context has changed. Neither Whitman's celebration of the universal heroic nor his intimate commerce with his self-selected readership translated easily into the modern intellectual's attempts to formulate a democratic model of community in an era of cultural standardization and mass manipulation. Escalating noise (in the sense of demands on attention) and expanding scale recast the problems of bringing democracy to birth. Woolf's recognition of mass democracy as the new specter to be faced is the subject she confronts in her representation of modern crowds.

"Thunder at Wembley" (1924)

The British Empire Exhibition at Wembley in 1924 was a landmark celebration of Britain's imperial achievement. So thoroughly did the Exhibition display the flora, fauna, artifacts, and products of much of the world under the British flag that a book with the somewhat immoderate title *Lies and Hate in Education*, published by Hogarth in 1929, used the Exhibition to mark the linking of geography to imperial history in British schools.[87] The Exhibition was also, we might say, a soundmark in mass communication. Not only was the inaugural speech of King George V heard, through wireless amplification, by an estimated 80,000 people in the Stadium; his closing message was immediately cabled around the world. The *Guardian* of the next day placed the first day's attendance at over 100,000, but it estimated that, in Great Britain alone, the speeches and music were heard by over 5,000,000 people.[88]

In both geographical and auditory space, the Exhibition epitomized mass democracy on its vast scale.[89] And Woolf's "Thunder at Wembley" reveals the Exhibition's message as inseparable from its mass packaging. Everything, she objects, is made easily consumable and digestible – nothing to overwhelm the imagination, nothing to shock, everything designed for the middle and to produce a middling, complacent response. But in her sketch, nature – precisely because it *is* uncontrollable – erupts in thunder to disrupt the Exhibition's reductive and regulatory control. The pomp and glory of Empire is magnificently dwarfed by a sudden storm – righting the balance between human and natural elements and suggesting diluvial wrath: "It is nature that is the ruin of Wembley... For that is what comes of letting in the sky" (*E* III:410, 413). In this fantasy of imperial devastation, the British flag seems temporal and transitory against the scope of time and space in the natural realm. Woolf's teaching of the relation between geography and imperialism suggests a rather different lesson from that in the schools.

But *human* nature also participates in the disruption. As the narrator veers toward disillusionment, the sight of the ordinary people visiting the Exhibition helps to restore her faith:

But then, just as one is beginning a little wearily to fumble with those two fine words – democracy, mediocrity – Nature asserts herself where one would least look to find her – in clergymen, school children, girls, young men, invalids in bath chairs... Each is beautiful; each is stately. Can it be that one is seeing human beings for the first time? (411, 412).

Once the content of the Exhibition is redefined as its visitors, their decency, their curiosity, their individuality make it impossible to construct them as "the mass." But the problem remains that the resistance to the commodifying and imperial discourse is all on the part of the narrator; beautiful as they are, the Exhibition's visitors (in this narrative) succumb to its spell, leaving the narrator shocked by their willing complacency: "How, with all this dignity of their own, can they bring themselves to believe in that?" (412). Overwhelmed by the Exhibition's powerful propaganda, humanity too flies to its doom and destruction in the violence of the storm. The packaging has caught the consumer, although there is a kind of patient heroic endurance in the "[c]lergy, school children and invalids" that elevates them above the wild exaggeration of the final apocalyptic release (413).

Woolf's essay thus challenges imperialist rhetoric; it also penetrates to a more disturbing level, interrogating not only what is there to see, but also the perceiver's ability to see it. For if the visitors have succumbed – at least until the storm – to the Exhibition's power, what of her reader? Woolf's fanciful narrative empowers the random personal observations that the Exhibition's regulatory discourse seeks to control, offering a liberating counter-discourse if the reader is open to its play. Imaginative flights resist rationalist control; imperial mapping and mass manipulation of media lose their dominance if the audience thinks back. But an irony is that the essay must distance the reader from the crowd in order to make visible what the crowd does not see: precisely themselves. And to grasp the implications, the reader needs time for reflection – not something that the exhibition space easily allows. Intelligent critical response might transform mass society into participant democracy, but only if there can be also be provision for crucial personal space.

"Abbeys and Cathedrals" (1932)

The modern crowd is more overtly the theme in "Abbeys and Cathedrals" and "This is the House of Commons" – two of the six essays Woolf wrote for *Good Housekeeping*, under the series' heading "The London Scene." Like "Thunder at Wembley," these essays are descriptive and impressionistic, although they provide more of the narrator's thoughts. Instead of exhibitionary space, however, these essays use relations between different spaces in London to expose the ambiguities and tensions of modern life. Superficially, the narrator is a tour guide, displaying some of London's famous historic buildings; but as modern London intrudes, the contrast between past and present becomes the dominant motif. The essays probe the differences between aristocratic and democratic eras, but the trail of shifting perspectives makes absolute polarization difficult to sustain.[90] Woolf's sympathies with common life bolster her antipathies toward the hierarchical and monumentalized past, but she also argues the need to recuperate individualism as an antidote to the standardization of modern life.

"Abbeys and Cathedrals" proceeds like a musical composition, conducting us through alternating spaces of order and chaos, quiet and noise. With a structure not unlike Mussorgsky's "Pictures at an Exhibition," the essay takes us inside a number of London's great landmarks – St. Paul's, St. Mary-le-Bow, and Westminster Abbey – with the connecting leitmotif of the busy street outside. As we enter each interior, the roar from the street is suddenly hushed, and we are enclosed within the reverberating stillness of the past: "Pause, reflect, admire, take heed of your ways," we are exhorted, and in response, "[m]ind and body seem both to widen" and "expand" (*LS* 31). In contrast, the busy street is all speed and movement: omnibuses, motor cars, and vans rush by; people "dive into tubes"; the crowds "scuttle and hurry" or "jostle and skip and circumvent each other" (30; 31). Everything is "hubbub"; everything is "helter skelter" (33). And the life of this street is both "democratic" and marked by sameness. Massified in units of a million, the "Mr. Smiths and Miss Browns... seem too many, too minute, too like each other to have each a name, a character, a separate life of their own" (30). Everything merges into "the hum-drum democratic disorder of the hurrying street" (34).

The spatial relation between historic church and contemporary street charts the difference between a past aristocratic, individual age and the present democratic age of the mass. The past, however, is not a better world to which the narrator longs to return, and Woolf challenges us to decide whether people have actually changed or whether the change has to do with the kinds of perception and interaction possible in a modern, mass society. If people now "*seem* to have shrunk and become multitudinous and minute instead of single and substantial," and "*seem*... too like each other to have each a name" (30; emphasis added), the essay pushes us to question the grounds of that seeming. Much of the perceived grandeur of the past has to do with the aura of rank, which the narrator succinctly punctures: "Often it is only the greatness of their birth that has exalted them" (33). Even the "more potent royalty," the "dead poets," show the effect of strain; their statues stand "transfixed" in "splendid crucifixion," like dead gods sacrificed to preserve a belief in the mind and the will (34). Correspondingly, the indistinguishability of the faces in the modern crowd has less to do with actual change than with the present lack of time and space for observation. Pointing to the eighteenth-century tomb of an ordinary citizen in St. Mary-le-Bow, the tour guide ironically contrasts "the space that the dead enjoy compared with what the living now enjoy," noting that the same area might now "serve almost for an office and demand a rent of many hundreds a year" (30, 31). But there is also a change in discursive ground that regulates different kinds of perception: the lengthy inscription on the tomb recalls an earlier world that allowed time and space for reflection, whereas the matter of rents foregrounds the economy of the fast-paced, modern business world: "The mere process of keeping alive needs all our energy. We have no time... to think about life or death" (31).

What happens then to individual human life, given the scale and speed of the modern world? Woolf answers with images of both merging and withdrawal. The next place in the tour, the church of St. Clement Danes, is yet another historical site, but – by virtue of its location on an island in the middle of the busy Strand – it sits directly in the flow of London traffic. And here the ceremony of tradition interfaces with the democratic hubbub of the city. Springing from a car, a bridal party speeds into the church and, in the integrated voices of the London soundscape, the "roar" of the bells – the famous chimes of Oranges and Lemons – harmonizes with "the roar of omnibuses" (35). What, from the Abbey, had seemed to be "the flood and waste of average human life" now, in the city, appears as "the full tide and race of human life" (34, 35). Although still with the anonymity imposed by the narrator's distant perspective, the bride and bridegroom testify to the endurance of human passions, even in a helter skelter world.

But there remains the question of contemplation. The tour, however, encompasses yet one more city space – this time, a quiet public garden on the site of an old graveyard, where the tombstones propped up along the walls further enclose the sheltered space. Removed, like the churches, from the noise of the city, the garden is nevertheless a place of democratic common life: its inhabitants are mothers, nursemaids, children, an old beggar scattering crumbs from his meal to the sparrows. It is also a place for a reader and for the reading, too, of long works: "Here one might sit and read *Pamela* from cover to cover" (35). The garden inserts a space, in the accelerated time of modernity, for private reflection; it juxtaposes to the business world the alternate discourse of the everyday. And, as an old graveyard, it is a reminder of different perspectives, different proportions, which need to be translated and transposed into modern life. The walk through London thus ends with a trope of substitution: the public garden in place of the public monument, the ordinary individual in place of the heroic statue. Furthermore, in this alternative democratic space, anonymity acquires a positive meaning; here finally is a place where "the dead sleep in peace" (36). Part of the natural rhythm of the garden, they resign "[u]nreluctantly... their human rights to separate names or peculiar virtues" (36). Part of the continuance of the natural world, they merge into the larger, communal life evoked by Whitman's cosmic consciousness. The garden is merely a little oasis – some might argue, an idyllic escape. But it argues the need to carve out personal space, for quiet living, for reading, in the midst of the modern mass democratic world.

"This is the House of Commons" (1932)

By carving out a space for reading and for everyday life, Woolf signals one means of fostering the individual in mass society. But since this portrait of the cultural democratic lacks a public dimension, the next essay turns to the parliamentary democratic by taking the tour group to the House of Commons. Again we encounter the swirling crowd, "passing and repassing... nodding and laughing and running messages and hurrying" and again we note the venerable and distinctive figures of the great statesmen of the past, memorialized in the imposing statues outside the House (*LS* 37). And the same tension between the distinctiveness of the past and massification of the present persists: although the proceedings in the House testify to the portentous victory that "we common people" won so long ago, there seems to be an enormous gap between the "[m]atters of great moment" in process of determination and the undistinguished and indistinguishable appearances of the men making the decisions (38, 41). Seeking the marks of individual life, the narrator questions, "how... are any of these competent, well-groomed gentlemen going to turn into statues?" (40).

Although the narrative point of view is firmly rooted in the "we" of the common people, the need for heroic models persists. Lacking the oratorical flourishes and idiosyncrasies of earlier political figures, the narrator complains, modern parliamentarians are no more impressive than the average man. But it was, we might wonder, precisely such lack of difference that Woolf admired in Whitman. Furthermore, the view now seems dangerously on the edge of class bias: the historical figures Gladstone, Pitt, and Palmerston all had fathers in the peerage, whereas, among the current parliamentarians, Stanley Baldwin was the son of an ironmaster and Arthur Henderson, the son of a cotton spinner. Yet the two contemporaries singled out as potential sculptor's material are William Jowitt and Ramsay MacDonald – the first from yet another mercantile family, this time in the wool industry, and the second, the illegitimate son of a servant. Woolf thus swerves away from class as a determinant and offers numerous other reasons to explain the prevailing machine-like stamp.

There is, to begin, the speed of modern life. In the past, there was time for individuality to unfold, time for the elaborate oratory that, however manipulative, nevertheless left an immense impression of individual skill. The faster pace is inseparable from the increased complexity of the proceedings; the scope of events now dealt with requires a devolution of personal power to the power of a committee, with the result that the "intricacies and elegancies of personality are trappings that get in the way of business"

(42). The modern audience is also larger, more diverse: these are speeches directed not to the "small separate ears" of those present in the House, but to men and women everywhere – "in factories, in shops, in farms on the veldt, in Indian villages" (43). Impersonality is, in this context, not a defect but a fundamental aspect of good parliamentary discourse. If statues then become increasingly "monolithic, plain and featureless," it is because the statesman's performance as an instrument of the state, rather than his personal character, is now the significant marker of success (42). Again, we are warned never to take Woolf's words out of context: she nostalgically recalls the desire for heroes but then dispels that desire by showing the different needs of a different time.

But the essay ends with a further shift, turning from the parliamentary members to the inclusive realm of the people. At the end of the tour, we pause by one last site, the vast space of Westminster Hall. Although originating as a place for royal entertainments in the reign of William II, this Hall held the first meetings of the Council that evolved into Parliament; it later housed the courts of law and was used for state trials; it had latterly become a place of public ceremonies. As a Hall of the people, it offers a fitting trope for Woolf's democratic modern age, marking the historical shift from the age of sculpture to the "age of architecture": "Let us see whether democracy which makes halls cannot surpass the aristocracy which carved statues" (43). And here modernity's expansion of scale is a positive change, since the vastness of the hall figures the inclusiveness of the whole.

But the new democracy can be anticipated with anxiety just as the old aristocracy can be rejected with regret. As we have seen, in his six-part BBC series (delivered just months after Woolf wrote "The London Scene") Leonard identified "standardization" as a disease that democracy must confront. In Woolf's Westminster Hall, democratic dreams are interrupted by the regulatory figures of policemen, reminding us that movement in the Hall is controlled. Conversely, as a place haunted by such heroic figures as Charles I, Thomas More, and Guy Fawkes, the Hall stirs old desires for individual life. Just as individual freedom was essential to Leonard's definition of democracy, so Woolf longs for a space for "the abnormal, the particular, the splendid" in hers (*LS* 44). However, although the future is not envisaged with unqualified optimism, the direction Woolf proposes is not resurrecting the past. Instead, she images the more complex and distant ideal of retaining the individualism that an aristocratic age fostered, but reconstituting it in a new democratic form. It may take a hundred years, or "some stupendous stroke of genius," but if individualism could be fused with inclusiveness and equality, then "both will be combined, the vast hall and the small, the particular, the individual human being" (44).[91]

Woolf's vision of a democratic future in the interwar period was more tempered and qualified than her fond recreation of Whitman's intimate relation with his common readers. She endorsed Whitman's communal democratic dream, but she had to confront the cultural parameters of her own world and the changing forms of organization and communication in her time. Was society capable of functioning in mass terms without succumbing to the forces of regulation and standardization? And if escalating scale meant increasing speed, what could be done to protect and foster the reflection necessary for individual thought? For Woolf, and for many writers and educators of her time, these questions placed additional stress on the intellectual's role. How could an intellectual culture, largely created by an educationally and economically privileged few, be passed on to a new audience consisting of the many? And how could the new audience become involved in the democratic creation of the intellectual culture of the future? In Woolf's approach to this predicament, she attempted a complex negotiation between rejecting the privilege inherent in aristocratic systems and retaining the advantages of individual freedom that such privilege often produced. And she insisted that the democratic world of the future could only be determined by an inclusive, dialogic communal voice.

"Memories of a Working Women's Guild" (1930; 1931)

In 1930, Woolf agreed to write an introduction for *Life As We Have Known It* (1931), a collection of narratives by Co-operative Working Women. But rather than a general introduction, Woolf wrote an open letter to her friend Margaret Llewelyn Davies, the editor who put the collection together. Since this publication gave Woolf a chance to address a larger and more inclusive constituency of common readers, her choice not to address a broad audience has been seen as her inability to go beyond her privileged position as a member of the literary elite.[92] She has been criticized for presenting her own, not always flattering, impressions of the working women and for focusing on literary issues rather than the women's lives – problems that were both raised by Davies and acknowledged by Woolf herself (*L* IV:286–87). Viewed another way, however, Woolf's use of the epistolary form allows her to avoid both the position of "foreign expert" and what we now term appropriation of voice. Her writing voice is personal and situated, rejecting the universalizing of discourse implicit in the standard preface. Even more important, given her concept of democratic community, the form of a letter establishes an equal relation between her words and those of the contributors to the collection. Her personal voice matches the personal voices of the women; possibly, too, since the last part of the book consists of extracts from the women's letters, Woolf's letter was meant as complementary to their own. For a balanced juxtaposition is essential to the argument she makes: the democratic art of the future must be made from an inclusive mix of voices in dialogue and exchange. Fraught as it may be, she must place her own writing voice in relation to the voices of others to prefigure the clashes and the cross-fertilizations that will arise from differing but interacting views.[93]

Opening with a flashback to a Guild meeting in 1913, Woolf situates herself as a member of a privileged class yet shows her position to be a source of irritation, frustration, and depression. Material grounds separate her from the working-class speakers and blatant inequality makes sympathy manufactured and honesty difficult. She is an outsider, cast into the ignominious role of "benevolent spectator" (*CE* IV:136). Writing from the perspective of 1930, however, she finds that distance enables her now to be ruthlessly direct about her views. She criticizes the way the working women imitated the discourse of the male establishment – including insignia of office – while they derided the less reprehensible manners of middle-class "ladies." She finds the stark prose of their political speeches lacking the unconscious suggestiveness that spins webs between minds. Yet she acknowledges that the luxury of valuing "detachment and imaginative breadth" (146) depends on the absence of material anxieties. Thought is not, Woolf reminds us, free; it requires time, let alone the basics of a dinner on the table at the end of the day. And for the kind of expansive holistic thought she has in mind, travel – even if it is simply the imaginative travel that comes from broad reading – is crucial. And so, as in *A Room of One's Own*, Woolf makes statements that, out of context, might seem to deny genius to working women, but again, her point is that material conditions bring genius to birth. As she made clear in the earlier work, her goal for both women and the working class is not subsistence living but enough money to nourish the imagination and, for genius to have equal access to such nourishment, the socio-economic conditions must be reformed.

At the same time, Woolf does not assume that middle-class or upper middle-class writing is the standard to which all writing should aspire. In her attempt to present a balanced relationship, she recognizes lack on her side as well. The dominant literature has become subject to middle-class convention, "to wearing tail coats and silk stockings and [being] called Sir or Madam" and in the process something "desirable, stimulating" has been lost (141, 140). What it lacks is precisely the imaginative vigor in the words of the working-class women. Even their political speeches contained "the quality that Shakespeare would have enjoyed," showing that these women were not "downtrodden, envious, and exhausted," but "humorous and vigorous and thoroughly independent" (141). It is probably impossible for Woolf either to criticize or to praise without giving offence, but her move is an attempt to establish a level ground with strengths and weaknesses on both sides. And to assert that equality, Woolf has to oppose the common denigration of the artist as one not living in the "real" world. She asks for space, in the democratic world, for her version of reality too: "no working man or woman works harder with his hands or is in closer touch with reality than a painter with his brush or a writer with his pen" (140–41). I do not think that Woolf is here carelessly eliding the differences between "crafts" and paid labor;[94] in the context I have been showing of a general cultural turn against the highbrow, she is claiming the equal value of different kinds of work, of different kinds of contact with the real. Trying to avoid the imputations of superiority to *either* side, she asks for equal exchange: "For we have as much to give them as they to give us" (141).

We see then, why Woolf in this essay focuses on writing, since it is literature, in her view, that holds the potential of bringing people together in a common community. Years after the Guild meeting and its speeches, when Woolf is given the collection of working women's autobiographical selections to read, the writings suddenly open to her the world that lies behind their earlier practical demands and statements of fact. Having shown the almost impenetrable barrier forged by class, Woolf shows how narrative eats through the barriers separating the two groups. In a combinatory vision, she suggests that, if the working women's vocabularies, their images, their scenes could combine with "the wit and detachment, learning and poetry" contributed by their middle- and upper-class sisters, together women might produce the great literature of the future (141). And Woolf images the force of these working-class women as the volcanic flame that will eventually burn through class distinctions, "melt[ing] us together so that life will be richer and books more complex, and society will pool its possessions instead of segregating them" (141–42). If a democratic future is possible, she suggests, it will be the power of the working-class women that will bring it about.

"The Niece of an Earl" (1928; 1932); "Poetry, Fiction and the Future" (1927)

The combinatory art of the future is the heart of Woolf's essay "The Niece of an Earl." Like William Morris's *News from Nowhere*, Woolf's essay connects the traditional form of the English novel to the capitalist system; however, whereas Morris's old grumbler argues that the spirit of competition and progress has given the novel liveliness and a sense of adventure, the benefit Woolf finds in class distinctions is the rich territory they have provided for satire.[95] Woolf's own satirical barbs, however, target the novelists themselves – the unquestioned assumption, for example, shared by Meredith and his unresisting readers, that a General would *naturally* give his coat an "extra brush" before proceeding to visit the "niece of an Earl" (*CR* 2:214).[96] Then, whereas in *News from Nowhere*, Morris pits the richness of the novel against the unhappiness and inequalities that are additionally the fruit of a competitive society, for Woolf, the cost of the "complicated comedy" is its toll in excluded voices (216). In British society, Woolf argues, novelists have come primarily from the middle class, since, in a capitalist economy, this is the one class to whom writing presents itself as an obvious, accessible profession. In consequence, the aristocracy are present as portraits, not voices, and the working class are generally reduced to signifiers for the "evils of the social system."

Woolf thus leads her own reader beyond her initial mockery of the content of class distinctions to a more fundamental critique of discriminatory discourse. Her most damaging analysis is that the class system in itself prohibits an inclusive demographic expansion of voice. Aristocrats contribute little since they seldom write novels, especially novels about themselves – the only social rank they understand. The middle-class writer is separated from the working class by the very conditions of success: "life is so framed that literary success invariably means a rise, never a fall, and seldom, what is far more desirable, a spread in the social scale. The rising novelist is never pestered to come to gin and winkles with the plumber and his wife" (217). For the aspiring working-class writer, the problem is even more insurmountable: acquiring the middle-class discourse of the novelist either produces a split-consciousness in working-class writers or distances them from their own communities: "For it is impossible, it would seem, for working men to write in their own language about their own lives. Such education as the act of writing implies at once makes them self-conscious, or class-conscious, or removes them from their own class" (218).[97]

It is important that we not mistake as universal judgment what Woolf intends as localized critique. The problem she identifies lies not in the abilities of working-class writers but with a discriminatory, hierarchical class system that privileges middle-class discourse as the prevailing literary mode. But future possibilities are not circumscribed by this present: "it may well be," she states, "that we are on the edge of a greater change than any the world has yet known" (218). Woolf's hopeful ending heralds a new paradigm so radically different that it is not thinkable in present paradigmatic terms. In her envisioned classless world, where there would be no generals, no earls, no nieces, maybe even no coats – a gesture to *Sartor Resartus* – certainly there is no need to imagine the continuance of the class-derived genre of the novel. But having said that a writer, in the English class system, "cannot escape from the box in which he has been bred" (216–17), Woolf refuses to confine the future to the box of her own definition. All she can ethically put on the page is a question mark: "The art of a truly democratic age will be – what?" (219).

Woolf's interrogative points, however, toward a form that would be more "elastic" and less "hide-bound" (218). In another essay, written just a year earlier, Woolf suggests that the new art of democracy will be one that transgresses borders, inscribes variousness, and gives shape to incongruities. "Poetry, Fiction and the Future" was initially a paper read to students at the Oxford University English Club; as a talk addressed to the "young" (*L* III:380), it seems designed to stimulate, to suggest possibilities, to open minds. Unfortunately, when Leonard posthumously reprinted this essay, he changed its title to "The Narrow Bridge of Art," inadvertently contributing to critical misunderstandings of Woolf's ideas. Woolf's statement that "You cannot cross the narrow bridge of art carrying all its tools in your hands" (*E* IV:438) occurs in a passage that acknowledges the inevitable omissions in even such a heterogeneous work as *Tristram Shandy*. Although Sterne, for Woolf, was a writer who could move easily and naturally back and forth between prose and poetry, his fanciful flights nevertheless entailed a sacrifice of daily life: he had to leave out the "more substantial vegetables" on the ground. Yet Sterne's limitation functions in Woolf's argument not, as Leonard's title implies, to urge selectivity but to explain constant experimentation. What drives the novel forward is the writer's incessant desire to include a little more than has been netted in the past: "Life is always and inevitably much richer than we who try to express it" (439).

The true subject of the essay is the discursive meaning of genre and the growing disjunction between prevailing genres and the perspectives, problems, and issues of the day. The poetic drama, Woolf suggests, was happily compatible with the Elizabethan mind; the lyric poem, with the Romantic. But neither form offers an adequate envelope for the "tumultuous" and "contradictory" experience of life in the modern, urban, technological world (438). Leading her audience on an imaginary walk "through the streets of any large town," Woolf directs attention to the compartmentalization and barricaded privacy of the dwellings, yet also to the cataclysmic reconfigurations of social space effected by radio broadcasting, now penetrating individual households with news from all over the globe (432–44). Sketching in a new mental mapping, Woolf indicates that the modern mind goes everywhere, but it also moves more rapidly and hovers in precarious balance on the borders of discordant territories.

Given the oppositions, the discordancies, the multiple modalities of this new life, Woolf turns to the novel, that most cannibalistic of forms (435), as the genre most able to adapt to modern sensibilities because it has the greatest potential for change. But this very capacity for protean transformation means that, in "ten or fifteen years' time," the novel will be scarcely recognizable by the same name (435). It will absorb poetry, it will absorb the drama, it will record the fact and trace the whisper: "It will take the mould of that queer conglomeration of incongruous things – the modern mind" (436). And, most pertinently for my discussion, Woolf construes this new hybrid form as democratic, in both its inclusiveness and its elasticity: "Therefore it will clasp to its breast the precious prerogatives of the democratic art of prose; its freedom, its fearlessness, its flexibility" (436). Historically, she has indicated, prevailing genres have expressed the sensibilities and ideologies of their times; the genre of the democratic age must accordingly give shape to diversity and difference. Since Woolf's own subsequent fiction moves increasingly toward hybrid experimental forms, this essay can easily be read as an articulation of her own aims. But we should not overlook Woolf's invocation of what is "scarcely visible, so far distant it lies on the rim of the horizon" (439). As its original title suggests, "Poetry, Fiction and the Future" looks forward to "what has not been expressed" and a future generation who will, in ways not possible to anticipate, find new forms to express it. Woolf may write *toward* her view of the democratic society. But until all voices have been added, democracy remains a question mark on the page.[98]

Democratic highbrow as a common goal

Virginia Woolf's ideal community of writers and readers is neither paradoxical nor logically inconsistent, however much it falls short of being fully imagined and achieved. Its basis is an educated people, united not in agreement but in dialogic discussion, equal in the opportunities to develop their minds and, as classless intellectuals, equal in exchange. As a concept, "democratic highbrowism" exists as a value, a goal to direct present work. Although it is the product of desire, it is the common desire that prompts most of us to imagine, in the words of Northrop Frye, "the ideal existence of a world beyond [our] own interests: a world of health for the doctor, of justice for the lawyer, of peace for the social worker, a redeemed world for the clergyman, and so on."[99] Woolf's ideal was certainly not an achievement for which her own writing was the prototype; it was in fact something that she knew she could not, by definition, model in her own practice. Highbrow writing can only become democratic with radical change, and change can only come about through communal effort – through the participation, in the making of highbrow culture, of voices previously occluded, marginalized, or suppressed. Woolf attacked the privilege ensconced within the existing high culture; she went further in using her own abilities and advantages in an attempt to strengthen other minds; but she did not presume to configure what the new inclusive intellectual world would be like. The achievement of democratic highbrowism would require the collaborative work of a much broader group of readers and writers than the literate intellectual community of her own time.

I do not suggest that Woolf's ideal was unproblematic, or that she saw it as being so, or that her writing practice, both private and public, was thoroughly and consistently congruous with its principles. But I do propose that, in bringing together the two apparently contradictory aims of democracy and highbrowism, Woolf confronted one of her era's most urgent public questions and, in doing so, refused to reduce its complex and challenging tensions to any simple schemata of opposing dichotomies. I began this chapter by citing Raymond Williams's belief that "[w]hat can really be contributed is not resolution but perhaps, at times, just that extra edge of consciousness." If we shift our own focus from advancing truth claims to confronting the challenges that Woolf's writings bring to light, we may indeed find "that extra edge of consciousness" in the "active relationships and conflicts" that make up our world.

CHAPTER 2

Woolf, English studies, and the making of the (new) common reader

But why teach English? As you say, all one can do is to herd books into groups, and then these submissive young, who are far too frightened and callow to have a bone in their backs, swallow it down; and tie it up; and thus we get English literature into ABC; one, two, three; and lose all sense of what its about.

Virginia Woolf, L v:450

I was glad to see the C.R. all spotted with readers at the Free Library.

Virginia Woolf, D v:329

BOOKS, PUBLISHING, AND READERS

Reading as a cultural issue in the 1920s and 1930s

If the democratic principle entails a commitment to classless intellectuals, then it also requires that education not be constrained or governed by class. But England in the early twentieth century faced innumerable barriers to the goal of such democratic education. Education had been the domain of a privileged class, and the universities had long been formed by those privileged classes. Verbal, written literacy was arguably at the core of the best education, but reading abilities and cultural literacy levels across the population were low. Mass production was flooding the market with inferior reading materials, while the cost of small-scale printing was soaring, so that quality publication was becoming harder to support. In this context, reading – and, more specifically, the question of how to educate the reader – emerged as one of the most pressing issues of the time.

The crisis of general literacy has been generally understood as a key social issue of the nineteenth century. In his ground-breaking study, *The English Common Reader: A Story of the Mass Reading Public, 1800–1900*, Richard Altick argues that concerns about reading provide "a strong link of continuity" between the nineteenth and twentieth centuries, to the extent that "the problems posed by the mass reading public of [the twentieth century] are essentially those of the nineteenth century as well."[1] But while the promotion of reading was not a new project in Woolf's time, the problems had become more complex. Although the nineteenth century had been able to achieve almost universal *functional* literacy, *cultural* literacy then became the immediate and more difficult goal.

At the turn of the century more people could read and write in England than ever before, with the proportion of assessed illiteracy constituting only 2.8 percent of men and 3.2 percent of women; however, the almost shocking reality was that, at the beginning of the 1920s, fewer than 10 percent of the children who attended elementary school went on to secondary education.[2] The acquisition of reading skills was demonstrably evident in the rapid growth in the sales of daily newspapers after the war, but a series of reports from the Board of Education raised significant concerns about the low levels of expression and understanding.[3] *The Way Out*, a study produced in 1923 by the British Institute of Adult Education, outlined "the deficiencies of the reading ability of the English public," arguing that the problem lay in "citizens not knowing *how* to read in order to extract meaning."[4] The ever-increasing volume of printed materials added to the difficulties. In 1899, Dr. Richard Garnett, the Keeper of Printed Books at the British Museum, graphically depicted the problem: the machinery required for newspaper production was "capable of producing more literary matter in an hour than all the scribes of Alexandria could have turned out in a generation." With such rapid acceleration in production, and the growing expansion of available texts by world literatures in translation (Garnett was writing an introduction to *The Universal Anthology*), the process of "[s]ifting and selection," presented itself as "an imperative necessity."[5] But how to achieve that selection was the fundamental problem. As the historian G. M. Trevelyan later put it, "Education...has produced a vast population able to read but unable to distinguish what is worth reading."[6]

In response to these widespread concerns, the period of post-war reconstruction witnessed the introduction of numerous measures to improve both secondary education and the dissemination of books. In 1918, the Education Act designed by H. A. L. Fisher (Virginia Woolf's cousin) raised the minimum school-leaving age from ten to fourteen (where it remained until raised to fifteen in 1947); in 1919, the Ministry of Reconstruction's Adult Education Committee produced an influential report arguing the need, as "an inseparable aspect of citizenship," for a wide range of educational opportunities that could be continuous and "lifelong."[7] In January 1924, the minority Labour government under Ramsay MacDonald approved funding to all non-vocational forms of adult education, and the first World Conference on Adult Education was held in 1929.[8] Organizations to promote books and reading included the National Book Council, established in 1925, the Book Society, formed in 1927 (one year later than the American Book-of-the-Month Club on which it was modeled), and the Book Guild, introduced in 1930.[9]

At a less institutional level, the 1920s and the 1930s were flooded with popular books and articles on reading, written for academic and non-academic audiences alike. Characteristic examples can be seen in W. E. Simnett's *Books and Reading*, which offered practical advice and direction for the users of public libraries, and F. H. Pritchard's *Books and Readers*, which presented vignettes in the history of readers and advice on how to read, accompanied by a photograph of the reading room in the British Museum. Another popular form modeled reading through personal narrative: Hugh Walpole's *Reading*, for example, provided an informal, accessible account of his reading life, sub-divided into three sections: "Reading for Fun," "Reading for Education," "Reading for Love." A more academic contribution came from Sir Arthur Quiller-Couch, whose collection of Cambridge lectures, *On the Art of Reading*, advocated the reading of English literature (along with a literary study of the Bible) as a way of interpreting "the common mind of civilization" and uplifting the soul. If Quiller-Couch was representative of an older, generalist discourse, Ezra Pound and F. R. Leavis of the younger generation turned to more rigorous methodological and canonical debate. Pound's *How to Read* and Leavis's *How to Teach Reading: A Primer for Ezra Pound* clashed over the merits of classical versus English canons and the values of technique versus meaning, each generating its own list of essential texts. Then there were the numerous self-help and self-study guides, such as the Pocket University's *The Guide to Reading*, which indexed a collection of inexpensive and transportable reading and included a daily reading schedule as well.[10]

Finally, public consciousness about reading was nowhere more evident than on the BBC. As a public and socially responsible institution, the broadcasting company assumed an informal educational role with a success that might be gauged through the response to Harold Nicolson's series of talks, *The New Spirit in Literature*, in 1931. As if casting Nicolson as an early Oprah Winfrey, the *Listener* reported, "His recommendation of Samuel Butler's autobiographical novel, *The Way of All Flesh*, has produced a phenomenal demand for copies of the book from booksellers all over the country. In fact, supplies are almost exhausted, and at the moment copies are

practically unobtainable." That *The Way of All Flesh* should, in 1931, achieve
the popularity of the Harry Potter books in 2000 may lead to some amusing
reflections on historical difference but the sell-out of Butler was, according
to the *Listener*, "but one indication of the stimulus which broadcasting is
giving to-day to bookselling."[11] Regular broadcast series included *Books of
the Week*, *Bestsellers of Yesterday*, and *Books and Authors*; regular reviewers
included, in addition to Harold Nicolson, Vita Sackville-West, Desmond
MacCarthy, and E. M. Forster.

In this context, Woolf's *The Common Reader* and *The Common Reader:
Second Series* are in no way unusual in their concerns, nor are her many
titles that refer specifically to reading: "In a Library," "Hours in a Library,"
"To Read or Not to Read," "Reading," "The Wrong Way of Reading," "On
Re-reading Novels," "How Should One Read a Book?," "All About Books,"
and her last two unfinished essays, "Anon" and "The Reader." Reading for
Woolf was crucial personal sustenance but writing about reading was part
of the public consciousness of her time.[12]

Reading, economics, and the highbrow press

All this activity around reading, however, speaks more to its threatened
survival than to its flourishing life. Despite Nicolson's effect on the sales
of Samuel Butler, Forster ended his 1932 broadcast series by reflecting anx-
iously on the encroachments of new media and his fear that microphone
and cinema are "turning us from readers into listeners and lookers."[13] In
addition, economies of scale in the publishing industry gave a decided
advantage to mass production and wide circulation, raising the cost and diminishing the visibility of limited-circulation, highbrow books. Following
his pessimistic statement about the general public's level of reading abilities,
Trevelyan gave voice to the commonly expressed fear of intellectual annihi-
lation by market forces catering to the tastes and abilities of the "half" and
"quarter" educated: "Whether in the twentieth or twenty-first centuries
the lower forms of literature and journalism will completely devour the
higher has yet to be seen."[14] Market forces caused an increasing migra-
tion not only toward entertainment but also away from the written word.
Q. D. Leavis, as part of her extensive documentation of declining intellectual standards, noted that the Readers' Library, first marketed through
Woolworth's in 1924, was initially an attempt to bring cheap accessible
editions to the working class; however, she continued, because it was necessary for each volume to sell "hundreds of thousands of copies," titles were

rapidly dominated either by novels that had been made into films, or film plots reconstructed into novels.[15]

We see, then, two separate though related strands in the discussion: promoting serious reading because it is a genuine public need, and defending serious reading because it is a threatened economy. The latter position dominates a series of articles run in the *Nation and Athenaeum* between February and May of 1927, subsequently published by the Hogarth Press as *Books and the Public*. The argument of this collection is that people need to buy more books, but the underlying concern is the survival of the highbrow press. The lead article by the editor, the economist Hubert Henderson, outlined the consequences of the low level of book-buying in England compared to countries such as New Zealand. As Henderson argued, publication costs had risen more than book prices, to the extent that the "large learned work" now required subsidy, while the short pamphlet, because it did not get reviewed, did not generate enough sales to be attractive to booksellers. Grappling with the problem of how to cope with mass commodity culture, Henderson launched a counter-argument for books as an important national resource. Urging that books should be considered basic necessities of daily life, he described publishing as "an industry which plays a much less important part in our economic system than coal or cotton or shipbuilding or iron and steel, but which in the long run affects our national life as profoundly as any of these." The succeeding article by Maynard Keynes argued that the low volumes of sales prohibited economies of scale, putting into jeopardy the livelihoods of booksellers, publishers, and authors. Setting perhaps the target figure that Virginia Woolf was to use one year later in *A Room of One's Own*, Keynes asked, "How many authors are there in England who can reckon on earning from their books above £500 a year on the average?" In a somewhat amusing adoption of oppositional stances, Basil Blackwell and Leonard Woolf debated the merits of advertising: Leonard argued that it added fruitlessly to costs unless timed to coincide with six or seven favorable reviews, Blackwell – perhaps as devil's advocate – proposed the use of "mass-suggestion" in the manner of advertising for cigarettes and whisky. Why not, he somewhat facetiously argued, employ an "expert in mass psychology" to appeal to "the wish to possess," adding that if one generation could be persuaded to buy books by the yard, the next generation might be persuaded to open them. Another contributor considered the threat to the "printed word" posed by the new technologies, warning that "[a]lready television hovers on the brink of becoming what is horrifically called a 'commercial proposition.'"[16]

Just how urgent, however, was the crisis confronting the highbrow press? As a later study undertaken by the Labour Research Board shows, the newspaper trade in the late twenties was flourishing and a publisher like Dent – with its popular Everyman series – was able, in 1926, to bring in a profit of eleven times the invested capital. Despite publishers' laments and threatened wage cuts, the report argued, printing supplies between 1924 and 1930 had dropped in price, no increases were evident in wages, but shareholders and controlling families were drawing in vast sums in the form of directors' salaries and share bonuses. Arguing, it is true, for the cause of improved wages and working conditions for the worker, the report nevertheless had sufficient documentation to conclude that "there is scarcely any other industry in Britain with such a sound financial basis."[17]

The situation at a small press like the Hogarth, however, was materially different. In 1926, the year in which Dent's profits totalled £108,761, Hogarth's net profits were £53.18.2½ – 50 percent of which went to the staff as bonuses.[18] For most of the 1920s, the Press was financially only marginally successful, with final profits below £75 until 1928. Although in 1927 *To the Lighthouse* would help to bring Woolf an income from her books for the first time of over £500 (from both British and American editions), Hogarth's final profit for that year was £64.2.0.[19] Although Altick states that "the 1890s saw the ultimate victory of the cheap-book movement," he is, after all, referring to cheap reprints of the classics or to novels, like Charles Kingsley's, that were viable in a million-copy run.[20] Novels by unknown or lesser known writers, volumes of new poetry, and intellectual pamphlets were a different matter, and Hogarth had, for their size, an expansive and varied list. Hindsight lets us know the comforting conclusion, but the situation in the 1920s augured vulnerability and risk. In consequence, there are two attitudes we might reasonably suppose the Woolfs to hold: a hostility to the mass production of middle and lowbrow literature and an elevation of the highbrow book to a status of special value deserving of its high price.

"Are Too Many Books Written and Published?" (1927)

In July 1927, a few months after the series in the *Nation and Athenaeum* – perhaps indeed spinning out of it – Leonard and Virginia Woolf as publishers broadcast on the topic, "Are Too Many Books Written and Published?"[21] The title clearly tapped into already widely publicized concerns: Was mass publication contributing to the decline of reading standards that were already too low? Was a commodity-driven culture going to ring the death knell for intellectual culture? These are fascinating questions for later press history, but what is most relevant to my discussion is what the modernists thought: How did the Woolfs' broadcast fit into the larger discussions on this matter and how can we relate Virginia's side of the argument to her work as a highbrow reviewer of books? (Note that to preserve clarity in discussing this broadcast, Virginia Woolf will be referred to as "Virginia.")

The radio audience, we must remember, was listening to a staged debate. Rather like the Basil Blackwell/Leonard Woolf exchange, the broadcast assumed deliberately polarized sides, a format common on the BBC, and the genre, for example, in which Harold Nicolson and Vita Sackville-West were later to shine. At the time of the Woolfs' broadcast, however, the BBC was still torn between the desire to stimulate thinking and the perceived need to keep a tight control over the debate. Although "talks" directors like Hilda Matheson tried to use radio as a means to involve the public in current issues, the nature of the BBC as a national institution demanded that it assume a standardizing, neutralizing role, to the extent that listeners' objections to alleged left-wing bias led to a ban on controversy in 1927. Spontaneity was considered too dangerous, so the general procedure for a talk show was that the participants would be invited to the studio for informal conversation, a typist would take notes from which a script would be produced, and the participants would then return to read from the script for live broadcast.[22] The Woolfs – perhaps because of their reputation as writers – were invited to prepare their own script, but it was composed in advance and approved prior to the broadcast.[23]

The existing typescript in the BBC archives uses separate – and therefore distributable – pages for each speaker. The typescript is produced in uniform style. However, only Virginia's papers are numbered, although their spaced numbers leave gaps for the insertion of Leonard's part. Most of Virginia's slight revisions are made in her own hand and over-typed, possibly on a different typewriter. There are a very few changes in a hand that is neither Leonard's nor Virginia's. The evidence suggests that the parts were individually produced and revised but collaboratively reviewed and approved. While likely imposed by the BBC, the debate format was not uncongenial to the Woolfs and they employed it again, in a more limited way, in their later Hogarth pamphlet *Reviewing*. There, although readers have sometimes been shocked by Leonard's apparent attack on Virginia's ideas, the opposition is clearly intended to create a dialogic form: Virginia's opening paragraph states, "The purpose of this paper is to rouse discussion" and Leonard's note opens, "This Pamphlet raises questions" (*CE* II:204, 215). The Woolfs did not avoid controversy and, as I show in the next chapter, the distinctive feature of Virginia's essays is their engagement of contradictory views. For them, however, the BBC talk was a genre not for reductive brow-beating but for complicating thought.

In "Are Too Many Books Written and Published?" the views are not transparently those of the speaker/writer, but polarized for the purpose of lively debate. Leonard is the pessimist, arguing that mass production is destroying the quality press; Virginia performs as the optimist, hopeful that mass circulation will stimulate more people to read and to write. Leonard states that writing has become a mechanical activity, that writers are driven only by vanity, and that the reading public is being diverted into the easier options offered by radio and cinema. Virginia suggests that the need is not for fewer books but for more writers producing fewer books each, and she proposes a fine (amended to a tax) for any author guilty of publishing more than thirty of them. She welcomes an overall increase in publication, however, as a way to broaden the field of writing, away from its current domination by the professional class. While Leonard complains that excess will swamp and obliterate the few valuable works, for Virginia, excess means appetite stimulation: beginning with light reading, readers will naturally progress to the more challenging; if people begin by consuming the sweets, they will soon desire "good beef and mutton."[24] And, to increase the amount of available reading, she urges a neighborhood sharing of individual private libraries. Furthermore, arguing that books should be as cheap to purchase, and as consumable, as a packet of cigarettes, she proposes that first editions be printed on "some perishable material which would crumble to a little heap of perfectly clean dust in about six months time." Books on shelves add to the never-ending work of house-cleaning; disintegrating books – in, it seems, an ecological way – would reduce to a nice little heap of organic waste. Although she allows that second editions "could be printed on good paper and well bound," time-destructing the first edition would reduce housework, give more writers a chance, and put more books into more readers' hands.[25]

The structure of the broadcast is not exactly dialectic, since the conflicts do not move toward synthesis; the pattern is more one of limited concession to the other's argument, followed by a further refinement or qualification that supports the speaker's own view. The speakers move into agreement about the existing state of the publishing industry, the explosion in published materials, and the dramatically variable, and indeed risky, outcomes. But they draw very different implications from the same scenario, largely because Leonard focuses on what has been lost from the past while Virginia speculates on what could be gained in the future. It is Leonard who mourns the loss of the Benjaminian auratic object, the carefully crafted and singular work, likening the change to the replacement of hand-made boots by the machine-made item – a provocative image given the publication of *To the Lighthouse* two months before.[26] It is Virginia who embraces the new economy of proliferation and excess, humorously indulging in rhetorical excess herself as she shifts from the factory to fishing, to gambling, to eating, and then to dirt and organic waste. And, in the interests of democratic production and catholic consumption, she actually advocates expendability and obsolescence. Her extraordinary scheme for disposable books is unlikely meant as a practical proposal (although it interestingly anticipates the advent of electronic books); nevertheless, her argument that books should be both cheap to buy and easy to throw away makes an important ideological point. Locating the book in the realm of everyday use challenges its permanent, sacralized status and demolishes, as she states, the practices of "reading seldom and . . . reading solemnly – both bad things as I think you will agree."[27]

Leonard has the last word in the broadcast, and ends by rather gloomily conceding that nothing can stop people from writing books. But in the debate overall, the Woolfs are fairly successful in stimulating the listener to consider both sides. In the interactive dynamic, it is true, Virginia gets the better role. Leonard appears as the static straight-man, nostalgically confined to the past, while Virginia moves increasingly toward a visionary future. Leonard largely complains; Virginia suggests a course of action. Yet while Virginia's view is the more energizing, I take the Woolfs' collaborative point to be that it is as naïve to ignore material and economic factors as it is unproductive to resist the new economy of excess. Jointly, their modernism is neither aloof from the "real world" nor simply antagonistic to its trends. But the views that Virginia individually expresses – however fanciful or exaggerated – are also fundamentally consistent with her general approach to reading, reflecting her belief, first, that learning can be self-generated and naturally progressive and, secondly, that literature should be part of our ordinary lives. Reading, as she presents it, initiates a process of growth and expansion, but, as the broadcast broadly hints, she sought alternative paths to the way such education was being conducted during her time.

From readers to students

In his sociological model of literary analysis, Pierre Bourdieu calls for an analysis of structural relations in what he terms "the field of cultural production," or the total environment or economy in which a literary or artistic text circulates. This comprehensive field includes not just the work but also "the production of the value of the work," which for Bourdieu involves the various means by which a particular society defines or legitimizes what constitutes writing, defining in turn which particular writers become invested with the greatest symbolic cultural capital.[28] Although Bourdieu focuses primarily on the power invested in the producer and the product, his approach can be usefully adapted to the cultural production of the reader during Woolf's time. The early twentieth century was a time when, as Peter Keating puts it, "readers – or at least one crucial group of readers – were being turned into students";[29] another force of cultural production, as we have seen, aimed to turn readers into buyers, whether of serious limited editions from the quality press or of inexpensive, ephemeral, mass-produced paperbacks. It is within this context of upheaval, transition, and redefinition that Woolf's idea of the common reader – or perhaps common reading – takes shape.

Woolf, I suggest, replaces reader as student and reader as buyer with her own construction of reader as eater. The touchstones of natural appetite and everyday use that we see in "Are Too Many Books Written and Published?" are pervasive throughout her work. Yet, while endowing the reader with an agency somewhat lacking in Bourdieu's model, she understands, at the same time, that our minds do not operate independently of social and physical space. In her expansive, comprehensive construction, the act of reading is a complex product of instinct, of circumstance, and of choice. Her field of cultural production extends broadly, as in pragmatism, to include the operations of "agent, other people, material things, social meanings and arrangements."[30] Such inclusive dynamics emerge clearly in her responses to three specific sites of reading that figured prominently in her time: the university, adult education, and the public library system.

WOOLF, ENGLISH STUDIES, AND THE UNIVERSITY

The institution of English studies

Virginia Woolf's hostility to the institutional practices of the traditional British university is well known. *A Room of One's Own* launches a radical critique of the exclusionary practices on which Oxford and Cambridge were founded, expressing Woolf's frustration as a woman at being locked out and depicting the deformity caused by the male fellows' being locked in. The university's competitive and hierarchical ideology is a target of biting satire in *Three Guineas*, where Woolf's resituating of a photograph of an academic procession in a series with other prominent public images exposes an ethos of dominance throughout British society not different in kind from the ideology driving the German nation to war. Her devastating portrait of Dr. Bentley, Master of Trinity College in the first part of the eighteenth century, exposes the life of the scholar as a mask for "aggression," "defiance," "arrogance," and "tyranny" (*CR* 1:191). She decries "the extraordinary spectacle of men of learning and genius, of authority and divinity, brawling about Greek and Latin texts, and calling each other names for all the world like bookies on a racecourse or washerwomen in the back street" (192–93) – actions which, to Woolf, "appear unhappily characteristic of the profession as a whole" (193). She cites no contemporary instances of learned scholars calling each other "maggot," "vermin," "gnawing rat," and "cabbage head" (194), yet her parting shot leaves progress in doubt: all this, she solemnly assures us, "happened many, many years ago" (195).[31] As for the study of literature, Woolf's position was equally critical. She considered academic reading practices to be as limiting and oppressive as the institutional policies of admission and the systems of honor and reward. In "Hours in a Library," she wrote that "to read on a system, to become a specialist or an authority, is very apt to kill what it suits us to consider the more humane passion for pure and disinterested reading" (*E* 11:55). A large part of the meaning of Woolf's "common reader" would appear to be "not an academic."

Woolf's objections to the academic study of literature, however, need to be read in the context of the embattled position of English studies during this time. At the beginning of the twentieth century, English was a relative newcomer to the university as an independent discipline. Although the first Chair of English Language and Literature in Britain was established in 1828 at the dissenting University College, London, throughout the second half of the nineteenth century, English remained a minor component in the curriculum, entering into university study largely through the newer colleges that were established in Manchester (1850), Leeds (1874), Sheffield (1879), Birmingham (1880), Liverpool (1881), and Nottingham (1881). Since the primary emphasis in these colleges was either technical and scientific or classical and theological, English came into the academy largely in the form of evening extension classes, with attendant assumptions of its peripheral rather than central character. The Merton Chair of English Language and Literature was not established in Oxford until 1885; at Cambridge, the first professorship in English literature finally materialized, after heated debate, in 1911. English did not become a Tripos subject at Cambridge until 1917 and did not qualify as a primary subject for a degree until 1926. The male cohort of Bloomsbury imbibed their English literature indirectly, through the study of history and classics.[32]

As the study of English literature entered the established academic sphere, its disciplinary identity was, not surprisingly, a contested site, plagued by challenges to its legitimacy and respectability. As Anne Samson states, "both the object of study and its methods were matters of dispute within the academic world."[33] In the early nineteenth century, the first Professor of English – the Reverend Thomas Dale – had attempted to introduce a skills-based approach, hoping to promote good reading habits, a literate populace interested in intellectual issues, and a more egalitarian democratic society; however, the pressure on the new discipline to acquire academic respectability rapidly turned its emphasis toward knowledge rather than skills.[34] The precise nature of such knowledge then became a subject of violent factional debate, divided primarily between philological and linguistic study (for many years the foundational approach at Oxford) and the history of English literature and thought (more characteristic of the approach at Cambridge). There were those like John Churton Collins at Oxford, and later Peter Lucas at Cambridge, who considered that English ought to rest, for clarity and rigor, on foundational training in Classics; in a different strain, following the influx into the student body of women and veterans after the First World War, younger faculty like I. A. Richards and F. R. Leavis argued for close reading and analytic textual study, the former for clarifying interpretative systems, the latter for determining and preserving cultural value.

What these controversies demonstrate is the pressure on English to define its institutional role and, in doing so, to negotiate between the older semi-amateur belles-lettres approach and a growing new professionalism. At the time when Woolf was developing her critical approach, the future of English – at least in the traditional universities – seemed to depend on establishing its legitimacy as a respectable area of study, and to do this it had to counter its image as the poor man's classics, overcome its lesser origins in colleges for dissenters, working-class evening colleges, Mechanics' Institutes, and redbrick universities, and refute the perception among the traditionalists at Oxford and Cambridge that it was "a soft option designed to accommodate the weaker students."[35] As Peter Keating points, out, however, the need to delineate disciplinary boundaries was not unique to English. In the process of change, the university was leaving behind old assumptions of unified cultural knowledge and embracing a new disciplinarity, led in the process by such emerging new areas as psychology, sociology, anthropology, and engineering: "It was an age of professionalisation and specialisation, and the study of English Literature followed both of these trends."[36]

But how much did Virginia Woolf know about the controversies surrounding the academic study of English? Her knowledge, as one located by sex and formal education outside the main current of the university, was understandably indirect. The only works on English literature that she reviewed by "professors" (as opposed to critics who occasionally gave university lectures) were Raleigh's *Romance, Two Lectures* (*E* II:73–76) and Clayton Hamilton's *Materials and Methods of Fiction* (*E* III:43–46).[37] And while she began to read I. A. Richards's *Principles of Literary Criticism*, her notes on it suggest she may have gone no further than chapter 1.[38] There is no evidence that she read the new periodicals written primarily for academic audiences – except for the occasional essay in *Scrutiny* – although their emergence dates from this time.[39] But Woolf's life constantly intersected with lives in the university. To select merely a few from a long list: she was acquainted with such renowned academics from the 1860s generation as Goldsworthy Lowes Dickinson, J. M. McTaggart, and Quiller-Couch, all at Cambridge, and she had frequent contact with her cousin H. A. L. Fisher at Oxford; in the next generation, she knew the Cambridge philosophers G. E. Moore and Bertrand Russell; her circle of friends included significant academics of her own generation such as Maynard Keynes, Gerald Shove, and J. T. Sheppard, all at Cambridge, and Arnold Toynbee at Oxford; and she was on intimate terms with two younger members in the new discipline of English at Cambridge, F. L. "Peter" Lucas and Dadie Rylands. Her connections with important women in the university ranged from one of the pioneers in the academy – Jane Harrison in classical archaeology at Cambridge – to the younger Joan Pernel in French and modern languages and Principal of Newnham College from 1923 to 1941.

While these were people whose backgrounds were primarily in history, philosophy, classics, or economics – and this is hardly surprising given the nascent state of English – they were certainly all aware of the controversies over the status of English in the curriculum. Leonard Woolf, for example, though reading classics at Cambridge, had written an undergraduate paper arguing that literary sensibility could not be taught, so rooted was it in one's views on life.[40] Years later, Virginia Woolf might seem to agree. Enjoying T. S. Eliot's mockery of a critic who attributed certain levels of meaning to his poetry that Eliot denied, Woolf recorded:

And we agreed about the infamy of teaching English; the idiocy of lectures; the whole hierarchy of professor, system & so on: at any rate I got him to go some way with me in denouncing Oxford & Cambridge. He learnt (1) self confidence at Oxford; (2) how to write plain English – thats all. I daresay though he will become Prof. of Poetry at Oxford one of these days.[41] (*D* IV:178–79)

This entry, however, occurs in the context of a conversation with Eliot in which Woolf was both impressed with his growing openness and annoyed by the "heavy stone of his self esteem" (178). Eliot's self-important references to "his writing" and his implicit conception of himself as a "great man" galled her, since there was no way she could talk about her own writing in those terms.[42] Pulling Eliot over to agree with her about professorships decreased his distance, but Eliot's discourse reflected precisely the problems in the teaching of English that she deplored.

Explaining "the infamy of teaching English," Woolf targets the "idiocy of lectures" (the construction of active, productive speaker and passive, receptive listener), the "whole hierarchy of professor, system & so on" (the institutional production of a scale of value), and the specific sites of "Oxford & Cambridge" (the inscription of privilege). The objections pertain to the historically situated university, but they are consistent throughout Woolf's career, if anything becoming stronger with the passage of time.[43] In 1935, she wrote to Julian Bell, who was teaching English at Wuhan University in China:

I hope you wont follow Dadies [Rylands] example; I see in the paper hes been made [Cambridge] University lecturer in English for three years. But why teach English? As you say, all one can do is to herd books into groups, and then these submissive young, who are far too frightened and callow to have a bone in their backs, swallow it down; and tie it up; and thus we get English literature into ABC; one, two, three; and lose all sense of what its about. (*L* v:450)

In October 1940, referring to professors from both Oxford and Cambridge, she powerfully summed up her view:

"The complete Insider" – I have just coined this title to express my feeling towards George Trevelyan; who has been made Master of Trinity: whose history of England I began after tea (throwing aside Michelet vol. 15 with a glorious sense of my own free & easiness in reading now). Herbert Fisher is another. So (with a "perhaps") is Maynard. They are Romans not Greeks. I like outsiders better. Insiders write a colourless English. They are turned out by the University machine. I respect them. Father was one variety. I dont love them. I dont savour them. Insiders are the glory of the 19th century. They do a great service like Roman roads. But they avoid the forests & the will o the wisps. (*D* v:333)

Direct and efficient, linear and end-oriented, rational and serviceable, modern academic discourse is, for her, the antithesis of the poetic, the suggestive, the fertile. It is also a segregating discourse, mapping the territories of inside and outside in a manner that, to look forward to Bourdieu, epitomizes the institutional production of cultural legitimacy.

Unfortunately, in Woolf's view, the younger academics showed no signs of improvement. Q. D. Leavis (well before her 1938 attack on *Three Guineas* for its class bias and "sex hostility") actually wrote a favorable review of the collection of working-class women's writing *Life As We Have Known It*, including the introduction by Virginia Woolf. But in forwarding the review to the book's editor, Margaret Llewelyn Davies, Woolf commented,

You may be amused by the enclosed letter and article which I've just had sent me by Mrs. Leavis. I dont know her, but am told that she and her husband represent all that is highest and dryest at Cambridge. So I rather feel from reading her article; but I suppose she means well, and I'm glad that she should feel sympathetic in her high and dry way to our book. (*L* v:425)

In terms rather more nasty and blunt, Woolf recorded her reaction for herself in her diary: "And Queenie Leavis also writes, a priggish letter, drawing attention to Life as we have known it, in that prigs manual, Scrutiny. All they can do is to schoolmaster" (*D* IV:337).

On the other academic side, F. L. "Peter" Lucas (one of the strongest opponents to *Scrutiny* and a long-standing friend of the Woolfs)[44] seemed to Woolf as tepid as the Leavises were dry. Woolf liked him personally, wrote fondly of his "charm & niceness," and described feelings for him of "love and respect," but as a critic he was to her a chilling model of the modern Cambridge don (*D* III:256–57; *L* IV:159). When the Woolfs, under pressure from Dadie Rylands, agreed to read Lucas's book on tragedy for the Hogarth Press, Virginia pejoratively labeled it "Academic" (*D* III:150). She thought his approach to literature cold and ascetic and described his writing as "frozen fingered" (*D* v:322). Full of "[i]ncessant similes" and "perpetual quotation," she considered he displayed "the rigidity, at 36, of a crusted college character" (*D* III:256–57).

But while most definite in her disapproval of academic practice, Woolf remained uncertain whether she had successfully achieved an alternative. In September 1940, thinking of her planned book on the history of reading, she self-reflexively critiqued her own criticism in relation to Lucas's approach:

Yesterday in the Pub. Library I took down a book of Peter Lucas's criticism. This turned me against writing my book. London Library atmosphere effused. Turned me against all lit crit; these so clever, so airless, so fleshless ingenuities & attempts to prove – that T. S. Eliot, for example is a worse critic than F.L.L. Is all lit. crit. that kind of exhausted air? – book dust, London Library, air. Or is it only that F.L.L. is a second hand, frozen fingered, university specialist, don trying to be creative, don all stuffed with books, writer? Would one say the same of the Common Reader? (*D* v:321–22)

The book she most likely took from the shelf was Lucas's *Studies French and English*, a collection of separate literary essays, arranged chronologically and ranging in subject from the Greeks to the modern world, and thus a collection in format not unlike *The Common Readers*. The essay to which she most likely refers is the penultimate one on "Modern Criticism," in which Lucas inveighs against the doctrinaire strain in current criticism, using T. S. Eliot as a primary example.[45] And similarly, both of Woolf's *Common Readers* end with essays that oppose doctrinaire critical practice: "How It Strikes a Contemporary" deals with the difficulty of making critical judgments of modern works, while "How Should One Read a Book?" concerns the need for different reading strategies for different kinds of literature.

Indeed, in ideas, there are numerous points of congruency between Lucas and Woolf. Lucas's choice of authors exhibits, like hers, a far-ranging and catholic taste: both include chapters on the essays of Montaigne and the letters of Dorothy Osborne. Lucas shares with Woolf a suspicion of experts, an antipathy to aesthetic "rules," a respect for the common reader, a belief in first surrendering to the text and judging afterward, a sense of the role of the unconscious in our response to literature, and an antipathy to dogmatism.[46] And they both similarly link authoritative and doctrinaire criticism to political dictatorship. There are echoes of *A Room of One's Own* and premonitions of *Three Guineas* when Lucas states, "Over a large part of Europe, indeed, bodies and souls are nationalised and rationalised already" and "We live, as it is, in a Europe brutalised with dictatorships of the Right and the Left; we need no Hitlers to adorn the republic of letters."[47] In addition, given the upsurge of a scientific, analytic, truth-oriented criticism, Lucas voices a Woolfian skepticism about the value of teaching English: "How far, indeed, English Literature should be taught in Universities is still an open question."[48]

But though Lucas condemns "the style of self-appointed censors and inquisitors," and finds "the assertion of superiority" more than "a little nauseous," these views seem not to affect his own tone when he disapproves.[49] Dividing critics into two categories – subjective, creative, autobiographical, and charming; and objective, scientific, rule-devising, and judgmental – he sets out to demolish the latter and two of its egregious examples, T. S. Eliot and Herbert Read. He mocks a quotation from Eliot as "this flower of criticism tossed us in a coy footnote"; he imagines Eliot's high esteem for Pope's poetry deflated by Pope's own laughter, rhetorically asking, "For how can any rational being make such enormous statements?"; he sarcastically turns Eliot's own words back on himself: "Mr. Eliot has himself observed that 'English criticism is inclined to argue or persuade, rather than to state.' It is possible that this may be a smaller fault than he supposes. Certainly he will be acquitted of it."[50] These are not scattered remarks; such sarcasm pervades the whole essay, from "So that it would perhaps be asking too much to expect that criticism, which has not much in common with charity in other respects, should begin at home" to "When the leaders of a movement allow themselves such orgies of certainty, it may be imagined what happens with the camp-followers."[51]

Virginia Woolf, as we have already noted from her comments on Lucas and Q. D. Leavis, could not be described as invariably kind. Readers are sometimes appalled to discover how devastatingly cruel her comments, particularly in her diaries, could be. But although Woolf was adept at direct sarcasm, in her published works and particularly in her essays, she usually handled opposition in a more subtle way. A discourse very different from Lucas's, for example, guides her treatment of the *Scrutiny* critics in her essay "All About Books."

"All About Books" (1931)

Deceptively simple, the title "All About Books" suggests the genre of fireside chat about reading so popular in the 1920s and 1930s. But Woolf's "all" is comprehensive in scope. The essay concerns the reasons why we read books and the problems of how to teach them, the relation between books of the past and the present, and the connection between living and reading. But even more significantly, the essay enters a critical battlefield in an unorthodox way. Woolf reviews a collection of essays, *Scrutinies II*, while managing barely to mention the essays at all; and she uses the genre of the letter to engage a discourse antithetical to the doctrinaire critical voice.

Edited by Edgell Rickword, *Scrutinies II* (a forerunner of the periodical *Scrutiny* established the next year) was dedicated to the goal, soon to be identified with F. R. Leavis, of raising the standards of criticism through rigorous attention to language and style and exacting evaluations of the ideas and attitudes in the literary text. There was less in this approach than in Lucas's criticism that was compatible to Woolf's views; but what horrified her in both critical practices was the self-righteous, "frozen fingered" academic style. The writers in *Scrutinies* are clearly impassioned about their calling; they are concerned about the absence, or mere mechanical presence, of form in contemporary literature and even more about the loss of the lyric spirit and the life-affirming creative will. The haunting spectre is the "Goddess Drab," against which they oppose the passionate life embodied in art: "only an emotional statement of life can be real."[52] The passion they display, however, is almost uniformly deprecatory and derogatory, as we see in the following pungent remarks:

I find that the scraps of quotation in the various languages he knows and the display of allusion is but a carapaceous covering, like that of the tortoise, containing itself no vital organs, but being merely an exaggerated form of protection. (Alec Brown, "The Lyric Impulse in the Poetry of T. S. Eliot")

A feminine tact, a feminine receptivity and impressionability, underlying and palliating the surface irregularities of his work, has become a worse than feminine hysteria. (Peter Quennell, "The Later Period of D. H. Lawrence")

"As we have remarked before, the irritating blemishes which might be overlooked in the earlier works now burst into a rash across *Elizabeth and Essex*. (Christopher Saltmarshe, "Lytton Strachey")

What I protest against is the consuming dullness of [*Ulysses*], a result of its interminable vomit of relevant sensation-associations and further back, fundamentally, of Joyce's failure to centralise his material. (Brian Penton, "Note on the Form of the Novel")

After such rebarbative commentary, it is not reassuring to learn from Rickword's foreword that, since the writers discussed in the present volume do not have the "sacrosanct" reputations of those discussed in the previous volume, readers should find volume II "less astringent" and less likely to rouse indignation.[53]

Woolf herself received a more tempered and careful critique from William Empson. Yet it is difficult today not to be amused by Empson's struggle with her apparent inconsistencies, broad juxtapositions, and inconclusive ending. The author of *Seven Types of Ambiguity* worries that the "arbitrary" connection of Clarissa and "the shell-shock case" provides no closure for our real curiosity, which is to find out what will happen between Clarissa and Peter. As for the difficulties of following all the overlapping, repeated motifs, the analyst suggests a cure: "if only these dissolved units of understanding had been co-ordinated into a system; if only, perhaps there was an index, showing what had been compared with what."[54] "All they can do is to schoolmaster," Woolf was later to write in her diary (*D* IV:337). And significantly, in reviewing this volume, Woolf chose a form of response that did not, like Peter Lucas, pontificate and schoolmaster back. "All About Books," as a fictionalized letter, makes full use of associative thinking, a personal narrative voice, and an inscribed reader in its text.

Woolf's essay-letter has roughly two parts: the first discusses the just-published 1765 *Journal* of the Reverend William Cole;[55] the second concerns the *Scrutinies* volume. There is no logical connection between the two sections, other than the fact that the disappointment experienced in reading what was written over one hundred and fifty years earlier prompts the letter-writer to turn to reading what is rather more hot off the press. But the associative link is that both works miss the whole point of experience, interested as they are in marking and cataloguing rather than the human heart. Cole's journal is a sites-oriented tourism that fails to be an observation of life; the *Scrutinies* critics subject reader and text to doctrinaire views. Instead of rebutting specific ideas, however, Woolf presents an alternative discourse, first by writing a letter and then by incorporating, within the letter, an allegorical narrative – a moral fable about the universities' production of learning and destruction of love.

To begin her allegory, Woolf imagines the younger generation as an advancing army: "No more respectable army has ever issued from the portals of the two great Universities" (*CE* ii:266). Its soldiers are attractive to behold, infused with vigour and energy but also dedicated to efficiency, regulation, and control: "there is not a single straggler or deserter among them; there is no dancing or disorder; no wild voice cries alone" (265). Their combative nature accords with their division of writing into fixed oppositional schools: "Camp is opposed to camp; the hostile parties separate, form, meet, fight, leave each other for dead upon the ground; rise, form and fight again. Classic is opposed to romantic; naturalist to metaphysic. Never was there such a sight since the world began" (266). And from this satiric military metaphor, Woolf slips into a story of origins, explaining how this new breed of critics, with its extraordinary uniformity and conformity, came about:

Some years since, for reasons unknown, but presumably of value, it must have occurred to someone that the arts of reading and of writing can be taught. Degrees were given at the universities to those who showed proficiency in their native tongue... And the teachers took the manuscripts of the young and drew circles of blue chalk round this adjective and circles of red chalk round that adverb... Hence it came about that... the young knew the whole course of English literature from one end to another; how one age follows another; and one influence cancels another; and one style is derived from another; and one phrase is better than another. (266–67)

The allegory exposes not only the production of critics but their production of criticism as well. The marriages between writers and words are all scientifically arranged: "tutors introduced the couples; lecturers supervised the amours; and examiners finally pronounced whether the fruit of the union was blessed or the reverse" (267). Such calculated breeding guarantees a certain improvement and the progeny is labelled "an erudite and eugenic offspring," but what is fatally absent is "the sound of the sea and the red of the rose" and "a voice speaking from the heart" (267).

On its own, Woolf's satiric fable may not escape the mud of critical in-fighting; "eugenic offspring" may be as much name-calling as "carapaceous covering" and "interminable vomit." But the form of the personal letter recasts potential vitriol as provocative performance, designed to entertain and amuse. Instead of the schoolmaster's elevated tones, Woolf adopts an ordinary conversational style. In addition, the letter-writer's modest self-positioning disarms us from taking offence: "A letter is not a review; it is not a considered judgment, but, on condition that you do not believe a word I say, I will scribble for an hour or two whatever comes into my head about books" (263). Finally, when the writer finishes her letter and goes off to bed without having opened the covers of *Scrutinies*, we can see her either as the older generation retreating from a confrontation with the forces of youth, or as a more vibrant soul going off to a richer world in her dreams. Such openness, it is true, makes for vulnerability. It is certainly possible for a reader to dismiss the essay as sentimental, lightweight, personal whimsy. But it is also possible to read Woolf's style as a stringent criticism of the *Scrutinies* critics, achieved by opposing their ardent, strident tones with suggestiveness and humor, by preserving the personal voice, and by establishing an intimate relation with the reader.

The epistolary form offers a further contrast to assertive critical discourse by inserting the reader into the text. Woolf's letter is presented as a response to a correspondent's request, giving her addressee a role in the motivation for her writing. Her interlocutor introduces the topic "all about books," almost as a call for help from an Alpine town:

Your last letter ends with the following sentence: "The cold profile of Mont Blanc; falling snow; peasants and pine trees; a string of stout fellows roped together with alpenstocks – such is the prospect from my window; so for pity's sake draw your chair to the fire, take your pen in your hand and write me a long, long letter all about books." (263)

The significance of the alpine climbers is overdetermined and many possible associations intrude: Wordsworth's Mont Blanc, Leslie Stephen's mountain climbing, the cult of endurance and the physical test, and the whole Victorian ethic of striving for a mental or spiritual goal. But within Woolf's text, the image functions first as a contrast: climbers pose an antithesis to readers, and the longing to hear about books expresses a desire for the reflective as opposed to the physical life. Yet, as Woolf shows, this very desire for difference is one of the motivations *within* reading itself. Woolf's brief survey of recent books of interest includes the memoirs of the Grand Duchess Marie of Russia, the diary of a nineteenth-century Somerset parson, and a book about British submarines during the First World War.[56] Opposing the uniformity and conformity of the *Scrutinies* critics is the reader's desire for contrast and variety, so that difference, rather than working to separate, actually serves – like the ropes linking the climbers – to connect. The initial bifurcation of physical and mental traveling resolves into a continuum of exploration, manifested in two different modes.

But the most important effect of the Alpine setting is that it constructs the unknown reader as *not* an academic, *not* a student – or at least, not one identified with those roles. If anything, the reader here is a traveler, cast in an exploratory, in-transit mode. And Woolf further constructs her reader as a writer, not only because the reader's quoted words open the essay but also because the epistolary genre encodes the possibility of the reader's writing back. In contrast to the pedagogical mode in Woolf's fable, in which the taught are herded into the willing ranks of followers, Woolf situates her discussion of books within a dialogic form.

Defining academic discourse

The dialogic form constitutes Woolf's greatest separation from the academic article as it was developing at this time. Beyond the hostilities, beyond the pitting of one view against another, academic discourse rested on the common assumption that one view – generally the view of the speaker – should prevail. Against this model, Woolf developed a reader-oriented approach that affirms a plurality of views. Her approach is also marked by another feature virtually absent in the emerging academic criticism: a self-reflexive questioning of her own approach. These qualities produce an elasticity of style that may seem capricious if its implications are missed; the lack of assumed authority can make her essays seem less serious than the academic mode. As a result, just at the time English was drawing its disciplinary boundaries, the most significant features of Woolf's approach situated her essays on the outside.

Disciplinary boundaries involved separating academic from non-academic writing. Profession was not an absolute determinant; the entry into the critical canon of T. S. Eliot and Percy Lubbock, for example, indicates that editors and writers could be included within the academic frame. Nor was site of publication necessarily a distinguishing factor: the "Summary of Periodical Literature" in *The Review of English Studies*, for example, included some, but not all, of the contributions to the *Times Literary Supplement*. The principles of inclusion/exclusion, however, are less than fully transparent. In volumes 1–5, covering the period from April 3, 1924, to

July 25, 1929, three of Woolf's *TLS* essays are included in the bibliographies but seven are not.[57] Furthermore, while her 1924 *TLS* essay "Joseph Conrad" was *not* included, the bibliography *did* list Jessie Conrad's *TLS* contribution of the same year, "Joseph Conrad: A Personal Remembrance," with the note that it "corrects some statements in Ford M. Ford's book by this title."[58] Even more strangely, Woolf's essay "Geraldine and Jane" – the leading article on February 28, 1929 – was not included, but letters responding to it by O. H. T. Dudley, Edith J. Morley, Ella H. Dixon, and W. H. Hutton on March 7, and by E. H. Woodruff on April 4, were.[59] The bibliographical inclusion of the letters was presumably because many of them purported to correct factual errors or faulty impressions in Woolf's work; the exclusion of her essay may have been accidental, or perhaps her depiction of the friendship between Geraldine Jewsbury and Jane Welsh Carlyle was judged to be too close to fictional narrative. Factual detail qualified as academic; historical recreation apparently did not.[60] Although the *TLS* and its readership did not suddenly change, the essays altered in cultural significance: they would now divide (until 1948, when the *TLS* was dropped altogether from the survey) into those that would be included in the scholarly bibliography and those that would not. The rise of the scholarly journal compounded this bifurcation, producing in turn a bifurcation in reading practices, even within the same physical readership, into specialist and non-specialist kinds of reading.

It was not the venue of publication, then, but the style of Woolf's essays that located them outside the academy, distinguished from the new professional article that was beginning to emerge. And to a large extent, through her hostility to the discourse of academic English, Woolf placed herself on the outside as well. There are indications in her work, however, that she conceived the narrowness of specialization not as inherent in university study but as specific to the new academicism of her time. In *A Room of One's Own*, the narrator nostalgically recollects the sound of a "humming" under the breath in the conversation of a pre-war and pre-professional university, evocative of a more suggestive and fertilizing mode (*R* 19–23, 151). A diary entry in 1923 similarly suggests she endowed Cambridge with a more idyllic past: "I had romanced so much about Cambridge that to find myself sitting there was an anti climax. No one else was excited" (*D* 11:230). Despite the deflation she experienced in the present, her expectations invoke an anticipated world of exciting, exhilarating conversation. That at least some academics shared her nostalgia for a different kind of academic discourse is evident in Peter Lucas's similar remark: "It [reading Proust] recalls to me the first intoxication, in undergraduate days, of Cambridge talk – a rapture, alas, departed."[61] Whether such discourse can survive within the academy is a question I suggest we have still to resolve; for the present, we shall turn to see how it fared, in Woolf's time, in the reading world on the outside.

WOOLF, ENGLISH STUDIES, AND ADULT EDUCATION

Class, culture, and education

During Woolf's time, to return to Keating's phrase, "readers – or at least one crucial group of readers – were being turned into students"; and, as we have seen, in Woolf's view, the university student was being turned into a camp follower. Drilled and trained for efficiency and assertiveness, ordered to serve under the banners of legitimacy and competitiveness, this student was losing the natural appetite for and close intimacy with books that, for Woolf, formed the essence of the reading experience. What, then, of a different type of reader coming into being – the new student of adult education? Given that adult education presented an alternative to a university degree, did it also then offer an alternative educational mode? The new readers make their appearance in fictional characters such as Leonard Bast and Septimus Smith; the new teachers hover in the background in figures like Isabel Pole and Doris Kilman. But the narrative outcomes expose once again the limitations of the educational system.

In the early twentieth century, adult education, like the university study of English, was experiencing the uncertainties of emergence and definition. Much of the complexity of adult education, however, came from the fact that its nineteenth-century antecedents were numerous and scattered, exhibiting various degrees of formality and institutionalization and encompassing a diversity of aim. The nineteenth century saw various attempts to establish separate institutions dedicated to working-class education: the Adult School movement, supported by the Society of Friends, for non-denominational religious instruction; the Mechanics' Institutes, created to provide technical training and scientific instruction for workers; lectures and classes organized by the Co-operative Societies, with a special focus on co-operative life; and Working Men's Colleges, expanded by the end of the century to include both men and women, with general cultural education as their goal.[62] And it was the last of these, drawing most of its teachers from the upper middle class, that was best known to Woolf.

One of the colleges Woolf would have known was the Working Men's College in London, established in 1848 by F. D. Maurice and others from

King's College, London. Like many Cambridge graduates, E. M. Forster taught at the Working Men's College – in Forster's case, for more than twenty years, beginning with weekly classes in Latin in 1902.[63] Another important London institution was Morley College, which held its classes in the Old Vic Theatre in the Waterloo Road. Established by Emma Cons and endowed by Samuel Morley – a millionaire hosiery manufacturer and philanthropist from the Midlands – it was open equally to women as well as men.[64] Woolf's brother Adrian Stephen taught both at the London Working Men's College and at Morley (*L* 1:311; 210). Woolf herself taught classes in history, literature, and composition at Morley for three years, from 1905 to 1907.

Forster and Woolf appear to have been dedicated teachers, both in their preparation for class and in their interest in the students as individuals.[65] The working-class college indeed promoted comradeship between pupil and teacher as the basis for effective learning. In the words of F. D. Maurice, "What we wanted was, if possible, to make our teaching a bond of intercourse with the men whom we taught."[66] At least two of Forster's students became his close friends, one of them going to Cambridge on a scholarship obtained with Forster's help.[67] As for Woolf, her first experience of Morley College appears to have been an informal "soirée," where she talked "with nice enthusiastic working women who say they love books" (*PA* 218). Her classes were small, apparently ranging from four to eight students, and her years of teaching relatively few, yet the experience left her with a vivid sense of her students and, in particular, with an appreciation of the tie between economic circumstance and intellectual work.

The one surviving account of that experience (another earlier report has apparently been lost) leaves a strong impression of the intellectual hunger of her students contrasted with the limitations of their circumstances. The student who appears initially to be the "least interesting" turns out to possess "a higher level of intelligence" than the others, to be absolutely committed to the class in her attendance, and to be the "germ of a literary lady" herself. But she also gives Woolf an important insight into the pragmatic world of writing for money. As a reporter and book reviewer for a "Religious paper," the student, Miss Williams, is under such pressure to churn out words rapidly that she is little more than "a writing machine to be set in motion." She has no opportunity to advance her own opinions; she must accept the editor's direction to write a favorable or unfavorable notice, and then, without time to read the book, cull a few quotations from it to support the verdict. Another student, apparently taking up Woolf's suggestion, tries to write an account of her own life but is hampered, not by difficulties with grammar or logic, but by stilted language, affectation, and cliché. She too appears to Woolf as someone who might have been a writer "in other circumstances"; as it is, any potential for original work is lost in the student's conventional attempts to mimic the style she thinks she ought to have.[68]

What is particularly interesting is that Woolf sees little problem with basic literacy and she objects to the college's focus on teaching composition. The problems, in her opinion, arise from class and circumstance: lack of opportunity, lack of time, and lack of comfort and familiarity with knowledge, so that it is either treated with too much respect or discounted out of fear and ignorance.[69] And some of the inhibiting circumstances are the conditions of Morley College itself. In 1905, in her first year of teaching, Woolf seems torn between her frustration with the college for preferring "the safeness of mediocrity to the possible dangers of a high ideal" and her despair about the impossibility of her task. On the one hand, she objects to a focus on numbers: Morley, in her view, places too high a priority on offering popular subjects to large numbers and not enough on making ambitious study available to the highly motivated few. On the other hand, Woolf struggles with the fundamental difficulty of bridging the gap between her students' lives and her historical materials. Quickly learning not to read her lectures but to talk from notes, and making use of pictures and narratives to bring English history alive, Woolf still agonizes about her task: "I used to ask myself how is it *possible* to make them feel the flesh & blood in these shadows? So thin is the present to them; must not the past remain a spectre always?"[70] This comment would be blatant class prejudice if she meant that her students' lives were empty because they lacked the exposure to intellectual culture that she herself had had. But Woolf seems rather to be referring to her difficulty, as a teacher, in finding intellectual hooks; she had certainly learned from Miss Williams's accounts of Grub Street that her students experienced dimensions of life beyond her own ken. And Woolf's difficulties reflect one of the basic problems in adult education of the time: despite the fine ideals of fellowship, the education was situated in the discourse of the educated upper middle class, reinforcing inequalities between teacher and student and placing the materials of study in a realm above and beyond the student's world. The effects were felt not only in the failures in the learning experience but also, unfortunately, in its success.

Whether or not they fully understood the cause of the problem, both Forster and Woolf sensed the error in the way "culture" was constructed in the education of the lower class. According to Furbank, in Forster's later life, "'educational' became for him a term of abuse" and despite his enthusiastic involvement in college activities, he "had his reservations about the College and was not sure it worked entirely for the good."[71] And both writers expressed their concern in fictional depictions of the effect of education on a man from the lower middle class. In *Howards End*, love of music occasions a meeting between the upper middle-class Schlegels and the clerk Leonard Bast, but they remain separated by the different ways "culture" relates to their lives. For the Schlegels, art is a familiar language that they adapt to their own experiences; each constructs the Beethoven symphony in a way congenial to his or her individual cast of mind. But for Leonard, art exists in a realm of romance that must be kept separate from his life to prevent it from becoming contaminated. And so to think in the language of his reading is to be false to himself; it is only when he breaks away from his quotations and uses his own eyes that his words ring true. What rouses the Schlegels' interest – and Forster's – is that he "troubled to go and see for himself."[72] When Leonard eventually dies in a "shower" of books, it is culture as well as mechanization that claims its victim. In his story, it is true, there is something of Forster's own "romance" of the lower class as an idealized release from the repressive conventions of middle-class culture. But there is also an indictment of the construction of that culture as an elevated superior realm above the lower-class student's life.

Woolf's Septimus Smith takes Leonard Bast's victimization to the next stage. If reading for Leonard produces a distanced, abstract worship of beauty, for Septimus, the ideal of beauty becomes wedded to an equally abstract ideal of England, with the terrible and ironic result that spiritual, cultural abstraction draws him into an all-too-physical field of war. And in Woolf's novel, the system of adult education is more clearly implicated in the guilt. Septimus has been a student at Morley College, drawn, in his immense desire to "improve himself," to "Miss Isabel Pole, lecturing in the Waterloo Road" (*MD* 129). A link to Woolf's own experience at Morley is suggested by references in her letters to a student named Cyril Zeldwyn, whom she describes as "a good working man" and "a socialist of a kind, and a poet," and for whom she tried to find employment in December 1907 (*L* 1:321). And Zeldwyn is most likely the same student whom she describes in October as "my degenerate poet, who rants and blushes, and almost seizes my hand when we happen to like the same lines" (313). But if Septimus has origins in Leonard Bast and Cyril Zeldwyn, by 1925 Woolf has moved this figure forward in time to expose the connection between education and the war. Because the teaching of English literature became permeated with the ideal of recovering a lost organic society, and because the ideal of manliness became invested with the ethic of sacrifice in defence of that society, Septimus tragically and naïvely goes to war "to save an England which consisted almost entirely of Shakespeare's plays and Miss Isabel Pole in a green dress walking in a square" (*MD* 130–31). With regard to the literary effects of Septimus's education, the novel is non-committal. But with regard to the social effects, the text is bitingly negative, figuring education as both manipulative and destructive. The system dangles knowledge in front of Septimus like a bait and then swallows him up in the patriotic trap. His initial "intoxication" with Shakespeare's language is transformed into a vision of Shakespeare's disgust with the body's corruption; culture, the education of the feelings, ends by annihilating them. It is not Septimus who is to blame but a misconceived pedagogy, and the consequent victimization in *Mrs. Dalloway* is much more thorough and endemic than in *Howards End*.

It is impossible for us to know the full effect of Woolf's teaching at Morley or the reason why she left. Not many letters survive from 1906, the year of her brother Thoby's death, and the only diaries we have from 1906 and 1907 are those she kept when away from London. From some dissatisfaction she expressed near the end of 1907, it seems likely that her exit from teaching was largely a result of Morley's expectation that she teach on Monday evenings when she wanted to be free (*L* 1:312). But though Woolf left few records of Morley, we can trace its effects on her critical practice. Beth Rigel Daugherty has argued persuasively that the challenging experience of addressing Morley students (who predated Woolf's *TLS* readership) shaped Woolf's understanding of how to write for an unprivileged audience and prompted her insight that "conversation teaches more effectively than lecturing." In Daugherty's view, the Morley experience laid the foundation for Woolf's continuing pedagogical commitment, witnessed in her "decision to keep writing essays long after the financial reasons for doing so had ended." Furthermore, Daugherty links Woolf's comments on her teaching to her later development of a distinctive critical style in which "readers and writers become partners in active reading, where readers become equally amateur, where learning, not hierarchy, is paramount, and where class barriers can be crossed."[73]

Woolf's pedagogical style in this respect shows a development quite different from Forster's. Furbank similarly considers teaching to have had a formative influence on Forster's style, but one less equitable in its assignment of speaker and audience roles. According to Furbank, Forster "had a way of simplifying issues and putting them into words of one syllable, which was often effective and charming but on occasion could sound like 'talking down'; and it was through these adult-education activities that he came by this habit." In the Clark lectures, Furbank notes, this tendency on

Forster's part to present "complex matters in the homeliest and most 'bread-and-butter' terms" delighted much of the Cambridge audience, though it enraged Leavis – a response that, in its division, reflects the prevailing tensions over academic style.[74] But the style that Woolf developed was much more than gracious, apt, and accessible. As I show in the next chapter, her critical voice shapes itself according to her imagined reader's response and she negotiates differences among readers who inhabit different discourses – in particular, the differences separating readers who were part of the privileged hegemony from those who were not. Perhaps one of the most crucial lessons Woolf learned at Morley was to avoid "talking *down*," and to strive for the alternative pedagogy of "talking *to* or *with*."[75]

Woolf's Morley experience led her to see that adult education was significantly hampered by an academic approach that did not emanate sufficiently from the point of view of the taught. And, in the pedagogical world of Woolf's time, it was precisely this problem that prompted objections to the university extension lecture, and that led to the formation, in 1903, of the Workers' Educational Association.

The Workers' Educational Association

In the 1870s, the universities significantly increased their involvement in adult education by mounting programs of extra-mural lectures which rapidly became the primary mode of University Extension. These programmes did much to advance the cause of higher education, but they were also plagued by serious limitations: the need for each locality to initiate a request and provide financial support, the reliance on itinerant lecturers, the lack of continuity between lectures and, most important, the failure to reach the working class. In 1903, in response to these problems, Albert Mansbridge instigated the formation of the Workers' Educational Association (the WEA) to bring together the University Extension Movement, the Co-operative Movement, and the Trade Union Movement with the goal of promoting closer cooperation between the universities and working-class organizations. Over the next years, the work of the WEA was undoubtedly controversial, and a rancorous division developed between the liberal education sought by the WEA and the ideologically Marxist education demanded by the radical Plebs League, founded in 1908. The WEA was never the exclusive voice of the working class nor was it always unanimous in forming its policies. In the larger social sphere, however, the WEA played a crucial role in bringing concerns about the nature, goals, and methods of adult education into the realm of public discussion. For the distinctive and foundational accomplishment of the WEA was the introduction of an alternative to the extension lecture: the University Tutorial Class. The motivating factors underlying the formation of tutorial classes continued to be subjects of public debate well into the next decade, constituting one of the first probing analyses of the ideological implications of pedagogical form.

From the beginning, WEA policy endorsed generalist, non-specialized education – education that was neither vocational in orientation nor designed for material advancement or class mobility. As one of its first initiatives, in 1907 the WEA sponsored a national conference of working-class and educational organizations, which led in turn to the appointment at Oxford of a "Joint Committee of University and Working-class Representatives on the Relation of the University to the Higher Education of Workpeople." The 1909 report of this committee, after stating as its first principle that no one should be excluded from the universities on economic grounds, listed, as its second and third principles, that education should not necessitate a change of class and that a general, as opposed to technical, education was as much a right and need for the working class as for any class.[76] Quoting the "words of a workman, a student and a Trade Unionist," the report argued that

the education required is not a mere bread-and-butter education, which will only make the worker into a more efficient wealth producer . . . The time has come for the working man to demand a share in the education which is called "liberal" because it concerns life, not livelihood . . . But in this, as in many other things, the working class has been for long a disinherited class, and the national Universities . . . have been regarded as the legitimate preserves of the leisured class. This state of things has not only wronged the working class; it has to a great degree sterilized the Universities themselves.[77]

The committee thus defended general as opposed to technical education; it also argued the need for a reconfiguration of academic education in response to working-class ideas and experience. Unlike the vocational training necessary to perform a job, general education would prepare workers to be effective members of society in a self-governing nation, but the report implied that the existing culture of the university was too removed from general life, and *not sufficiently disinterested*, to meet this need: "But it is undoubtedly the case that workpeople feel, and feel with justice, that there are certain departments of knowledge in which something more than the best academic training is needed for the attainment of comprehensive and impartial views; and they are sometimes inclined to suspect teachers of

displaying in these subjects an unconscious class bias."[78] University extension as it existed, the report argued, evidenced the need for the involvement
of working-class representatives in both the design of the classes and the
selection of teachers.

The specialized and class-based nature of university education became a
continuing subject of discussion in *The Highway*, the journal of the WEA
which began publication in 1914. The Labour historian G. D. H. Cole –
who taught in the WEA from 1913 to 1931 and served as their national
Vice-President until 1938 – was strongly of the opinion that the prevailing university-style education was unsuitable for the working class. Cole
dismissed criticisms of the tutorial class that judged its success according
to existing academic standards, explaining that "the basis of experience,
the way of approach, and the interests of the [WEA] students differ fundamentally from those of undergraduates." Furthermore, he argued that
the academic approach was too limited in scope: "Most University education is," he stated, "largely vocational in *aim*, if not in method," whereas
the tutorial movement was "largely free from vocationalism...and wholly
free from examinations, rewards, and distinctions."[79] In another article, he
noted that Robert Peers, Director of Extra-mural Education at University
College, Nottingham, made "a new and startling point when he looked
to adult education as the means of saving the humaner studies amid the
onrush of vocational training that is overwhelming the newer universities and sweeping their arts departments into an unregarded corner of the
curriculum."[80] For Cole, workers' education should be neither assimilation
into a "high" cultural tradition outside their class nor vocational training
for their class position; culture was to be regarded as a rightful possession
of the working class and education was to be the opening of a "Broad
Highway" helping the workers "to bring their own ideas to birth."[81] More
recent cultural analysis has tended to construct the tension between vocationalism and personal growth as a class issue in which the latter represents
a bourgeois humanism that can afford to neglect the material products of
education. But it is interesting to note that, in the early twentieth century, a high percentage of the working class claimed the right to personal
intellectual development without any implications of class mobility or professional advancement, regarding vocationalism as a limited concern of the
establishment. It is also important to recognize that the goal of intellectual rather than social advancement posed no contradiction to the often
accompanying goal of social critique and reform.[82]

At the same time, however, the aims of the WEA diverged from the
ideological agenda of the more radical group within the working class.

The policy of the WEA was to work in co-operation with the universities, to benefit from what they had to offer, and to transform what needed change; the Plebs League, on the other hand, viewed the universities as instruments of capitalism, and believed the working class should pursue its own course in isolation and devote itself to the cause of preparing workers to engage politically in class struggle. For the WEA, this self-styled "Proletcult" differed from education in the way that propaganda differs from critical thinking; for their part, the Plebs considered the WEA to be tainted with bourgeois, capitalist ideology. Moderates like G. D. H. Cole tried to defuse the tensions, arguing for the acceptance of the activities of the Plebs League as an alternative for those who were dogmatically inclined. But he just as strongly asserted that the WEA liberated its students for more effective Marxist or socialist work by equipping them to do their own thinking.[83] An article in *The Highway* in 1920, for example, likened the workers' use of academic people to a professor's use of a plumber: in both cases, the employed were invited to perform a specialized job, not to control the design.[84] The WEA claimed access to culture while they simultaneously disclaimed complicity in the ideology of the privileged group that had been for so long identified with the possession of cultural knowledge.

It is not difficult to identify large areas of commonality between the principles supported by the WEA and Virginia Woolf's critical approach. Woolf did not have the opportunity, like the WEA, of working closely with the university, nor did she seek it; nevertheless, the cultural work performed by her essays strongly accords with the pedagogical goal that *The Highway* promotes. Like the WEA, Woolf raised concerns about the university's narrow specialization and professionalism, its inculcation of a competitive ethic, its exclusionary nature, and its bias toward the assumptions of the privileged. Woolf's common reading was fundamentally an advocacy for broad, generalist reading as opposed to academic study, and it was a defense of reading for such personally directed goals as pleasure and intellectual stimulation rather than such professional purposes as publication and accreditation. And embedded in her pedagogical project was a process for achieving a genuinely democratic society. All these ideals she shared with the WEA; but the parallels assume a more concrete form in the commitment to conversation and dialogue over the lecturing mode.

Dialogue versus lecture

One of the significant achievements of the WEA, as I have noted, was the introduction, in 1908, of the Tutorial Class. Although extension lectures continued to be offered, many believed that small on-going classes were preferable to lectures that were expensive, lacked systematic planning, and challenged the endurance of people who had already put in a hard day's work. But the WEA also looked for a change in the mode of instruction. Most instructors lectured on the university model, with little alteration of material or manner for the different audience. The distancing effects can be well imagined, although, in Richard Altick's opinion, "[m]any of the handicaps might still have been overcome had the art of popularization been understood."[85] The WEA, however, wanted not less rigor but more. In their view, the tutorial class enhanced learning potential by providing longer, more intense, and more unified periods of study, by ensuring smaller classes (limited, by 1924, to twenty-four students), and by requiring a substantial amount of written work.[86] The WEA sought further to improve the content of the course, not by striving for "popular" appeal, but by engaging the students' experiences and the students' ideas. They sought, and for some time continued to seek, a method of instruction that relied not on lecturing but on discussion.

The new pedagogical model attracted a good deal of public attention, as can be seen in a series of articles that appeared in the fall of 1922. Reviewing the Conference of the Tutorial Class Tutors' Association held at Leeds in September, Cole declared that the conference "went straight to the root of the matter by discussing the fundamental problems of tutorial class teaching and making it plain that our essential purpose in our classes must be, not to convey the maximum quantity of information, but to equip our students with the power both to get information for themselves and to base upon it courageous and scientific judgements of their own."[87] In the same month, he published an article in the *New Statesman* reporting on another recent conference on adult education, held again at Oxford. Under the header "The Doubtful Value of Lectures in University Education," the article charged that, with a few notable exceptions, the university representatives at this conference seemed to take it for granted that "the teaching methods they have been used to apply to their own students are of necessity the right methods for adult education." On the contrary, Cole argued, the substance of most lectures could be better acquired by reading a book and he proposed that instructors look to the American universities where progress had been made in "supplementing the lecture with group-study." Cole argued that the most effective moments in education arise from "the close unorganized contact of mind with mind" and yet, he continued, such contact was almost entirely absent in adult education. The university itself, Cole went further to state, might itself benefit from the critiques, coming from adult education organizations, of existing pedagogical modes.[88]

The next issue of the *New Statesman* published five letters expressing sympathy with Cole's critique, although three of the letters – those with university addresses – all claimed that the universities themselves shared Cole's skepticism about the lecture method. The letters, however, pointed out various practical complications: the "tyranny of written examinations" that made students anxious for lectures that spell out the course material; the need for "increased staff" to allow the time for "conversation"; and the lack of the "time and energy" needed to undertake the significant work of change. There was recognition that the problems were greater at the newer universities, pressured as they were to handle larger numbers of students, than at the older universities where the tutorial was an established tradition. And one letter strikingly conveyed the diversity of method within the university – indeed within any one professor's teaching – by suggesting that "no teachers are more sceptical and less uniform than University teachers."[89]

The following month, Arthur L. Dakyns, writing in *The Highway*, welcomed the exchange in the *New Statesman*, but he pointed out, too, that support from within the university came mainly from those who were, or had been, tutorial class tutors. And *The Highway* continued to urge pedagogical change. In 1923, Cole embarked on a series of articles outlining the "Achievements – Needs – Prospects" of workers' education "with a view rather to setting ideas to ferment than to the settling of problems." He vociferated against "the faith in lectures which prevails even in the WEA," and advocated a "widening of our methods to include other forms of education besides the class and the lecture," including "dramatic societies, musical clubs, and other auxiliaries." University lecturers or professors, he further claimed, too often lacked understanding of the "special needs and character" of adult working-class students; the result was a give and take approach in the classroom instead of "an essentially democratic and co-operative method of give and give between tutors and students" in which the students would not be constructed as passive learners but as active participants with knowledge related to their own experiences to contribute.[90] Significantly, when two years later Cole took up a position as Reader and Fellow at Oxford, his introduction of a question period following his lectures and his creation of the "Cole group" for informal discussion created a stir.[91]

As a whole, the controversies show that the debate was not polarized as a conflict between adult education and the universities.[92] Nor was the debate limited to educational publications and committees; the issues were circulating in an open public forum, and one that Virginia Woolf would know. Both Leonard and Virginia were reviewing for the *New Statesman* at this time; Leonard knew Cole as a member of the Fabian Society and the Labour Party, and he later published a good many of Cole's works.[93] The Woolfs were also familiar with *The Highway*. A flyer inserted in *The Highway* in September 1923 advertised a special subscription to *The Nation and The Athenaeum* that included, free of charge, *A Revision of the Treaty* by J. M. Keynes and Virginia Woolf's *Jacob's Room* (value 7s 6d each). Woolf herself published in *The Highway* in the summer of 1924, in a "Symposium" on the topic "What is a Good Novel?" As I show in the next chapter, her contribution strongly supports educational practices that teach students how to think, aligning with the arguments in the WEA for a pedagogy of empowerment rarely found in the extension lecture. And in *Mrs. Dalloway*, if Morley College's Miss Isabel Pole is unwittingly implicated in Septimus's excessive idealization of culture, Miss Doris Kilman, the teacher who does "a little Extension lecturing" (*MD* 187), is more damagingly associated with conversion and the forcing of the soul.

THREE ESSAYS ON EDUCATION

"A Professor of Life" (1926)

Woolf's opposition to the lecturing mode stretches throughout her career. In 1906, in her days of teaching at Morley College, Woolf published a review in the *Speaker* (the anti-imperialist precursor to the *Nation*) of Canon Ainger's *Lectures and Essays*, in which she asserted that "anyone who has had the misfortune to be lectured knows that certain defects are almost inherent in the form" (*E* 1:83–4). The lecture, Woolf observed, has to adapt itself to the least intelligent of the audience and to make its points more obviously than the written essay. Just over thirty years later, Woolf's outrage with the lecture, and the university system formed around it, is yet more clear: "If we are asked to teach," she declares "we can pour mild scorn upon chapels, upon degrees, and upon the value of examinations... If we are asked to lecture we can refuse to bolster up the vain and vicious system of lecturing by refusing to lecture" (*TG* 43). To some extent, Woolf was launching a semiotic critique of pedagogical methods, exposing the unequal dynamics of speaking and being spoken to. Yet her objection was grounded even more specifically on the way the lecture in her society was being used. In practice, as Woolf implied through Miss Kilman, lecturing was closely tied to cultural domination – a problem that Woolf diagnosed, just the year after the publication of *Mrs. Dalloway*, as infecting Sir Walter Raleigh's academic career.

Woolf had not always taken Raleigh as representative of domination. In 1917, she reviewed his recent work on Romance, praising his lectures for their rejection of fixed critical categories and their suggestive, flexible approach: "He touches his subject with life, and invests it with all the uncertainty, the possibility, and the vagueness of a living thing" (*E* 11:73). But in 1926, having read Raleigh's letters, Woolf sees a very different side. Written for *Vogue* rather than the *TLS*, "A Professor of Life" mounts a strongly feminist critique, exposing the culturally encoded military and imperialist values driving Raleigh's career. As I noted in chapter 1, this review becomes an intertext in her essay "Middlebrow," in which Raleigh's off-hand references to "Bill Blake" and "Bill Wordsworth" trope his reductionist feminization of intellectual culture and his celebration of a masculinized aggression instead.

Once alerted to Raleigh's values, Woolf also comes to a different view of his pedagogical mode. Raleigh, she satirically notes, lectures – frequently, ubiquitously, indiscriminately, repetitively, mechanically:

On a certain Wednesday in March 1889 Walter Raleigh, then aged twenty-eight, gave his first lecture upon English literature in Manchester. It was not his first lecture by any means, for he had already lectured the natives of India on the same subject for two years. After Manchester came Liverpool; after Liverpool, Glasgow; after Glasgow, Oxford. At all these places he lectured incessantly upon English literature. Once he lectured three times a day. He became, indeed, such an adept at the art of lecturing that towards the end "sometimes he would prepare what he had to say in his half-hour's walk from his home at Ferry Hinksey." (*E* IV:342)

Now, instead of "touch[ing] his subject with life," Raleigh's style appears as an automatic activity dependent on reiteration rather than thinking. In India, his lecturing bears the taint of colonial discourse; later, enthusiastically supporting the Boer War and the advent of World War I, he infuses his lectures with the discourse of battle: "He was coming to feel that there is some close connection between writing and fighting" (346). Despite Raleigh's profession as a professor of literature, his true apotheosis comes through the heroic, masculinized forms of patriotism, militarism, and factual writing: "He drilled. He marched. He wrote pamphlets. He lectured more frequently then ever; he practically ceased to read. At length he was made historian of the Air Force. To his infinite satisfaction he consorted with soldiers" (346).

Woolf's condemnation is clear, but what is not so readily understandable to her is Raleigh's apparent success. For she acknowledges that "[p]eople who heard him said that his lectures stimulated them, opened their eyes, made them think for themselves" (342). If this was so, then lecturing was not, as Cole argued, antithetical to the desired goal of critical thinking. Woolf's critique does not ignore this difficulty: "Yet there is no doubt, Walter Raleigh was one of the best Professors of Literature of our time; he did brilliantly whatever it is that Professors are supposed to do. How then shall we compose the difference – solve the discrepancy?" (343). But then Woolf twists that little phrase, "whatever . . . Professors are supposed to do," so that it interrogates itself. "In the first place," Woolf continues, "the Professor of English Literature is not there to teach people how to write; he is there to teach them how to read" (343–44). A few months earlier, Woolf herself had given the talk to the girls at Hayes Court School that was to become her essay "How Should One Read a Book?" But Raleigh's subject, Woolf suggests, was not books: "And they went away loving something or other. Perhaps it was Keats. Perhaps it was the British Empire. Certainly it was Walter Raleigh. But we should be much surprised if anybody went away loving poetry, loving the art of letters" (344). The problem with the "Professor of Life" is that he separated life and literature, and redefined life as himself.

Woolf is particularly alert to the loss for general audiences and extra-mural students, for whom this experience could have opened a doorway to books: "Moreover, those people include city magnates, politicians, schoolmistresses, soldiers, scientists, mothers of families, country clergymen in embryo. Many of them have never opened a book before. Many will seldom get a chance of opening a book again" (344). Woolf's list of potential common readers does not, it is true, include clerks and manual workers, though it may have appropriately reflected the audience for *Vogue*. But the crucial point is that her attention is on unskilled, uninitiated readers and the way that Raleigh's entertaining but self-referential style neglects their real needs. And it is not just literature he has failed to give them; his works fail to break down the barriers of conventional thinking and to open new windows on the world. For Woolf makes an extraordinary statement about literature's potential, in pinpointing just what Raleigh missed: "He never pressed on over the ruins of his own culture to the discovery of something better" (345). As for relational dynamics, the lectures suffer the same lack as the letters: "But when one looks for the unprofessional talk, the talk which is talked among friends when business hours are over, one is bewildered and disappointed" (343). Again Woolf's views accord with Cole's advocacy of the "close unorganized contact of mind with mind." This contact is sadly lacking, for Cole, in adult education, and sadly lacking, for Woolf, in Raleigh's approach.

Clearly Woolf sees Raleigh's writing in gendered opposition to her own; in addition, in the context of the recent articles in *The Highway*, Raleigh appears similarly antithetical to the aims of the working class. The WEA was not arguing for the use of slang or other such popularizing techniques and, while they opposed the elevation of culture as a superior world passed down from the class above, they wanted not to disparage culture but to claim it as their natural right. And despite the predominance of male contributors to *The Highway*, literature, music, and drama – as witness Cole's endorsement of dramatic societies and music clubs – do not appear in its pages as the feminized other. Writing for *Vogue*, and as a self-termed educated man's daughter, Woolf nevertheless comes closer to the aims of workers' education than does the supposed leader in the development of English studies (the subtitle of Raleigh's *Letters* is "A Brilliant Commentary on the Life and Work of a Great Professor of English Literature").

Ideologically, Woolf was thus in agreement with the pedagogical arguments of the WEA and in particular with Cole's views on lecturing; she was not, however, strongly taken by Cole himself. Her reactions to him were ambivalent: impressed by his cleverness, determination, and energy, she was nevertheless alienated by his pugnacious, aggressive, and self-assured manner. When he and his wife dined with the Woolfs in 1919, she responded negatively to their militant style: "A positive domineering young man he seemed; & she, with less force, equally sure of herself... Who gains, even if they do win their victories" (*D* 1:268). And she connected the domineering element to the absence of stimulating effect: "no speculative or contemplative or imaginative power seems to be left in them" (268). On a later occasion, Woolf found Cole, a Balliol graduate, to be in manner no different from any other academic insider: "Never," she wrote, "was there such a quick, hard, determined young man as Cole; covering his Labour sympathies, which are I suppose intellectual, with the sarcasm & sneers of Oxford" (*D* 11:41).[94]

Woolf's criticism reminds us that sharing a view is one thing and sharing a language is another. Although Cole was an advocate, like Woolf, for a co-operative dialogic mode of education, his manner of promoting it was combative and coercive. Virginia Woolf, for her part, developed a suggestive style designed to stimulate the reader's own thoughts. She enacted the "give and give" that she and Cole both considered the desired pedagogical approach. But it was an approach that, at least for her time, was situated outside the classroom and the institutional sphere.

"Why?" (1934); "The Leaning Tower" (1940)

Woolf's belief in empowering student voices is strongly evident in two essays about educational matters that she wrote for primarily student audiences. "Why?" was written in 1934 for the second issue of *Lysistrata*, a magazine published by the students of Somerville, the women's college at Oxford. "The Leaning Tower" was a talk that Woolf read to the Brighton Workers' Educational Association on April 27, 1940; it was published later that same year, in a slightly revised form, by the Hogarth Press.[95] Both audiences were outsiders to the traditional university system (Somerville did not receive full status within the university until 1957). Both audiences included a high proportion of students or people who had at least attended a class. And in both works, Woolf tried to offer interactive exchange as opposed to authoritarian instruction. But while neither essay adopts the conventional lecturer's tone, Woolf employs her subversive alternative discourse differently for each group.

Titles are often good indicators of approach. "Why?" conveys a predominantly interrogative mode; "The Leaning Tower" reflects the development of an extended metaphor. These titles further differentiate the manner of Woolf's assault on the privileged establishment. Her message to the Oxford students is to question everything: the status quo, all aspects of public and social life, and, most particularly, the pernicious system of lecturing on English literature. "[W]hy lecture, why be lectured?" she asks, and further, "why learn English literature at universities when you can read it for yourselves in books?" (*CE* II:279, 281). Her appeal to the WEA is instead to ask them to visualize three images, representing the past, the present, and the future: the erect tower of the nineteenth-century privileged class; the leaning tower of those now self-conscious of and uneasy about that privilege; and the flat playing field of an imagined future of equality and democracy. Both essays, however, move similarly from tropes of elevation to tropes of leveling: "Why?" replaces the figure of the lecturer mounted on a platform with the composite image of the teacher talking to *and listening to* the students, everyone situated "naturally and happily, on the floor" (281); "The Leaning Tower" tumbles the writer and intellectual out of his "raised chair" of expensive education down to the "common ground" where all readers and writers assume equal responsibility for the making and the preserving of literature (*CE* II:168, 178). The essays are therefore similar in message, but Woolf "performs" more radically for her university audience than she does for the WEA. "Why?" subjects the reader to a barrage of questions whereas "The Leaning Tower" guides its audience smoothly through a well-articulated argument. But the greatest difference lies in their approach to the inscribed reader – the reader that the textual discourse both presumes and creates.

In "Why?" Woolf describes the lecture as "an obsolete custom which not merely wastes time and temper, but incites the most debased of human passions – vanity, ostentation, self-assertion, and the desire to convert" (*CE* II:281). She herself then writes in a polyvocal, destabilized mode. The opening paragraph employs what I have elsewhere called Woolf's "trope of the twist" – a settling and then subsequent unsettling of the reader, usually by shifting ideological ground.[96] The first sentence delivers an initial shock by pronouncing a negative judgment on the magazine: "When the first number of *Lysistrata* appeared, I confess that I was deeply disappointed" (278). According to traditional assumptions, the remark would suggest a lack of quality, the disgrace of not being up to standard. But the twist is that Woolf's disappointment is provoked by the "established, prosperous" appearance of the magazine. To understand the different inflection, we have to shift to the subversive ideology that constructs mental freedom as more desirable than public and social power. Reversing our assumptions, we see "power and prestige" as inhibiting markers and the "respectable dailies and weeklies" as constraining, unfertile sites (278). Internal power depends upon the ability to question, the freedom of taking nothing for granted – all of which an investment in the establishment represses and kills.

Having alerted us, somewhat humorously, to oppositional ideologies, the essay then uses fictional modes to dramatize multiple voices. The voice of an imagined monologic lecturer is counterpointed with circuitous meanderings in the mind of his listener; questions themselves are animated as various subversive hauntings in the writer's brain – an unruly, uncontrollable, "screaming and crying" lot (281). The writer's mind becomes a performative site, with the writing voice comically playing the role of a calm parent trying to assuage a group of clever, rebellious children. The essay ends with a further imagined dialogue, this time with an exasperated reader of academic manuscripts who, in total disgust, whizzes one across the room. Woolf is playful, funny, and quite thoroughly non-academic, deliberately subverting the authority presumed in a university publication. And, given the magazine's title, Woolf's essay appropriately demonstrates the overturning of the supposedly strong (warriors and answers) by the supposedly weak (the women of Athens and Sparta, and questions).

The most striking difference of Woolf's talk to the WEA is the even seriousness of its tone. The structure follows the development of an argument through clear separate stages, asking questions but always providing answers. The writer's voice is stable throughout. While the tower image is developed with multiple connotations – it is the ivory tower of the university, the stucco tower of middle-class comfort and respectability, and the golden tower of wealth – the dominant mode is that of theoretical exposition, supported by illustrative quotation. Woolf does undercut the authority that adheres to the stable speaking voice, but with more straightforward techniques than the subversive performatives of "Why?" Woolf qualifies her views with provisionality: "It is only a guess, and a rough guess" (*CE* 11:165); she acknowledges her bias and partiality: "These then, briefly and from a certain angle, are some of the tendencies" (176); and she presents her conclusions as incomplete and undeveloped: "These then are a few reasons, hastily snatched, why we can look forward hopefully" (179). She diminishes distance between speaker and listener by frequently employing the pronouns "we" and "us." Perhaps most importantly, she repeatedly undercuts the whole process of theorizing: theories are "dangerous things," only to be hazarded with a great deal of "risk." And she assumes the further risk of deconstructing her own argument: "the germ of a theory is almost always the wish to prove what the theorist wishes to believe" (163).

But there is a final inevitable risk, in her hour's talk,[97] of becoming implicated in the very discourse she is trying to oppose: the hierarchical, authoritarian discourse represented by "Hitler's voice" and the voice of "the pedagogic, the didactic, the loud speaker strain" (164, 175). For, no matter how modestly framed, Woolf's talk still required the audience to listen to a monologue, and to a manner and accent that would necessarily interfere with her intent of uniting with her audience as similar outsiders to privileged education.[98] It was still, in many ways, a lecture. But one clear way to counter the central "I" down the middle of her text[99] would be to bring in other voices and so Woolf concludes by urging the audience to become participants – reading for themselves, criticizing for themselves, constructing their own theories. And she shifts from writers and what they have written to readers/critics and their responsibility to formulate opinions, and then further to the way formulating opinion begins to place the reader in a writer's role. For the "writer" who is distanced in Woolf's opening words as the other is at the end what "we" must become: "in future we are not going to leave writing to be done for us by a small class of well-to-do young men... We are going to add our own experience, to make our own contribution" (181).

"The Leaning Tower" is ultimately a rhetorical performance designed to shift empowerment away from the traditional, privileged establishment and over to the working-class students. Using Roman Jakobson's model of communication, we might say that Woolf's focus is less on message than on contact, that her words signify less for their referential than for their phatic function. Taken as literary history, Woolf's overview might well seem strange and tenuous: is there not something highly selective about her claims that nineteenth-century writers took class divisions for granted, that writing before the First World War was apolitical, and that contemporary poetry is all didactic "oratory"? But if we read her lecture as contact with her audience, then her critical history functions as political praxis, undermining the cultural tendency to construct literature as hallowed, sacred ground and opening it up for repossession. "Let us trespass at once," Woolf declares, mapping literature as "common ground" and urging her listeners to "make that country our own country" (181).[100] In criticizing past and present writers, she models a critical voice, establishing her audience's right to critical opinions. While the qualifiers attached to her monologic voice help Woolf to avoid the plot of conversion Clarissa attributes to the extension lecturer Kilman, Woolf's critical practice helps her to avoid the false elevation of culture associated with Miss Isabel Pole.

Woolf's narrative of the pivotal literary "turn" in 1914 is, like her linear evolutionary history of women's writing in *A Room of One's Own*, cultural work rather than essentialist history, designed more to clear a space for the future than to fix the past.[101] And in this way, too, her lecture is an attempt to reach a large audience without engaging the regulating and homogenizing effects implicit in mass culture. For part of Woolf's message is that equal educational opportunities will eradicate the "featureless mass" because people will be able to develop their individual qualities, "their humour, their gifts, their tastes" (179). The purpose of her closing "peroration" is to engage those individual, multiple voices, and to replace her own voice with the voices of her audience: "Try it for yourselves" (180). Woolf ends with an inclusive democratic gesture, calling on her audience, and indeed the larger audience of all readers, to engage in the work of constructing a meaningful past and writing a hopeful future. Utopian though it may be, Woolf's concluding vision claims for literature a significant political role. At a time of immense political threat, she presents literature as a site for modeling a new social reality: "It is not cut up into nations; there are no wars" (181). The hedged geography of nations and classes is reconfigured as a borderless community of readers and writers standing together on common ground.

THE RECEPTION OF "THE LEANING TOWER"

The listening audience

It is one thing to ask for questions; it is another to get them. Despite Woolf's call for audience participation in her talk to the WEA, her letter to Sackville-West the next day suggests that her audience responded with silence. On April 28, Woolf wrote, "I lectured for an hour yesterday: 200 betwixt and betweens – you know how they stare and stick and won't argue" (*L* VI:394). Writing to T. S. Eliot on May 15, Woolf was even less charitable: "Dear, how I'd like to discuss poetry with you! And not with the WEA at Brighton" (*L* VI:398). But here Woolf is voicing her exasperation, her frustration, her failure to elicit the response she desired – all of which, by May 29, erupted in her diary into anger:

Then the [Women's Institute] plays rehearsed here yesterday. My contribution to the war is the sacrifice of pleasure: I'm bored: bored & appalled by the readymade commonplaceness of these plays: which they cant act unless we help. I mean, the minds so cheap, compared with ours, like a bad novel – thats my contribution – to have my mind smeared by the village & WEA mind; & to endure it, & the simper. (*D* v:288)

This is precisely the kind of remark that, out of context, shocks and offends, seeming as it does, too, to belie Woolf's publicly professed encouragement of these very same minds.[102] But the passage that follows explains the reason for her disparaging words. Woolf's objection is not to nature but to culture; further, her anger is not at working-class culture but at middle-class attitudes imported into working-class minds. For Woolf proceeds to qualify what she has written and then not to qualify but to explain:

But this is to be qualified – only theres Miss Griffiths [Hogarth press clerk] coming for the weekend – all simper & qualification. So, if Margaret Ll. Davies says, how insolent we middleclass women are, I argue, why cant the workers then reject us? Whats wrong is the conventionality – not the coarseness. So that its all lulled & dulled. The very opposite of "common" or working class. (*D* v:288–89)

If the aim of adult education was to help the workers "bring their own ideas to birth,"[103] the unquestioning elevation of culture constitutes a repressive idealization for students like Leonard Bast and Septimus Smith. Woolf's irritation here is not with any native lack of intelligence, but with an ac-culturation process in which the aspiring working-class mind serves as a reflection of all that is worst in middle-class conventionality, complacency, and unthinking acceptance of inherited valuations. Woolf's WEA audience was probably puzzled, perhaps taken aback, by her criticism of poets and novelists they admired or expected that they ought to admire; very possibly a respect that she did not want them to feel made them "stick and stare" and prevented their arguing back. As "betwixt and betweens," they were not yet the new classless society; they were the victims of inhibiting middlebrow. Their failure to respond to Woolf's talk was a failure in the system as a whole – the system that had Woolf lecturing to two hundred people, the system that put the audience in the position of sitting metaphorically at her feet instead of talking equally to her on the floor.

Writers write back

There were other responses to Woolf's lecture, however, though unfortunately not comments that she was ever to see. "The Leaning Tower" was published in *Folios of New Writing* in the autumn of 1940; the succeeding spring number included three invited replies, plus a postscript to the exchange by John Lehmann. Though her intervening death may have occasioned some hesitation, Lehmann decided to publish these views, "believing she would have preferred the argument to go on, with her love of all debates and new ideas."[104] *Folios of New Writing* was a journal devoted to new voices, with a particular emphasis on writers unlikely to be found in traditional venues. It included a high percentage of working-class writers and very young writers – often students – publishing for the first time. It was therefore a highly appropriate place to debate Woolf's revolutionary call.

Woolf's three respondents were Edward Upward, a schoolmaster, novelist, and critic who had recently published the novel, *Journey to the Border* (1938), B. L. Coombes, a farmer's son who had worked most of his life in the mines of South Wales and who had recently published his autobiography *These Poor Hands* (1939), and the poet Louis MacNeice. Not one of them disagrees with her argument that the tower is leaning, that it should come down, and that writing must include more voices of the working class. But each writes back, understandably, from his own position. The result is an interesting difference: the two middle-class writers react largely with self-defense of their own group; the working-class respondent picks up where Woolf leaves off and takes her approach to a further stage.

Upward and MacNeice (the first a graduate of Cambridge, the second of Oxford, and both now listed in the *Oxford Companion to Literature*) focus on the middle section of Woolf's essay, the section concerning the leaning-tower writers. Both read her essay, in Jakobson's terms, for its message, not its contact, and both are concerned with defending the leaning-tower group against what they see as her attack. Upward sees that Woolf criticizes this group for expressing bitterness toward bourgeois society while taking advantage of its benefits, but he claims he has problems understanding her point. He wonders if she wants to protect bourgeois society, or if she thinks (simply but wrongly) that bitterness is not an emotion that should be expressed in literature. Then agreeing that there is some truth in her criticism of their "half-hearted" commitment, he explains that it is their lack of full commitment to socialism that is at fault. He thinks that they should focus their attacks on more important bourgeois figures and that they should portray their socialist heroes more heroically. But his main proposal is that they should supplement their writing with political activism, even subordinating writing to political work. Thoroughly committed to the value of propaganda, he fails to grasp Woolf's point about its limitations. He sees no problem in the writing of the leaning-tower group except for thinking that increased social activism would produce better work.

MacNeice writes a more formally analytic article, taking Woolf to task point by point for her over-simplifications and errors. He does not, it is true, call her "maggot," "vermin," "gnawing rat," or "cabbage head,"[105] but we definitely hear the aggressive tones of professional competition. In MacNeice's view, Woolf is wrong that nineteenth-century writers accepted a class-based society, wrong that social upheaval is antithetical to the production of good literature, wrong that good writing is not didactic, wrong that the writing of the 1930s was solely didactic, wrong that it was filled with self-pity, and wrong that it was focused on destruction. She is not wrong but inconsistent about language, since she cannot make up her mind whether language should be purified or hybridized. As for the leaning-tower poets, they were right and if there was anything wrong with their position, they learned from it. There is a strong sense of going into battle to demolish the enemy. And again, there is no sense that Woolf is concerned about writing; MacNeice, like Upward, thinks that her problem is with their political views.

These criticisms are worth examining, since they represent a view of Woolf that has always been strongly entrenched: Woolf as aesthetic, sentimentally attached to tradition and privilege, and opposed to political work. If we think that Woolf was attacking the political subject matter of the leaning-tower group, then there is some justice in this view. Or if we understand Woolf's objection as pertaining simply to the style of leaning-tower writing, she will emerge as a writer concerned about aesthetics and not about life. But Woolf's analysis – which today we might define as semiological – has to do with the "subjects" of writer and audience that such writing constructs.

One problem Woolf identifies with "the pedagogic, the didactic, the loud speaker strain" (*CE* II:175) is that it constructs the human subject as conscious mind alone. A dominating political self-consciousness has excluded the unconscious – and its fertilizing richness – as part of the writer's world: "The inner mind was paralysed, because the surface mind was always hard at work" (176). And, in a further domination, the compulsion "to preach," like the compulsion to lecture, inscribes the audience as a passive undifferentiated herd: "We are in a group, in a class-room as we listen" (175). In contrast, the suggestivity of poetic discourse stimulates the individual mind: "We listen to [it] when we are alone" (176). The cultural value of such discourse is, on the level of the human subject, to liberate the whole of the mind and invest it with agency;[106] on the social level, the value is to enable a dialogic, democratic community. Woolf's brief reference to Hitler's voice on the wireless implies the connection between the "loud speaker strain" and the totalitarian state, whereas her brief though enigmatic reference to excluded voices points to the loose thread that could unravel repressive regimes – whether of thought or of political organization: "And that influence [the influence of the leaning tower], let us remember, may well have excluded from that string of names the poets whom posterity will value most highly, either because they could not fall into step, as leaders or as followers, or because the influence was adverse to poetry, and until that influence relaxed, they could not write" (170–71). These alternative voices simply puzzled Upward, whose notions of engagement were tied to conventional political work: "One passage in her paper seems to imply that the best modern writers are those who have remained immune to the 'influence' of the major social realities of our time. Which writers she means is not quite clear."[107] Woolf, however, did not urge aloofness from social reality; she meant aloofness from leaning-tower consciousness. In the context of 1940, the marginalized poetic voices are those that, unable to "fall into step," resist the marching armies and, remaining on the outside, create an alternative space to the war.[108]

Far from espousing an aesthetic ideology, Woolf's essay concerns the cultural value of poetic discourse and asserts that writing is cultural work. Her object is the political liberation of both the working-class voice and of the undermind, both in her time suppressed and disempowered. Such liberation, if we read semiotically, is also the meaning of a spatial analogy following her famous statement about human nature changing "on or about December 1910" (*E* III:421). In describing the difference between the Victorian cook living "like a leviathan in the lower depths" and the Georgian cook moving "in and out of the drawing room" (422), Woolf does not literally mean that the Victorian cook never came "upstairs." She is describing a shift in the locations of power, from hierarchical orderings to a flat plane, and suggesting a shift in both class and mental structures. Upward and MacNeice, however, become so involved with correcting what they see as her simplified construction of their own circle that they fail to see that she is asking them to think in different terms. Since they focus only on message content, they fail to grasp her underlying argument that a way of writing – that is, a discourse – inscribes a human subject, the communicative dynamics that define social relationships, and in turn a society's political map. On their side of the coin, there are justifiable grounds for their charge that Woolf relies on partial evidence. On her side, there is every evidence that she demolishes their literal politics in favor of a discursive politics that is both more subtle and more percipient.

As the mining son of a farmer, Coombes not surprisingly approaches Woolf's essay for what it says about the working class. Focusing on Woolf's final section, he virtually ignores the earlier parts. He begins with a minor correction, challenging Woolf's separation of the working class from "The Poor" (*CE* ii:165) by indicating how easily the first can slip into being the second. But his primary aim is to take her argument further, to respond with the "Yes, but" dialogics that Leavis endorsed, if he did not perform.[109] Agreeing that the issue is the empowerment of working-class writing voices, Coombes delves into further problems that Woolf did not raise: the almost insurmountable difficulties blocking working-class writers, hampered as they are by low levels of literacy, lack of education, and physical exhaustion.[110] He agrees with Woolf in his desire that "education – as well as opportunity [be] made free and equal for all," but he then raises a crucial conundrum embedded in the concept of working-class writer.[111]

Woolf had written "it is death for a writer... to be forced to earn his living in a mine or factory" (*CE* ii:172). She is suggesting the reason why the leaning-tower group did not give up their capital even though it pinned them down, yet it is one of those passages in Woolf's writing that, because of her frequent use of free indirect discourse, is difficult to assign to an unambiguous point of view. Is this Woolf presenting her own view, or Woolf as ventriloquist articulating the leaning-tower group's thought? Coombes himself is uncertain, just as he notes a possible difference between literal statement and intent: "If one accepts the statement by Virginia Woolf as it is written it means that no one who works at manual labour can ever hope to be a writer. She may not have thought of it that way but the result must be so."[112] But then Coombes uses the slippage between intent and implication to uncover an apparently self-defeating paradox; if the worker continues in manual labour, he has no time or energy for writing; if he leaves his work to write, he ceases to be working class. And the latter is no mere technicality; at stake is the writer's access to language and community. For Coombes points out that, if a writer like Woolf visited a working-class home, she would be given a friendly reception, but it would take place in the parlor with all the formality of a Sunday afternoon; his own visit would be in the kitchen, in the midst of daily life. Coombes thus responds with his own spatial and geographic mappings, as he simultaneously reinforces Woolf's point about the object that is absolutely crucial for the writer to keep in sight: "human life" (*CE* II:162). Strongly informed by Woolf's way of thinking, Coombes does not so much prove her wrong as to show how her being partially right prompts him to go further to disclose the "catch 22" dilemma of a writer in the working class.

But Coombes has no easy resolution to propose. The working-class writer must learn everything about language that the educated writer knows and at the same time preserve all ties of access to, and familiar intercourse with, the speech of the working class. And indeed it is Woolf's sense of this necessary conjoining of languages that explains the apparent inconsistency that MacNeice thought he detected in her work. In her view, the "bastard" language of the leaning-tower group is language that has been severed from part of its lineage, whereas a "pool[ing]" of vocabularies and dialects would recover for language its extended family ties (*CE* II:176,179). Similarly for Coombes, such commingling is, while not the solution, the course of action that he recommends. Advocating co-operation and mutual exchange, Coombes states that he "would like to learn" from the leaning-tower writers all that their professional training has given to them; at the same time, he asserts, "Very probably I could tell them of things that they have never seen and they should benefit by that telling."[113] Like Cole's vision for the tutorial class, Coombes imagines not a "give and take" but a "give and give" situation. And, if Woolf has stimulated Coombes's own thinking about the way exclusion from education affects a writer, he, on his part, gives to Woolf the kind of dialogic talking back that she continually sought.

The discussion of "The Leaning Tower" is rounded off with John Lehmann's postscript, which balances the attack upon Woolf by those "writers who felt themselves misjudged and misrepresented in her arguments" with his knowledge of her many years of supporting and encouraging young writers at the Hogarth Press.[114] What Lehmann further understands about Woolf is that she could only be truly supportive by not falsifying her own position or suppressing her own views. She gave to younger or less experienced writers what she could; at the same time, she did not pretend to give them what she could not. Lehmann's perspicacity on this matter is such that it is well worth quoting his words:

> Virginia Woolf was neither insensitive to the difficulties and discoveries of younger writers nor to the great injustices in the way the world is arranged. She was a socialist, and no one could doubt her sympathy with the struggles of working-class people, particularly working-class women, and her belief in the value of their long, historic effort to make themselves articulate, who has read her Introductory Letter to the volume of reminiscences of Co-operative working women called *Life As We Have Known It*. But, as that essay brings out very clearly, she was always conscious of belonging to another class, and felt that it was impossible for her to be more than a sympathetic observer, that an element of insincerity would inevitably creep in if she were to make out that their hopes and hates were hers in equal measure . . . She knew that the working classes were beginning to find their voice, but she wanted them not to imagine that the qualities arising from more direct contact with the hard facts of existence which they could contribute would ever be enough. Her belief was reconciliation, mutual enrichment.[115]

Lehmann goes on to quote from Woolf's Introductory Letter, or "Memories of a Working Women's Guild," choosing a passage on language in which she speaks of the words, images, scenes, and sayings known to the working women but not to her, and from which the middle-class writer has much to gain. But Lehmann also continues the quotation to show that Woolf does not shrink from pointing out that, for their part, the working class can learn from the literary knowledge and experience that the middle-class writer has acquired. He quotes the words I have already emphasized: "For we have as much to give them as they to give us."[116]

FROM LECTURE TO PUBLIC LIBRARY: IN SEARCH
OF COMMON GROUND

Dynamic lecturing and the example of Roger Fry

As we have seen, Woolf subjects the genre of the lecture to devastating critique. And given the prevalence of the lecturing mode in educational practice during her time, her views are strongly anti-establishment, even hostile, it would seem, to the practical demands of mass education. But it is a mistake to assume that Woolf categorically condemned the format of one teacher addressing a large number of students. Although to some extent Woolf launched a semiological analysis of the classroom – exposing the hierarchical ordering of the lecturer raised on the pedestal and the students down on the floor – it is the mirroring of this physical ordering in the traditional discourse of the lecture that lies at the heart of her critique. Woolf tried to subvert the lecturer's implied authority in her talk to the WEA but her scattered self-qualifiers did not sufficiently encourage her audience to speak. Merely stating that your ideas are not authoritative is not enough; what is required is a different lecturing style. As a public speaker, Woolf may not have had the ability to rouse audience response, but she recognized that the lecture did have positive potentials, through the example of Roger Fry.

Beginning in 1894, and largely because of the need to supplement his income, Fry took up the work of extension lecturing and, over time, developed into a successful public speaker who could fill London's Queen's Hall (*RF* 88–89; 261). In Woolf's descriptions of Fry's lectures, however, we are in a totally different realm than at the feet of Sir Walter Raleigh, "professor of life." The sound of Fry's voice, Woolf recollected, conveyed his love for the works of art, and the proximity of art work and audience brought his ideas alive: "The audience stimulated him, and the picture on the screen in front of him helped him to overcome the difficulty of finding words; he improvised" (89). In reciprocal fashion, his informal, spontaneous manner made the audience feel that they were experiencing a present event: "And then in a flash he found the word he wanted; he added on the spur of the moment what he had just seen as if for the first time. That, perhaps was the secret of his hold over his audience. They could see the sensation strike and form; he could lay bare the very moment of perception" (262–63). And the audience's engagement was evident in the way that, after the lecture, they sought him out (264). Nor did Fry exploit popularizing methods for his success. His excitement was all for the challenging works: "The success of the lectures surprised him. Perhaps he had misjudged the British public. Perhaps in its queer way the public had more feeling for art than he allowed. At any rate there was the fact – 'under certain conditions the English public becomes interested in 'highbrow' stuff'" (263). Fry as a lecturer thus achieved the double display of subject and object that is similarly the goal of Woolf's essays: he illustrated for his audience the processes of his own thinking and in the process convinced them to see for themselves.

Fry showed there was nothing inherent in the form of talking to a large group that legislated against audience involvement; but Woolf could see that to achieve immediacy in such a recalcitrant form required enormous energy and great skill. Furthermore, Fry's particular talents were not the most appreciated by the establishment. The Slade professorship that he hoped for was repeatedly denied to him until finally, almost belatedly, offered just a year before his death. Commenting on the way he had been passed over in 1910, Woolf wrote, "Roger Fry's energies were made no use of, officially, to teach the young to use their eyes" (*RF* 151). Despite the life that Fry breathed into the lecture, this kind of life was not what the academic establishment of the time most desired.

For both personal and practical reasons, then, even the dynamic, process-oriented lecture could not serve Woolf as a pedagogical form. Fry was an inspiring example, but his success depended on his charismatic temperament. And if even Fry existed precariously on the margins of the educational institutions, there was little likelihood that Woolf, with her background of self-education and her female status, could exert a pressure on the institutions to reform. Writing, on the other hand, did not require the same institutional sanction as lecturing, and writing was more conducive to her complex dialogic approach. At a time when public concern had highlighted the need for adult education and attention to reading, Woolf conceived a non-institutionalized, alternative pedagogy. The informal essay or review, published through a private press, and made available through free libraries, was her way of taking pedagogy to the street.

The library as alternative pedagogy

In "The Leaning Tower," speaking to the WEA, Woolf constructed herself as a commoner standing with her audience on common ground. She held her alternative pedagogy up in her hand, saying "This book was not bought; it was not hired. It was borrowed from a public library. England lent it to a common reader" (*CE* ii:180). She encouraged her readers to read it; she encouraged them to "point out any defects" – indicating ironically that she did not refer, as the librarian's notice did, to physical damage. Her point was, as usual, not about respect for the book, but respect for the reader's mind. The reader must feel free to write back. If England has lent you books, she told her audience, in return you must "make yourself critics" (180).

The public library adds a significant component to the audience for the highbrow press, complicating the usual assumptions about its small, exclusionary nature. As Hermione Lee states, "All her life [Woolf] celebrated the democratic function of the public library as the university of the non-specialist, uninstructed reader; it is the reading room for the common reader."[117] John Mepham similarly notes Woolf's sympathy with "the hunger that working people felt for books, art and travel, and the importance to them of such sources as exist, for example, the municipal libraries and the WEA."[118] Woolf's sketch in her diary for the WEA talk shows how clearly she saw the library as the link between writing and a democratic social goal. After noting the limitation of the leaning-tower poets, she wrote,

Is the best poetry that which is most suggestive – is it made of the fusion of many different ideas, so that it says more than is explicable? Well thats the line; & it leads to Public Libraries: & the supersession of aristocratic culture by common readers. Also to the end of class literature: the beginning of character literature; new words from new blood; & the comparison with the Elizabethans. (*D* v:267)

Like the communal sharing she had recommended in "Are Too Many Books Written and Published?" libraries would open culture to all, and an open culture would mean a more democratic world.

As opposed perhaps, to the democratic yet policed and regulated site, Westminster Hall, the public library signified inclusiveness, freedom, and common ground. Woolf's essay "The Lives of the Obscure" begins by evoking a precious moment in a "faded, out-of-date obsolete library," where the lives of those forgotten to history are reclaimed from the dusty shelves. Her essay "How Should One Read a Book?" declares the library as a site of common reading: "To admit authorities, however heavily furred and gowned, into our libraries and let them tell us how to read, what to read, what value to place upon what we read, is to destroy the spirit of freedom which is the breath of those sanctuaries. Everywhere else we may be bound by laws and conventions – there we have none" (*CR* 2:258). The public or free library – as opposed to the circulating library, with its subscription method, or the British Museum, with its reader's ticket – required no payment of fees, no letters of introduction, no accompanying Fellow of the College.[119] Ideally, the library would be inclusive in content, unrestricted in thought, and open in admission.

Public libraries in Woolf's time, however, had not exactly achieved equitable access. At the beginning of the century, methods of book borrowing were still nothing short of intimidating. A common procedure required borrowers first to look up a book to find its assigned number, then to pass the number on a little slip of paper to an assistant ensconced behind a metal grill, and finally to receive in return a book they had until then not been allowed to see or touch. The formalities, one librarian wryly commented in 1922, served to keep books "in working order and unpilfered," safely out of reach of "the reading proletariat."[120] The report on Oxford and Working-class Education did celebrate the establishment of public libraries "in over 500 places," stating that "their educational possibilities cannot be over-emphasized." But their marginally welcoming nature was betrayed by the modesty of the praise: "In some towns, according to a growing custom, readers are permitted to go among the books and handle them."[121]

Even the library, then, tended to treat the book as a sacred object of veneration, and censorship still influenced the selection of books.[122] But Woolf also saw, through her work for the Women's Service Library, the possibilities for a more welcoming, reader-friendly approach.[123] As she wrote in *Three Guineas*, "For you have a library, and a good one. A working library, a living library where nothing is chained down and nothing is locked up" (*TG* 73). Woolf was a constant advocate for the ordinary life of the book, and it is hardly surprising that, taking down one of her own books in a public library, she was delighted by the signs of everyday use. In October 1940, Virginia Woolf went to the library in Lewes and looked up their copy of her *Common Reader*; in her diary she recorded, "I was glad to see the C.R. all spotted with readers at the Free Library" (*D* v:329). The spots left by her common readers were to her not a defacement but a sign of life – a sign, moreover, of her book's life in the public realm. Markings on library books are still unappreciated by librarians but, in 1940, Woolf's reaction to those spots reflects a progressive, democratic attitude to the status of the book. A book spotted with common readers claims the book as a possession of the people, there to be handled and used.

The tower and the common ground

To what extent, then, did Woolf stand with her common readers on common ground? Despite everything Woolf said about equal relations between writers and readers, and her support of libraries, and her advocacy of a use-oriented approach to books, her life was nevertheless marked by personal privilege. Despite all the discrimination she experienced as a woman, she was Leslie Stephen's daughter and she spent much of her life interacting with some of England's best-trained minds. This background, and Woolf's ability to use it defensively and territorially when threatened, needs to be recognized, but it also needs to be studied as one of the subjects of Woolf's probing thought. We need to move beyond the polarities of attack and defense of Woolf's "privilege" to heed what she herself was saying about it in her published works.

Woolf was a highbrow and to be a highbrow was – and still is to a large extent – to have benefited from certain kinds of privilege, if nothing more than the privilege of having had the time to learn to read books. But rather than disdaining the results of privilege, Woolf modeled a future world in which the attainments traditionally reserved for a privileged few would be available for all. Democratic highbrowism was her ideal – not to be confused with what she claimed herself to have achieved. But if making books and knowledge accessible to all on an equitable basis was one reform to be achieved, the other equally important revolution was to eradicate the prejudice against the intellectual approach. As I have argued, Woolf's projected ideal of equitable exchange includes her own world too.

Misunderstandings and criticisms of her goals, however, came from a variety of quarters in the months following her talk to the WEA. In August, she received two challenging letters from Ben Nicolson – letters that perhaps expressed the usual youthful rebellion against the older generation but that reiterated the long-standing dismissal of the reality of her work. Another "sneer" came from David Cecil, probably in an article published the next January, which, according to Woolf, categorized her work, along with Strachey's, as "withdrawing from life to cultivate their art in quiet" (*D* v:352). The next February, Desmond MacCarthy's book column in the *Sunday Times* reviewed the volume of *Folios of New Writing* in which "The Leaning Tower" had appeared. Although noting Woolf's hope "that, the privileges of wealth having been abolished, the literary qualities which wealth produced will be within reach of many more talented people," MacCarthy, albeit reluctantly, claimed she was wrong to think that creativity could thrive without wealth. Forgetting that Woolf was rejecting privilege not money, and forgetting that she had argued for the comfortable though not exorbitant wage of £500 per year, MacCarthy failed to grasp the classless, equitable society that Woolf was urging as a goal. Rather than reading Woolf's "we" as rhetorically invoking a shared democratic project, MacCarthy retreated to the old class positioning, concluding, "I think that, except as a sign of sympathy, she ought not to have used the pronoun 'we' in addressing an audience of working-men."[124]

Woolf wrote back to her challengers, trying different strategies for asserting her views. With her old friend Desmond MacCarthy, she was direct and lively, assailing him with questions to remind him of the difference between his insiders' and her outsiders' education, and teasingly pointing out how, when it came to privilege, she stood in relation to him: "Of course I'm not on the ground with the WEA but I'm about four thousand five hundred and fifty pounds nearer them than you are" (*L* vi:468). Her short, friendly note contains a signal, however, about her seriousness: she lets MacCarthy know her letter follows three hours of argument between her and Leonard.

With the younger Ben Nicolson, Woolf confronted a more difficult task, and the three letters she wrote to him stand as a magnificent testimony to her consciousness of, and sensitivity to, her reader's response. In the first letter, Woolf abandons argument for dramatization, prompting her reader to construct in his own mind the image of the writer in the real world. As in "All About Books," the semiotics of letter-writing are, to a large extent, what this letter is about. Woolf foregrounds the scene of writing, presenting herself in the midst of air-raid sirens and falling bombs, going on with her work, the work that is writing a letter to Ben. While explaining some of the ways Roger Fry faced "disagreeable actualities," she *performs* her own commitment to writing, with the disagreeable realities of German raiders passing overhead. The attempt at communication, the respect that the writing self declares for the reading other, the goal of stimulating the reader's ability to see – all assert the value of the artist's reality against the opposing reality of war.

Nicolson's reply, however, betrays his inability to shift position, so that Woolf's first response is to rebut his arguments with a straightforward explanation of her views. Against his posited construction of Bloomsbury's select and rarified audience, Woolf makes clear her opposite goal: "I did my best to make [my books] reach a far wider circle than a little private circle of exquisite and cultivated people" (*L* vi:420). To Nicolson's claim that "[y]ou must educate your public" if they are to understand such sophisticated work, Woolf adds the next, more challenging level: "What is the kind of education people ought to have? That it seems to me is the problem we have got to solve" (420). She and Roger and Leonard had done their best to assist people's education but were limited by the educational institutions, which only the politicians can change. Yet ultimately the letter is less a defense of her own position than an attempt to get Nicolson to reflect on his own: "but I cant find your answer in your letter, how it is that you are going to change the attitudes of the mass of people by remaining an art critic" (420–21). Artists and politicians have equally important but separate roles, the letter suggests, and Nicolson should stop scapegoating and define what his own goal will be.

But this heavily revised draft was never sent; it was replaced by a mildly questioning, somewhat self-deprecating, even rather flattering response, expressing the hope that Nicolson would be able to do what he claimed others had not. The final version is a considerate letter, one that makes allowance for the reader's youth, one that at the same time sounds a note of hopelessness about the prospect of getting this particular young man to entertain alternative views. And it, too, indicates that the letter-writer is writing while an air raid is going on. Taken as a whole, the three letters leave no doubt about Woolf's intellectual project: as a writer she had done what she could to bring her views to the broad public, just as she does what she can – however limited its success – to open Ben Nicolson's eyes. Empowering her reader was for her ultimately more important than winning the argument, and was a way she, as a writer, could oppose the subjugation of the other she considered to be the backbone of war.

Woolf's claim that she would "go down with [her] colours flying" (*D* v:358) was a final assertion of her belief in the "real work" set out by the artist's goals. But the extent to which she had achieved them – created, that is, her dialogically empowered audience – was always for her an area of uncertainty and doubt. Toward the end of her life, enveloped by reports of increasing war casualties, Virginia Woolf wrote in her diary, "No echo comes back. I have no surroundings. I have so little sense of a public that I forget about Roger [her biography of Roger Fry] coming or not coming out" (*D* v:299). The next month she continued, "[t]here's no standard to write for: no public to echo back" (304); a little more than a month before her death, she wrote, "But shall I ever write again one of those sentences that gives me intense pleasure? There is no echo in Rodmell – only waste air" (357). On October 10, she referred in her diary to "Ben's attack"; on October 12, she jotted her note about seeing the C.R. spotted with readers. Was her visit to the Lewes library not a reality check? Was she not listening to Ben's criticism and considering the possibility he may have been right?

Impelled by curiosity, I decided to try to locate that *Common Reader* all covered with spots. Could the spots be marginalia, I wondered? Would I find Woolf's readers talking back, as she so hoped they would? The old Lewes library, I discovered, has been converted to other uses, and the new library is filled with colorful new books. But the librarians assured me that the contents of the old library were safely stored in archives and that if I would return in four or five days, they would produce the book. Waiting for me indeed was a 1929 copy of the first *Common Reader*. The librarian's note read, "The book appears to have had heavy use, as evidenced by the dates on the labels, and at some time before 1955 was rebound in its present (and now very worn) blue cloth."[125] Opening the book, I found, to my surprise, *literal* spots splattered over a great many pages: smudges that appeared to be thumb marks but also orange spots, brown spots, pink spots – looking like tea, marmalade, jam, and lipstick. The spots were the marks of everyday life, and I thought of the way in which Woolf, in her letters to Ben Nicolson, performed the integration of life and art by interspersing descriptions of air raids and falling bombs. I was reminded of Woolf's introduction to *Life As We Have Known It* and her descriptions there of the women reading while cooking or while eating their meals. "They read at meals; they read before going to the mill," Woolf had written; "They read with the indiscriminate greed of a hungry appetite, that crams itself with toffee and beef and tarts and vinegar and champagne all in one gulp" (*CE* II:144–45). I was delighted that Woolf – who so frequently used the metaphor of eating to describe her own reading – should have herself been delighted by the literal tokens of eating on her page. Perhaps, I thought, there is no better sign for her work as a democratic highbrow, working for the integration of literature into our daily lives.

PART TWO

Critical practice

CHAPTER 3

Woolf and the theory and pedagogy of reading

For the desire to read, like all the other desires which distract our unhappy souls, is capable of analysis.

Virginia Woolf, "Sir Thomas Browne" (*E* III:368)

So we reveal some of the prejudices, the instincts and the fallacies out of which what it pleases us to call criticism is made.

Virginia Woolf, "An Essay in Criticism" (*E* IV:455)

WOOLF AND COMMON READING

The pedagogical history outlined in the last chapter helps to explain the difference between the "English Common Reader" as Altick employs the term and the "Common Reader" as conceived by Virginia Woolf. Altick alternately names his common readers the "mass reading public," meaning by this term the group of new readers or potential new readers that, in the nineteenth century, emerged from the artisan and laboring classes. The "revolutionary social concept" that he identifies as a belief in the "democracy of print" had, as its object, the extension of cultured reading beyond the upper classes down to what, in 1858, Wilkie Collins referred to as the "Unknown Public" – the great number of people who were then just learning how to read. Defined oppositionally, the nineteenth-century common reader is thus "not the relatively small, intellectually and socially superior audience for which most of the great nineteenth-century authors wrote."[1] In contrast, Virginia Woolf distinguishes her common readers from the "mass" audience and does not tie them to identifiers of class. Her common reader is identified by an active, intelligent reading practice, motivated by a desire for broad, inclusive knowledge and expanded human experience. Defined oppositionally, Woolf's common reading is not professional reading pursued in order to acquire specialized learning or to prove a theory; it is equally not complacent conventional reading, designed not to disturb the comforts of "middlebrow" life. Most crucially, as representative of a kind of reading rather than a defined segment of the reading public, the identity of Woolf's common reader is self-selected, and therefore potentially open to all. While Woolf tried to encourage more involvement in intellectual culture from the working class and, at times, from the aristocratic upper class, common reading as she presented it could be a form of reading practiced by the professional and academic classes as well. Linking the common reader to a mode of reading rather than a social being, however, signals a changing pedagogical dynamic. The nineteenth-century goal of conveying a putatively superior culture to the lower classes is replaced by the twentieth-century work of developing the skills and abilities of anyone able and willing to participate in collective cultural activity.

To be pedagogical, however, Woolf's democratic project must pose intellectual challenges. During Woolf's time, newly literate readers might have found her assumption of knowledge daunting, as – with our changing reading habits – most readers probably will today. Yet the essays are readily accessible even if we are not familiar with the books being discussed. The essays either prompt us to reexamine our previous understanding, or prepare us for reading new works with specific questions in mind. A greater challenge may lie in the imagistic suggestiveness, the shifting perspectives, and the ironic subversions of Woolf's style. The problem is not that such features make the essays difficult to understand but that their form runs counter to, and thus encounters the interference of, the expectations established by linear expository prose. At a time when impersonal, objective, analytic criticism was gaining ascendancy, especially in the new discipline of English studies, even skilled readers – or perhaps skilled readers in particular – were not likely to look for theoretical depth in Woolf's informal and elastic prose. As Graham Good argues, her "both/and" thinking and her "'soft' rhetoric of empathy and changing viewpoint" were less amenable to prevailing academic thought than T. S. Eliot's "either/or" thinking and "'hard' rhetoric of precise judgment and stern rejection."[2] Additionally, as David McWhirter points out, the "frank heterogeneity" of Woolf's eclectic approach was less academically containable than Eliot's canonical orderings, with their "neater and perhaps...more marketable package."[3] A third challenge in reading Woolf's essays is that we must pay close attention to their structure to grasp what they are about; we must follow an ongoing process of thinking that undergoes alterations and even reversals in direction. Both Virginia and Leonard Woolf concurred with Montaigne's emphasis on the "journey" not the "arrival," and in Virginia's essays, how we think, rather than what we conclude, is the continuing focus of her approach.[4] Whatever our starting position as readers, her essays offer, in effect, a training in literary thinking through exercises for the mind.

In this respect, the essays serve, like Woolf's fiction, as occasions for stimulating and liberating the reader's thought processes; correspondingly, the need for active reading practices surfaces as a theme in Woolf's fictional works as well. Susan Stanford Friedman argues, for example, that "the narrative of *The Voyage Out* is fundamentally pedagogical, motivated by the protagonist's education into the ways of the adult world," and that "[r]eading functions in the novel as a trope for education." Friedman also posits Rachel as the "'common reader's predecessor," glimpsed in an early, still vulnerable phase: Rachel's lingering investments in authority and her propensity for a total submersion of self in her reading are replaced, in the common-reader essays, with reading practices that both engage with and resist the texts being read.[5] It is of course impossible *not* to be struck by the way Woolf's kinetic and dialogic approach to reading anticipates later theory, particularly the interactive constructs of interpretation advanced in reader-response criticism and poststructuralist formulations of the reader's activity in "producing" the text. Pamela Caughie has admirably demonstrated the way Woolf's process-oriented approach anticipates postmodernist thought in its inscription of "the conception of art as activity rather than property."[6] Yet the social relevance of Woolf's criticism resides in its functional significance in its historical, *modernist* context. The pedagogical may be what most distinguishes her essays from recent writing on the literary text, for Woolf's interest lies not in articulating a theoretical model, but in modeling critical thought.

Closer to Woolf's own time, the theory with which she has most in common is Louise Rosenblatt's transactional approach to the relation between reader and text. Rosenblatt first published *Literature as Exploration* – now in its fifth edition – in 1938, just at the end of Woolf's career; however, Rosenblatt's roots lie in the American pragmatism that, contemporaneously with Woolf, urged the links between education and democracy discussed in chapter 2.[7] Rosenblatt, perhaps regrettably, seems to have noted only Woolf's description of unconscious processes in reading; had she read more widely in Woolf's essays, she would have undoubtedly been struck by the close similarity between Woolf's dialogic reading practices and the transactional theory of reading. The parallels could easily be the subject of a separate study: a defense of common reading, an advocacy of active, self-reflexive reading practices, the concept of a reading community linked by conversations about their reading, and the significance of such practices for a democratic community. More theoretically, Woolf and Rosenblatt both promote a mutually informing relation between the ordering power of the text and the reader's self-ordering activity, in a way that avoids the binary opposition of textual authority, on the one hand, and proliferating relativity, on the other.[8] Such commonalities say much about shared twentieth-century concerns and continuities between British and American modernist thought. But the distinctiveness of Woolf's approach is again that she conveys theory through critical practice. By modeling reading, she makes it a living subject always under examination and always a process that occurs in time.

Woolf relates, as Caughie suggests, stories of her reading and, in doing so, Woolf conveys the kinetic experience of reading in time. She contrasts, for example, expectations before reading with reactions during the reading process (*E* iii:22–25); she traces the development of the reader's (or playgoer's) reactions, noting the difference between her response when a play begins and her views as it reaches its conclusion (*E* iii:246–49); she compares immediate and retrospective responses, reconsidering a work or returning to read it a second time (*E* iii:235–38; *E* iii:336–46). And – because reading is an interactive process between the text of the book and the text of the self – she acknowledges that our readings change over time: "To write down one's impressions of *Hamlet* as one reads it year after year, would be virtually to record one's own autobiography, for as we know more of life, Shakespeare comments upon what we know" (*E* ii:27).

Not surprisingly, the journey appears in Woolf's essays as a frequent trope for reading, but with an emphasis on movement rather than destination. Reviewing Middleton Murry, she asks, "Does he give us what after all matters so much more than the end of any journey or the truth of any argument?" (*E* iii:55). Her discussion of John Evelyn is cast as "Rambling Around Evelyn" (*CR* 1:78–85); another essay ventures into "that jungle, forest, and wilderness which is the Elizabethan drama (*CR* 1:48). She adjures us to be travelers, not tourists; we are warned not "to make museum pieces out of our reading" (*CR* 2:13), and told "[i]t is no use going to the guide-book; we must consult our own minds" (*CR* 2:81). In discussing the "Americanness" of American fiction, Woolf draws a parallel to the traveler's limited (or "orientalizing") constructions of cultural otherness: "Excursions into the literature of a foreign country much resemble our travels abroad...in our desire to get at the heart of the country we seek out whatever it may be that is most unlike what we are used to, and declar[e] this to be the very essence of the [foreign] genius" (*E* iv:269). The journey metaphor emphasizes Woolf's process-oriented approach, while the activity of rambling expresses her resistance to the categorical ordering of knowledge. And, given what we would now call her critique of the touristic consciousness, her link between traveling and reading asserts the provisionality and the partiality of the observer's view and its susceptibility to change.

By inculcating mental agility and flexibility, the essays thus encourage readers to shift from conventional realist reading to modernist self-reflexive practices, perhaps even educating readers for their encounters with modernist fictional texts. But if the essays make modernist literature more accessible, they also perform a transformative social function: they cultivate active minds in opposition to the normative and regulative influence of authoritarian discourses. As a literary critic, Woolf thus testifies to what I regard as the central issue underlying this whole discussion: the potentials for a specifically literary intervention in the formation of public culture. For the question, What is the public work that Woolf's literary work did in her time? is intimately related to the question, What is the public work that literature can do? I hazard to say that most people are drawn to literary discourse because it does *not* reduce to single meanings, even though it then frustrates critical attempts to explain what it means. And perhaps we are today once again at a point where we need to reassert the importance of *literary* value. Writing in a forum about the future direction of English studies, Margery Sabin writes that "literary study has in the past distinguished itself from the social sciences by allowing more space for the language of texts to talk back, to exert pressure back on what readers bring," as opposed to current tendencies to "coerce the text into a priori analytic structures."[9] J. Hillis Miller similarly calls attention to "the irreducible otherness of the work" and argues that a "work's force as an event bringing cultural value or meaning into existence depends on a certain performative use of language" that "always exceeds the referential or mimetic dimension."[10] In her own time, Woolf's intervention in the public forum on literacy and adult education called attention to that region of excess, to that realm of proliferating interpretation, not to retreat to an aesthetic sphere but to insert the values of literary language into the public issues of the day.

The crucial opposition Woolf posed to standardizing, regulating discourse was her commitment to literary discourse as an active, not static, mode. Plasticity and elasticity are words that she frequently used to describe the qualities she sought in her own writing, and they serve to describe the kinds of reading practices she advocated as well. Woolf's dynamic and pluralistic approach to reading, however, makes it a difficult process to define. Its nature is chaotic, and not particularly amenable to analysis, but its very unruliness, Woolf asserts, is its life:

reading, you know, is rather like opening the door to a horde of rebels who swarm out attacking one in twenty places at once – hit, roused, scraped, bared, swung through the air, so that life seems to flash by; then again blinded, knocked on the head – all of which are agreeable sensations for a reader (since nothing is more dismal than to open the door and get no response), and all I believe certain proof that this poet is alive and kicking. (*HL* 231)

The corollary is that any schematic organization of her ideas will necessarily be partial and reductive. In what follows, I isolate four elements in the reading process for closer examination: unconscious, dialogical, historical, and evaluative modes of reading. But I do not mean to suggest that Woolf approached these elements as independent, separable processes in the reading experience. As is clearly evident in the way she models reading in her essays, this highly complex act never proceeds along any one single strand.

READING AND UNCONSCIOUS PROCESSES

Perhaps the most difficult aspect for a pedagogy of reading to address is the realm of unconscious processes. Not surprisingly, the overt questions Woolf poses about reading pertain to the conscious part of reception and the intellectual, retrospective reflection that completes the reading experience. At the same time, as we have seen, she objected to the new academic criticism because it suppressed the personal and emotive dimension of literature and its rich pluralities of affect. She missed what she described in *A Room of One's Own* as a "humming under one's breath," and she sensed a declining appreciation of literature's appeal to the associative powers of the unconscious mind. On the most basic level, Woolf undoubtedly included unconscious processes in her discussion of reading because she knew the role they played in her own experience, yet addressing the unconscious for her also functioned as a crucial antidote to the scientific model that privileged the conscious alone. Woolf valued the plasticity and fluidity of language, seeing its effect on the unconscious as both fertilizing and liberating, in stark contrast to the increasingly analytic and monolithic tendencies of the new professional discipline of English studies. Experience at this level, however, is not easily conveyed in standard critical prose.

Unlike Freud, Woolf was not attempting to theorize the unconscious. Instead, she focused on the evocative possibilities of unconscious response, and to do so, she wrote in metaphoric, imagistic, and highly suggestive ways. In "The Perfect Language," for example, she describes the reader's experience of almost instant understanding as a moment in which "we seem not to read so much as to recollect what we have heard in some other life" (*E* ii:115). In "'The Cherry Orchard,'" she tropes unconscious response – as she frequently does – as a descent into water: "we seemed to have sunk below the surface of things and to be feeling our way among submerged but recognisable emotions" (*E* iii:248). Describing the writer/reader relation in the essay "Fishing," her language itself mirrors the fertilizing, generative transaction she envisions: "Now, if the art of writing consists in laying an egg in the reader's mind from which springs the thing itself" (*CE* ii:301). The destabilizing provisionality and uncertainty ("*if* the art of writing"), the suggestive metaphor ("laying an egg"), the unnamed issue ("the thing itself") suggest a process that defies or eludes logical definition. Woolf's sentence enacts its own meaning, requiring its thought to be completed in the associative caverns of the reader's mind.

Correspondingly, throughout *The Common Reader*s, the quality of "suggestion" is like a ground bass reminding us that literature works in subliminal ways. While praising Dorothy Wordsworth for her exacting descriptions, Woolf nevertheless writes that in them "one feels the *suggestive* power which is the gift of the poet rather than of the naturalist, the power which, taking only the simplest facts, so orders them that the whole scene comes before us, heightened and composed" (*CR* 2:167). Using Hardy to explain what Charlotte Brontë lacks, Woolf comments, "As we read *Jude the Obscure* we are not rushed to a finish; we brood and ponder and drift away from the text in plethoric trains of thought which build up round the characters an atmosphere of question and *suggestion* of which they are themselves, as often as not, unconscious" (*CR* 1:157). A more evocative prose is the direction she envisions that Jane Austen's art would have taken had she lived to write more fiction: "She would have devised a method, clear and composed as ever, but deeper and more *suggestive*, for conveying not only what people say, but what they leave unsaid; not only what they are, but what life is" (*CR* 1:145). In yet another essay, using again the trope of a submerged world, Woolf declares that in reading Dorothy Osborne's letters, "we are deep in this world, seizing its hints and *suggestions*" (*CR* 2:65). And, in discussing De Quincey, Woolf proposes that the effect of his writing is simultaneously to still the conscious and liberate the unconscious:

If we try to analyse our sensations we shall find that we are worked upon as if by music – the senses are stirred rather than the brain... Our minds, thus widened and lulled to a width of apprehension, stand open to receive one by one in slow and stately procession the ideas which De Quincey wishes us to receive... The emotion is never stated; it is *suggested* and brought slowly by repeated images before us until it stays, in all its complexity, complete. (*CR* 2:133–34. All emphases above added.)

As a writer, Woolf conceived the unconscious as modernism's consuming subject: "For the moderns 'that,' the point of interest, lies very likely in the dark places of psychology" (*CR* 1:152). As a critic, however, Woolf was more interested in opening her readers' susceptibility to this dimension of reading than she was in specifying or defining how it works. There are only a few passages in which she directly broaches the interrelation of conscious and unconscious processes, and these are not entirely consistent in view. The shifts perhaps reflect her reluctance to attempt definition and perhaps also her sense that there are different ways of looking at, or explaining, the issue. In "How Should One Read a Book?" for example, she isolates unconscious immersion in a book as a separable, independent stage of reading, prior to conscious criticism:

The first process, to receive impressions with the utmost understanding, is only half the process of reading; it must be completed, if we are to get the whole pleasure from a book, by another. We must pass judgment upon these multitudinous impressions; we must make of these fleeting shapes one that is hard and lasting. But not directly. Wait for the dust of reading to settle; for the conflict and the questioning to die down; walk, talk, pull the dead petals from a rose, or fall asleep. Then suddenly without our willing it, for it is thus that Nature undertakes these transitions, the book will return, but differently. It will float to the top of the mind as a whole. (*CR* 2:266–67)

The passage shows Woolf's characteristic use of evocative imagistic language to suggest the mode by which reading gets assimilated into the unconscious and her repeated figuration of the unconscious as a submerged world. But her need here to distinguish two different mental operations leads her to construct a fairly extensive system of binaries. Unconscious response is first, followed by conscious articulation; the unconscious feels, while the conscious judges; the unconscious surrenders, while the conscious distances. It is passages like this that lead Kate Flint to identify a duality in Woolf's essays between empathetic and intellectual approaches to reading, which Flint then further equates with a dialectic of alternating submission and resistance on the part of the reader.[11] But a closer scrutiny reveals Woolf's sense of a more complex dynamic.

The notion of suspending judgment and waiting for the book to float up to the top of the mind may suggest submission but, in the above passage, the passivity – or suspension – is in the *conscious* mind. The unconscious – which is forming and returning the book to the conscious mind – is envisioned as an active, creative mode. In *A Room of One's Own*, Woolf states, "it is in our idleness, in our dreams, that the submerged truth sometimes comes to the top" (*R* 47). Similarly, in "The Leaning Tower," she writes, "Unconsciousness, which means presumably that the under mind works at top speed while the upper mind drowses, is a state we all know" (*CE* II:166). Furthermore, in a complex description of reading Dostoevsky's "The Eternal Husband," she elaborates upon the relation between conscious and unconscious processes, suggesting an almost undetectable but nevertheless crucial interdependence:

From the crowd of objects pressing upon our attention we select now this one, now that one, weaving them inconsequently into our thought... and the whole process seems both inevitable and perfectly lucid. But if we try to construct our mental processes later, we find that the links between one thought and another are submerged. The chain is sunk out of sight and only the leading points emerge to mark the course. Alone among writers Dostoevsky has the power of reconstructing those most swift and complicated states of mind, of rethinking the whole train of thought in all its speed, now as it flashes into light, now as it lapses into darkness; for he is able to follow not only the vivid streak of achieved thought, but to suggest the dim and populous underworld of the mind's consciousness where desires and impulses are moving blindly beneath the sod. (*E* II:85)

The passage is an extraordinary replay of the mind in slow motion, detecting, as in chronophotography, intervening movements too fast for the naked eye. Using the model of Dostoevsky's prose, Woolf's analysis of thought processes proposes that barely perceptible gaps in the chain of logical thought are in actuality filled by the insertions of the unconscious, emanating from that "dim and populous underworld." Here unconscious assimilation is not prior to conscious apprehension; it is an ever-present, formative participant enabling the *apparent* seamlessness of conscious thought. The "vivid streak of achieved thought" is, under microscopic examination, made of a chain of conscious and unconscious links.[12] The unconscious is thus not, in Woolf's construction, a passive container or a deterministic mechanism; it is an active and creative participant in thought. Furthermore, it is not purely personal in its contents. In what is perhaps Woolf's most extensive – if most poetically rendered – description of the unconscious, she represents the unconscious as the repository, not of personal memories, but of the communal past.

"The Fascination of the Pool" (1929)

As a brief sketch, possibly not for publication, "The Fascination of the Pool" resembles a painter's study, yet it may offer Woolf's most detailed anatomy of the mind. In this fictional essay – or essayistic fiction – an unnamed viewer/narrator looks into a pool, describing first the reflection of a dark "fringe of rushes" around the edge and then, in the center, the reflection of a white sign advertising the sale of a nearby farm. Looking more deeply, beyond the pool's surface, the viewer then describes faces and voices that emerge from its lower depths. A pool, a viewer bending over it, a reflection, faces in the pool, one of whom drowned – the sketch rests upon accumulated fragments of the Narcissus myth. It is also the implicit allusion to Narcissus which explains the last voice, the mysterious unidentified voice that cries "Alas, alas."

The myth of Narcissus is of course a charged allusion for representations of the mind, especially in the work of a female writer. In both critical and literary traditions, Narcissus has commonly been applied in pejorative ways to the female psyche, signaling such limited parameters as vanity, solipsism, and a self-enclosed world.[13] But as part of her feminist revisioning, Woolf inverts the myth to suggest a positive epistemology in which identification with the watery reflections yields an extension and expansion of self through its access to the collective unconscious.

By positing identification as a route from the self outward, Woolf's figuration of the unconscious is similar in its dynamics to a model of reading recently proposed by Isobel Armstrong. In "Textual Harassment: the Ideology of Close Reading, or How Close is Close?" Armstrong suggests that the "close reading" of New Criticism, in its objectification of the text as a site of verbal analysis, is really "distance reading"; similarly, she argues, poststructuralist theory constructs the text "as outside," in its effort to reject "what de Man called the 'aesthetic ideology' and the 'mirror-like structure' of reading, with its 'seductive powers of identification.'"[14] In contrast, Armstrong argues the need for a holistic critical practice, not to revive "appreciative criticism" but rather to situate "the power of affect, feeling, and emotion in a cognitive space." Such criticism would include the "suasive, somatic elements of a text" and, following Emanuel Levinas, would challenge the ensconced binaries of thought/feeling and conscious/unconscious. Drawing further on Levinas, Armstrong engages his redefinition of narcissism, proposing that the reader's "'narcissistic' moment of identification" may be an essential response to texts and a prerequisite of critical reading."[15] In this transformative refiguration of the Narcissean myth, the mirror image is read not as a projection of self but as an alterity that draws the self outward to identify with and become something other.

Armstrong thus locates identification as part of a process by which a text engages its readers in a relation with what is other than the self. In similar fashion, Virginia Woolf outlines a process that depends on an identification that is, at the same time, an experience of alterity. "Do not dictate to your author," she urges; "try to become him. Be his fellow-worker and accomplice"; by so "steep[ing]" ourselves in the book, we will be brought into "the presence of a human being unlike any other" (*CR* 2:259). Such identification is neither projection nor appropriation; it is a movement toward a relational engagement with the voice, or rather voices, in the text. For Armstrong, and for Woolf, this is not simple empathetic sympathy; it demands a willingness to displace one's own thinking and to participate in "how the text thinks."[16]

"The Fascination of the Pool" conveys both this sense of displacement and a complex interplay between conscious and unconscious perceptions. We slip first of all through the conscious surface of the mind:

Round the edge was so thick a fringe of rushes that their reflections made a darkness like the darkness of very deep water. However in the middle was something white. The big farm a mile off was to be sold and some zealous person, or it may have been a joke on the part of a boy, had stuck one of the posters advertising the sale, with farm horses, agricultural implements, and young heifers, on a tree stump by the side of the pool. The centre of the water reflected the white placard and when the wind blew the centre of the pool seemed to flow and ripple like a piece of washing. One could trace the big red letters in which Romford Mill was printed in the water. A tinge of red was in the green that rippled from bank to bank. (*CSF* 226)

In this passage, objective reality – the world beyond the pool – is imaged only in the watery medium that both contains it and alters it. For the mind is not a passive reflector; the perceived world acquires its identity from the reflecting medium. The first transformation is that the referential meaning of the images becomes subordinated to painterly relations of form and color. The dark image of nature (the rushes) contrasts with the white of the world of human toil and possessions (the sign), but the way in which the first mass relates to the second as a frame or border conveys balance rather than opposition. Similarly, the red of the sign intermingles with the complementary green of the water, further integrating the two realms. In such painterly perception, with its emphasis on design and correspondence, the distinctions between the world of the pool and the world outside the pool become blurred; the external world is both contained within the mind and part of its texture.

But perception influences what external reality signifies. The viewer knows about (although does not actually read) the words on the poster "advertising the sale, with farm horses, agricultural implements, and young heifers" and observes that "one could trace the big red letters" – they would be, of course, in reverse – "in which Romford Mill was printed in the water." Words evoke the workaday world, the world of practicality and economics, the world in which language defines and contains meaning. In the pool world, however, words are subjected to fluidity, motion, instability, reversal: the white placard seems "to flow and ripple like a piece of washing" and the "big red letters" become merely "a tinge of red... in the green that rippled from bank to bank." Words cease to be stable and definitive, becoming slippery (multiple and ambiguous) and diaphanous (allusive and associative). In Woolf's next paragraph, the provisionality of language becomes explicit: "the red and black letters and the white paper seemed to lie very thinly on the surface, while beneath went on some profound under-water life like the brooding, the ruminating of a mind" (226).

However, although the solidity of the rational logical world of language is disrupted as we descend into the unconscious, the narrative proceeds not through sharp opposition but by gradual transitions, accomplishing not a rejection of language but its redemption through a revisionary perception of the fluidity of words. Conscious and unconscious processes are separable, but not in conflict. The surface of the pool becomes an entrance to deeper layers, as Woolf moves the mind of the viewer easily from reflected images to images in the depths. And this deeper world is not a solipsistic retreat, but a reservoir of historical and communal memory.

The pool is the inheritor of centuries of thought, of multiple communal voices which, transformed in this fluid medium, function paradoxically in a realm beyond language:

Many, many people must have come there alone, from time to time, from age to age, dropping their thoughts into the water, asking it some question, as one did oneself this summer evening. Perhaps that was the reason of its fascination – that it held in its waters all kinds of fancies, complaints, confidences, not printed or spoken aloud, but in a liquid state, floating one on top of another, almost disembodied. (226)

The voices, as "not printed or spoken aloud," are detached from the limitations and restrictions of time and place. Released from their isolated identities, they inhabit a larger, freer world: "The charm of the pool was that thoughts had been left there by people who had gone away and without their bodies their thoughts wandered in and out freely, friendly and communicative, in the common pool" (226). In this last phrase, "common pool," words expose their slipperiness: "pool" evokes the double association of the fluidity of the unconscious and the sense of shared, collective possession; "common" involves a conflation of "shared" and "ordinary," as it does in *The Common Reader*. The passage implies that collective life exists in a realm beyond the conscious mind and beyond language, yet is communicated through language once we respond to the suggestive, rather than definitive, nature of words.

In this sketch, then, the pool world is a repository of a communal collective past, and the recuperative work of memory – perhaps the involuntary memory – is a mode of understanding through unconscious processes. So in *Orlando*, memory sinks to "the dark hollow at the back of the head" where "everything [is] partly something else," dissolving in "a pool where things dwell in darkness so deep that what they are we scarcely know" (*O* 290). The radical work of the unconscious supplants normalized rationality; furthermore, the multiple selves encountered in the pool are linked by a view of human continuity that resists conventional public constructions of value.

As in the "Time Passes" section of *To the Lighthouse*, the pool world records events of conventional historical significance, but resituates them, as it were, in parentheses. The first three voices in the pool are attached to times of importance in the public and political realm; all are associated with nationalism and two with war. The first self conjures up the technological and economic progress of the Victorian age: a whiskered man in side boots and top hat tells how he came to the pool "in 1851 after the heat of the Great Exhibition" (*CSF* 226). The second self, a girl, came to the pool in the summer of 1662. While the girl's world is not political, her context is, and the background of recent civil war and religious tension is ominously figured in the reference to the soldiers who were unable to see the girl and her lover where they lay. The third figure – a boy coming to fish – is a similarly "common" figure, yet likewise placed in his time (1805) by a political background: "We never caught the giant carp but we saw him once – the day Nelson fought at Trafalgar" (227). Woolf thus alludes to "important" historical occurrences – occurrences of "primary" significance in a patriarchal view of society – but deflects the usual emphasis. In the pool world, the event is now "all gone, all crumbled" (227); the ordinary human emotion is what endures. The three voices link to each other, and to Narcissus, through their common sense of loss – whether it be an amused chuckle over the passing pomp of the Victorian age, the despair of lost love (for, we learn, the girl eventually drowned herself), or the haunting poignancy of the quest for the ever-illusive mystery (for no one, legend has it, was ever to catch the giant carp).

Loss and longing, imaged with increasingly mythic overtones, lead down to a voice that seems to "come from the very bottom of the pool." This is the voice left unidentified, but the one that has greater power than all – the voice that promises to lead to an ending:

Alas, alas sighed a voice, slipping over the boy's voice. So sad a voice must come from the very bottom of the pool. It raised itself under the others as a spoon lifts all the things in a bowl of water. This was the voice we all wished to listen to. All the voices slipped gently away to the side of the pool to listen to the voice which so sad it seemed – it must surely know the meaning of all this. For they all wished to know. (227)

The cry of this voice, "Alas, alas," repeats the words of Narcissus grieving for the unattainable, the words repeated, in Ovid's original telling, by Echo. In Woolf's retelling, the disembodied cry – like the anonymous third voice in *Between the Acts*, the "other voice" that is "no one's voice" and hence everyone's voice (*BA* 211) – signifies the imagined consolation of continuity in the collective human unconscious. Yet the cry in itself is inconclusive; rather than marking the end of the journey, it dissolves into a continuous series of replacements and substitutions:

One drew closer to the pool and parted the reeds so that one could see deeper, through the reflections, through the faces, through the voices to the bottom. But there under the man who had been to the Exhibition; and the girl who had drowned herself and the boy who had seen the fish; and the voice who had cried alas alas! yet there was always something else. There was always another face, another voice. One thought came and covered another. For though there are moments when a spoon seems about to lift all of us, and our thoughts and longings and questions and confessions and disillusions into the light of day, somehow the spoon always slips beneath and we flow back again over the edge into the pool. And once more the whole of its centre is covered over with the reflection of the placard which advertises the sale of Romford Mill Farm. That perhaps is why one loves to sit and look into pools. (*CSF* 227)

The passage draws the reader into a moment of unification and sharing, enacting a liquid merging of different selves as the narrator slips from one pronoun to another: "one," "another," "all of us," "our," "we," and back to "one." The water seems thus to function (to push the metaphor) as lubrication, reducing the friction of the barriers of consciousness – perhaps, too, as the gender-neutral pronouns suggest, the barriers of gendered consciousness. Furthermore, though elusive and unreachable, the voices in the unconscious do not signify permanent loss. The lack of resolution becomes instead the source of continuing motivation: one will ever continue "to sit and look into pools."

Woolf's refiguration of the pool of Narcissus as a metaphor for the mind thus replaces gendered oppositions and hierarchical orderings with a dynamic that is integrative and relational. She writes over the pejorative, limiting associations of narcissistic desire with women's self-absorption to posit a new epistemological mode that, by descending into the "dark places of psychology," expands outward to a continuum of human experience. And the larger world accessed through the individual's unconscious is both the writer's source of inspiration and the reservoir on which she draws. As Woolf wrote in "The Old Order," "All great writers have, of course, an atmosphere in which they seem most at their ease and at their best; a mood of the great general mind which they interpret and indeed almost discover" (*E* ii:168).

In this sketch, the viewer – Narcissus – is in one sense the artist, like the playwright La Trobe who sinks down through the pool of private vision to the mud of collective experience that then bubbles up into words. In another sense, Narcissus is the reader, reading words through a plurality of associations that have accrued over time. For Woolf's collective unconscious is a historical inheritance transmitted through language, as opposed to the genetically encoded archetypes conceived by Carl Jung. Perry Meisel fittingly describes Woolf's construct as a "textual unconscious"; in his words, it is "less an unconscious pool of instinct...than a linguistic or textual unconscious in which a word's semantic inventory, like a psychic memory trace, gets 'stored.'"[17] Woolf's *textual collective* unconscious helps to explain her notably less anxious view of associative connections in reading in comparison to her contemporary I. A. Richards. In *Practical Criticism*, Richards presented what he called "protocols," or sample student analyses of sight poems, exposing "mnemonic irrelevances" such as "erratic associations" as a problem for criticism because they introduced personal, idiosyncratic ideas, tangential to the text.[18] For Woolf, words trigger associations with recollected words absorbed through our reading, with the corollary, of course, that the ideal unconscious has assimilated the entire literature of humankind.

This idea of a linguistic communal consciousness came to Woolf very early, as we can see in one of her earliest records of the sensation of reading: "I feel sometimes for hours together as though the physical stuff of my brain were expanding, larger & larger, throbbing quicker and quicker with new blood...I think I see for a moment how our minds are all threaded together...It is this common mind that binds the whole world together; & all the world is mind" (*PA* 178–79). And, in her late essay-broadcast "Craftsmanship," she spoke about the associative dimension of words, telling her listeners, "[i]n reading we have to allow the sunken meanings to remain sunken, suggested, not stated; lapsing and flowing into each other like reeds on the bed of a river" (*CE* 11:248). It is precisely this level of response that Woolf considered had been, in her culture, derogatorily feminized and suppressed, and her well-known tropes of androgyny bring conscious and unconscious together in "swift marriages" reconjoining two arbitrarily divided sexualities of the mind (251). In "A Letter to a Young Poet," protesting at one and the same time the gendered body and the gendered mind, she wrote,

there is a malcontent in me who complains that it seems to him odd, considering that English is a mixed language, a rich language; a language unmatched for its sound and colour, for its power of imagery and suggestion – it seems to him odd that these modern poets should write as if they had neither ears nor eyes, neither soles to their feet nor palms to their hands, but only honest enterprising book-fed brains, uni-sexual bodies and – but here I interrupted him. For when it comes to saying that a poet should be bi-sexual, and that I think is what he was about to say, even I, who have had no scientific training whatsoever, draw the line and tell that voice to be silent. (*HL* 232)

But of course by saying what she should not say, Woolf has said it.

The bisexuality of the mind thus signifies – at least in relation to the present discussion – an openness to both conscious and unconscious processes. It was her culture, not Woolf, that gendered the polarities, and her culture that located them oppositionally. In Woolf's construction, their relation is one of on-going interplay, which, in the act of reading, makes it crucial to employ the whole range of the mind. As we shall see, for Woolf, the unconscious has a particularly important role in evaluative judgments; but we must turn first to the conscious processes that are the complementary other side of the coin.

READING DIALOGICALLY

Woolf's "turn & turn about method"

In contrast to her evocative allusions to the work of the unconscious, Woolf directly addresses conscious processes and subjects them to theoretical investigation. Her approach, however, is similarly to emphasize the active and dynamic nature of reading and to focus on the empowerment of the reader. As always, her goal is not to schematize literature but to stimulate the reader's growth. Woolf concentrates on the dialogic relation between reader and text, prompting the reader not simply to be receptive to the literary work but to engage in conversation with it. The give and give relation that G. D. H. Cole articulated as the ideal relation between teacher and student is for Woolf the ideal relation between text and reader. In a further extension of the dialogic principle, Woolf writes about literature in a way that leaves room for her own reader's intervention and response.

As I have indicated, Woolf's essays usually begin by posing some question or problem, which she then explores in relation to specific literary works, often pursuing different possible approaches in the course of a single essay. She might suggest an answer or offer an opinion, only to change or even reverse it, or she might view a work through different and even conflicting lenses. She presents her own views and judgments, but she simultaneously examines the processes through which her ideas were formed. By fore-grounding her process of thinking, Woolf conveys a theoretical approach that is speculative and open-ended rather than definitive and conclusive. She also presents the literary text as dynamic and changeable – acquiring its meaning through its interaction with the context in which it was writ-ten and the context in which it is read. When Woolf praised Sir Walter Raleigh's approach to literature – before she discovered his less than literary agendum – it was for "touch[ing] his subject with life" and "invest[ing] it with all the uncertainty, the possibility, and the vagueness of a living thing" (*E* ii:73). Her words perhaps best describe the animating force behind her *own* critical work. Approaching literature as a living thing, she directs our attention to the multiplicity and plurality of a text's meanings, to the on-going, developing process of the critic's thinking, and to the dynamic dialogic relation between writer and reader.

Correspondingly, Woolf objects to monologic prose because it forestalls and prohibits such negotiation. Literature's essential life, she argues, is cur-tailed and suppressed when discourse employs an authoritative, impersonal, didactic mode. In *A Room of One's Own*, discussing a hypothetical male novelist, Woolf imagines that the authoritative and privileged voice of the patriarchal writer darkens his text with a "shadow shaped something like the letter 'I'" (*R* 150). Woolf's objection is not just to the implicit egotism; more crucially, it is to the suppression of active creative dialogue between writer and reader. The absence of interaction leaves the reader vulnerable to domination – the political consequences of which become clear when Woolf ridicules the concept of a "Fascist poem" as a contradiction in terms (155). Fascism – the subjugation of the crowd to the desire of the leader – is antithetical to poetry – liberator, through its multiplicity and sugges-tivity, of the minds of the common readers. But the further consequence is that, if monologism is tyrannical in form, dictators also stimulate re-bellion. Reviewing a book that aimed to stir children to a revolutionary passion "to redress the wrongs of the world," Woolf points to the limitation of the writers' well-intentioned but simple-minded didactic approach (*E* II:196).[19] Since our ideas, she asserts, tend to develop through reaction, she humorously suggests that "[t]he truth may be that if you want to breed rebels and reformers you must impress upon them from the beginning the virtues of Tories and aristocrats" (196). Her serious point, however, is that imposed instruction pushes its recipients into either submission or resistance, locking them into either passive or oppositional roles.

The more threatening dynamic, then, of monologic prose, is its potential for provoking confrontation. Reviewing *Joan and Peter*, a novel by H. G. Wells, Woolf faults the novelist for being so caught up in his attack on the educational system that he forgets the primacy of narrative, of fiction, of character. As a result, Woolf argues, his passionate cause deteriorates to a harangue by a man who is "sore and angry and exaggerated and abusive" (*E* II:294). Wells's attempt to embody his "fiery passion for the rights of youth" in a realized fictional world gives his "hybrid" book some "relation to a work of art" (296), but ultimately the diatribe deadens his characters into pasteboard figures, with the result that Woolf sees no life for the book beyond the immediate relevance of its ideas to current issues. But the most fascinating part of Woolf's review is the first paragraph where, as is often the case, she prefaces her discussion of literature with some question of a general theoretical nature – and here the theory concerns what we might call the interpersonal dynamics of conflict talk:

The moralists of the nursery used to denounce a sin which went by the name of "talking at," and was rendered the more expressive by the little stress which always fell upon the "at," as if to signify the stabbing, jabbing, pinpricking nature of the sin itself. The essence of "talking at" was that you vented your irritation in an oblique fashion which it was difficult for your victim to meet otherwise than by violence. (294)

Woolf directs our attention to the way discourse defines the possibilities for reply. To harangue is to stab or jab; it pushes its recipient into a corner and provides no opportunity for reasonable response. As I have variously shown, Woolf continually encourages a reading practice of "talking back" but, on the writer's side, her implication here is that the approach of "talking *to* or *with*" – as opposed to "talking *at*" – is preferable not because it lends a "nicer" construction to the speaker but because it converts confrontation into dialogic negotiation.

The "moralist of the nursery," it is true, is inculcating Victorian – and more specifically, feminine – politeness and, perhaps because Woolf once posited the origins of her *Common Reader* essays in her "tea-table training," some readers have equated her style with feminine charm, employed to be gracious and entertaining. But we should be warned against such simple interpretation by Woolf's own ambivalence: "the Victorian manner," she writes, "is perhaps – *I am not sure* – a disadvantage in writing" (emphasis added).[20] While deploring the role assigned to the Victorian "Angel in the House," Woolf was able to use elements of the "tea-table" discourse to create a supple, sensitive, and responsive speaking voice.[21] What must be rejected in this tradition is the tendency to side-step controversial issues; what can be gained is a discourse that empowers all voices at the table. Just as Woolf could reject the hierarchical principle embedded in aristocracy without disparaging all its characteristics, so she could select and reconfigure, from the wreckage of Victorian convention, the attributes that could make for a more humane world.

Dialogic discourse defines a space for exchange and negotiation. The form has critical antecedents in Plato's dialogues and Dryden's "An Essay of Dramatic Poetry," but in Woolf's distinctive treatment, the conversation is designed not to lead the reader to a final truth but to prompt the reader's critical thinking by juxtaposing equally justifiable views. Woolf, as we have seen, used this form twice in constructed debates with Leonard: "Are Too Many Books Written and Published?" and the pamphlet *Reviewing*. It was also the form that Woolf proposed as the underlying structure of *The Hogarth Letters*, a collection of imaginary letters from diverse perspectives that she had hoped would stimulate literary debate.[22] It might seem contradictory for Woolf to court intellectual disagreements while, as we have seen, objecting strongly to the BBC series "To an Unnamed Listener," a series that she said had taken its inspiration from *The Hogarth Letters* (*L* v: 83). But for her there was a great difference between brow-beating and conversation. Conversation does not give the victor's crown to the dominant view; its aim is to expose the complexities of the situation and to provoke further thought.

Back in 1910, when Virginia Woolf was embarking on some "humbler" mechanical work for the cause of adult suffrage, she lamented, "How melancholy it is that conversation isn't enough!" (*L* 1:421). Out of that early tea-tabling training in the art of conversation, she went on to develop a rhetorical style that she defined, in June 1923, as her "turn & turn about method" (*D* 11:247). Conversation focuses on the exchange of different views – *conversare*: "to turn around frequently" – and it is such exchange that lies at the heart of Woolf's "turn & turn about method," or what I have called the "trope of the twist."[23] To write conversation is to engage other voices, and the technique is thus related to what we now call – after Bakhtin – the dialogic, or double-voice discourse. In 1929, in an essay entitled "Discourse Typology in Prose," Mikhail Bakhtin advanced the idea of double-voice discourse, expressing his views through formalist analysis and within a well-recognized tradition of expository argument. Six years before Bakhtin's essay, however, Woolf enacted a similar theory in a dramatized, fictionalized form.[24]

"Mr. Conrad: A Conversation" (1923)

In 1923, Woolf proposed her own version of the dialogic by casting a review of Joseph Conrad as a debate between two readers on the relative merits and limitations of Conrad's works. The essay presents a genuine exchange of equally valid views; furthermore, neither speaker adopts a unilateral or monologic position. The form was, in Woolf's eyes, a crucial breakthrough; she considered restructuring all the essays for *The Common Reader* as conversations (*D* II:261). Although she did not literally effect this plan, it gave her a crucial insight into her "turn & turn about method" as the informing method of her critical prose.[25]

The review, entitled "Mr. Conrad: A Conversation," presents two fictional common readers, Penelope Otway and David Lowe, in a garden setting, discussing the merits of Conrad's works. For Penelope, Conrad is a great writer who succeeds in dramatizing his internal conflict, pitting the subtle skeptical Marlow against simple, code-worshipping Captains. David, on the other hand, considers Conrad to be merely an aged romantic unable to come to terms with his disillusionment. There are certainly ways in which Penelope, as a woman educated in her father's library, resembles Virginia Woolf as a common reader, but it is David who echoes the judgment that Woolf had expressed in a recent review of Conrad's *The Rescue* (*E* III:229–33). Woolf thus begins by dramatizing two sides of herself through her two speakers, and she then proceeds to introduce a "turn about" into each view. David, who is dissatisfied with Conrad's plots, praises Conrad's prose; Penelope, who praises the plots, finds the prose often pompous and monotonous. Finally, reversing evaluative positions once again, David finds limitations in Conrad's lack of broad humor and the absence of women in his works, and Penelope counters with the view that Conrad's women are his ships – another idea from Woolf's earlier review, but one that she gives this time to Penelope rather than David. The overall effect of such constantly shifting opinion is to focus on the challenge of evaluating Conrad's works, and the debate is thrown open when

Penelope abandons her argument, suggesting the best recourse is to return to the novels and read Conrad yourself.

The debate, nonetheless, is not just an exercise in indecision. The repeated twists make it difficult for us to adopt any view of Conrad that passes a unilateral and comprehensive judgment on his works. An evaluation of his prose depends on the selection, and the decision whether or not Conrad's disillusionment is adequately contained in his ironies depends on the work. Furthermore, the intertwining of viewpoints helps us to see that the strengths of any method are inseparable from its weaknesses. The power of an idealism embodied in the heroic code of the sea depends for its impact on the necessary excision of other, potentially distracting, aspects of life. The reader returning to Conrad will now do so with such theoretical and critical complexities in mind.

Woolf wrote this review as she was hatching her plan to collect some of her essays in a single volume and she was excited enough about her new method to consider recasting the other essays in "Otway conversation" (*D* ii:261). But the success of any rhetorical strategy depends on responsive reading and Woolf's chatty, inconclusive style presumably lacked the obviously serious intent that readers in her day expected from critical prose. "Mr. Conrad: A Conversation" was greeted with deafening silence in Woolf's immediate circle; four days after its publication, she noted in her diary that the response was "purely negative – No one has mentioned it" (*D* ii 265). But the lack of reinforcement did not deter Woolf from her method. Quite the opposite: she recorded, "to be dashed is always the most bracing treatment for me... It also has the effect of making me more definite & outspoken in my style" (265).[26] And she wrote for the first time that the title of the projected volume was to be *The Common Reader*.

In planning this work, however, Woolf abandoned her scheme for using explicit dialogue – influenced sufficiently by the response to modify her approach.[27] Convinced that conversation was the right mode, she decided to be less literal in its application. To avoid the distracting intrusion of personalities and fictional settings, Woolf embedded the dialogue within the essayist's voice: "Characters are to be merely views" (*D* ii:265). But a less obviously mediated dialogue creates a greater challenge for the reader. No longer situated as a spectator witnessing a debate, the reader undergoes repeated repositionings; it is as if the reader gets comfortably settled in one easy chair only to be told to shift to another facing the opposite way. The different chairs are all presented as viable ideological locations, including the chair made from the stuff of conventional assumptions, traditional thinking, and patriarchal attitudes; however, as our positionality changes, each new perspective exposes an earlier one from a new angle. Repeated shifts then gradually foreground the process of shifting; that is, repeated re-definition prompts the reader to consider the significance of interpretative structures in the creation of meaning, in the assigning of value. Woolf's leap forward in her method thus led her to a new perspective on her sub-ject matter; in the same diary entry, she noted that "a new aspect, never all this 2 or 3 years thought of, at once becomes clear... To curtail, I shall really investigate literature with a view to answering certain questions about ourselves" (265). If "investigating literature" was her text, "answering cer-tain questions about ourselves" became her subtext. Shifting positionality emerged as the method and the matter of her critical approach.

"On Not Knowing Greek" (1925)

In an essay written expressly for this first *Common Reader*, Woolf develops her "turn & turn about method" precisely to excavate the relation between the text and its multiply situated readers. Approximately two months after her renewed commitment to the conversational method, Woolf notes that she is hard at work on her "Greek chapter" (*D* II:276), in which she ranges over the writings of Sophocles, Euripedes, Aeschylus, Aristophanes, Plato, and Homer. The ostensible subject of the essay is thus Greek literature, but its title "On Not Knowing Greek" reveals that her subject is equally our ability to read it. Located in its historical context, the title alludes to one of the pedagogical differences separating middle- to upper-class male readers from women and middle- to lower-class men: knowing, or not knowing, Greek. For despite the gradual introduction of English literature into the university curriculum, a firm grounding in the classical languages continued to be the educational foundation of the public boys' schools and the "Oxbridge" universities.[28] Education, as we have seen, produced different discursive communities according to class and gender, and Woolf's title plunges right to the heart of the power structure that placed different readers in hierarchically ordered locations.

The essay opens with an image of hierarchical ranking on a scale of knowl-edge and the writer's disarmingly candid admission that "our ignorance" places us "at the bottom of any class of schoolboys" (*CR* 1:23). Whether we read the first-person plural as editorial or consensual, Woolf's relation to her readers bifurcates according to two different reading communities. Readers who are conscious of the inadequacies of their knowledge of Greek are disempowered by their consciousness of "superior" readers but brought into community with the writer; the privileged reader who knows Greek is elevated above the text and allowed a measure of complacent superiority. But from this point on, the essay enacts a series of shifts, twists, and reversals that serve first to modify, then to question, and finally to undo the initial ordering.[29]

A close examination of the opening sentence shows how our feet are first firmly planted on a solid platform, only to experience first slight and then growing sensations of tremor:

> For it is vain and foolish to talk of knowing Greek, since in our ignorance we should be at the bottom of any class of schoolboys, since we do not know how the words sounded, or where precisely we ought to laugh, or how the actors acted, and between this foreign people and ourselves there is not only a difference of race and tongue but a tremendous breach of tradition. (23)

After its humble opening, the sentence embarks on a series of redefinitions that gradually alter and ultimately reverse the initial signification of "knowledge." At the beginning, "knowledge" refers to the acquisition of a foreign language, the knowledge any (privileged) schoolboy might be expected to have; the first subsequent definition – "how the words sounded" – could still be compatible with a schoolboy's training, except that even the specialist here must admit to a doubt as to the exact pronunciation of words. In the next definition, the word "precisely" signals even more clearly its ironic intent, since identifying humor is scarcely as precise as parsing a sentence. Each subsequent qualification takes us increasingly further from the area in which even classicists can claim knowledge, until the ignorance of *all* twentieth-century British readers is implied by the untraversable chasm of cultural difference – what we would now describe as a recognition of "otherness." The sentence thus encapsulates a distinctive feature in Woolf's "turn & turn about" technique: she adopts a focalization only to disrupt it, and this disruption alters the positioning of the reader in relation to the text.[30] In this example, the privileged reader, initially situated outside and above the educative competency of the implied author, is relocated to a position inside the same sphere: both are equally ignorant in the larger interpretative scheme. In reciprocal fashion, by the end of the sentence, the uneducated reader is no longer marginalized by her ignorance, since ignorance is shared by all.

In so maneuvering and exposing the different subject positions of different readers, Woolf's sentence strikingly prefigures the work of later speech-act theorists on multiple readerships. In "Ideology and Speech-Act Theory," for example, Mary Louise Pratt urges critics to move beyond the privatized context of "THE text" and "THE reader." She argues the need to analyze plural "readerships, kinds of readers, and kinds of reading," to examine "how texts are constructed to address mass or multiple readerships, or to place single reading subjects in multiple roles at once," and to analyze how speaking subjects are themselves positioned in a variety of ways. The effect of Woolf's text achieves precisely the goals Pratt describes: to question the norm of language as "representational and intentional" or as "the discourse of truth and falsehood," to recognize differing and multiple motivations and assumptions in both author and reader, and to situate our utterances within the complicating power relations that make conversation no simple "exchange" between equal participants.[31] Woolf's opening sentence both acknowledges a power structure among different readerships and works to undo it. And such destabilization is indeed Woolf's subject; in a further enactment of the twist, the essay on "*not* knowing" turns out to be about knowing – the whole vexed question of interpretation – and the reversal in her initial sentence is repeated on a larger scale in the structure of the essay as a whole.

By destabilizing the reader's relation to the text, Woolf foregrounds the role played by the reader in any interpretation of the text's meaning and, in the rest of the essay, *how* we interpret is the continuing theme. Most readers are unlikely to be fully aware of the rhetorical shifts in the opening sentence; the more probable reaction is a subliminal uneasiness, a premonition of uncertainty. But the narrative repositionings become increasingly overt as the essay progresses. The initially subservient role of the "ignorant" narrator is subverted when Woolf begins not only to quote Greek in the original but also to compare the effect of the original with its translations. Yet the "privileged" position of knowing the language is undercut when the essayist points out that no one in the twentieth century has firsthand knowledge of the society or the climate of ancient Greece, or – and now Woolf clearly goes beyond the issue of phonetic pronunciation – really knows how these words sounded when spoken in their original outdoor setting. But next, our inability to know the Greek world because of cultural and historical difference is overturned by the hypothesis that Greek literature transcends particularity to reveal the deeper truths of common, universal human nature. At this point, we seem to have returned to the stable ground of "knowing," abandoning the uneasy perch of a postmodernist theory of alterity for the comfortable chair of traditional humanist assumptions and the touchstone of "the stable, the permanent, the original human being" (*CR* 1:27).

But just as we have shifted position, Woolf again changes course to argue that, rather than revealing a universal absolute, our reading of Greek teaches us to know ourselves. Our passion for pure outlines and universal touchstones is merely our reaction to the "vagueness" and "confusion" of the twentieth century; we seek in the literature of the Other what we ourselves lack. From this perspective, "not knowing" refers to the subjectivity of all knowledge: "Back and back we are drawn to steep ourselves in what, perhaps, is only an image of the reality, not the reality itself, a summer's day imagined in the heart of a northern winter" (35). However, just as this image problematizes any attribution of "truth" to Greek literature, so the word "perhaps" casts uncertainty over any assertion of relativity. The constant turning-about means that any view can be interrogated by its opposite, so that Woolf's reading of Plato stands as a possible description of her own technique: "what matters is not so much the end we reach as our manner of reaching it" (32). The significance of the essay is not just that such questions are raised; it is equally important that they are raised through a process of settling and unsettling, as we are urged simultaneously to form opinions and never to allow opinion to harden into "truth." Ultimately the effect is to dissolve the conventional either/or oppositional relation between knowing and not knowing, and to hold these apparent opposites together in an ironic tension.

"On Not Knowing Greek" illustrates how Woolf transforms the literal dialogue of "Mr. Conrad: A Conversation" into a subtle technique that achieves the rhetorical effect of conversation by employing a single voice that undergoes constant shifts in focalization. The essay also clarifies the close tie between this rhetorical style and Woolf's theory of interpretation. The authorial voice in this "turn about" technique constantly defers its own authority and yet it neither compromises with, nor accedes to, the opposing view; conflicting views are incorporated into a new perspective and, in the process, reconstituted in new terms. Woolf both satisfies conventional scholarly expectations – advancing theories, for example, about the distinctive characteristics of Sophocles, Euripides, and Aeschylus – while, at the same time, she disempowers the authoritative stance by situating interpretation within an on-going process of provisionality and exploration. She confronts and acknowledges discriminatory differences in education relating to class and gender, yet also engages larger equalizing contexts that unite readers in what they share. In this light, the conversational shift – or "the trope of the twist"[32] – becomes a distinctive conflict strategy; it asserts its own views, even while it looks for common ground on which to accommodate difference.[33] As a genre of conflict talk, Woolf's method offers a productive alternative to the confrontational, assertive public discourse of her time.

Collaborative versus resisting readers: "The Plumage Bill" (1920)

As a rhetorical mode, the "turn & turn about method" is well suited to a woman writer who seeks an alternative to the authorial/authoritative dominance of patriarchal discourse.[34] However, to eschew authority is to incur vulnerability. Double-voice discourse assumes a co-operative and collaborative reader and, as a non-authoritarian mode, it is subject to the natural tendency of the already-dominant to maintain domination. Since conversation by its nature encodes opposing views, the culturally dominant view can easily be privileged by the resisting reader/listener who employs the single-voice discourse of competitive, unproblematized assertion. A published exchange between Woolf and a male editor illustrates the difficulties encountered when the reader refuses to "play."

In 1920, Woolf was involved in a male/female dialogue that developed as follows: Woolf published an article in the *Woman's Leader* challenging an editorial by H. W. Massingham ("Wayfarer") in the *Nation*; Massingham in turn wrote a letter to the *Woman's Leader* criticizing Woolf's article, and Woolf responded once again the following week. What is of particular interest here is Massingham's complete failure to "read" Woolf's first rhetorical strategies, and Woolf's switch to his mode of language in her second communicative attempt.

Massingham's original editorial concerns the defeat of a parliamentary bill to end the violently cruel trade in egret feathers. After decrying the cruelty and documenting the threat to the bird species, however, Massingham suddenly turns his attack on women, ending, "But what do women care? Look at Regent Street this morning!"[35] Picking up Massingham's words, Woolf takes him to task for his unconscious gendered assumptions, using at first her "turn & turn about" technique.

The opening sentence of Woolf's article, like the beginning of "On Not Knowing Greek," both adopts a focalization and subjects it to a wobble. In paraphrasable content, the meaning is straightforward, running something like this: "Even though I have since childhood always adhered to the principle of never contributing to the harm of the egret, after reading 'Wayfarer' I am angry enough to go and buy an egret feather and put it in my hat." But this apparently simple opening encodes contradictory implications. Although Woolf situates herself in angry opposition to Massingham, her constructed voice imitates the image of women in Massingham's text: emotional, irrational, self-centered, defensive of their right to fashion, offended at any imputation of blame. In Woolf's actual sentence, however, linguistic twists signal that this "voice" is simply a role: "If I had the money and the time I should, after reading 'Wayfarer,' in the *Nation* of 10 July, go to Regent Street, buy an egret plume, and stick it – is it in the back or the front of the hat? – and this in spite of a vow taken in childhood and hitherto religiously observed" (*E* III:241). The phrase "If I had the money and the time" separates Woolf from the shoppers on Regent Street; her abrupt question about the feather's placement, plus the crude words "stick it," further transgress Massingham's construct of women by establishing both ignorance of and disdain for fashion, and in a not entirely ladylike way. Thus, although Woolf poses as the traditional "woman," at the same time she subverts and disrupts the markers that inscribe this woman's role. The result is a double positionality: Woolf takes the part of the fashionable, leisured women, while she repudiates their acts.

The multiple implications of the sentence are further complicated by the question of multiple readerships. Since Woolf's article was written for the *Women's Leader* at the request of Ray Strachey, the primary audience – unlike that of the *Nation* – would be female and feminist, followed by male readers concerned about equality between the sexes and issues "of special interest to women."[36] But since the article was also a reply to Massingham, another significant readership is the male – or possibly female – reader who has yet to arrive at any perception of the problematic nature of gender assumptions. In addition, the general readership might well include the women whose purchase of egret feathers initiates the debate.

Woolf's multilevel discourse allows these different readers to enter her text from different positions. Let me try hypothetically to sketch their most likely reactions. The woman of fashion would be brought into complicity with the writer through shared anger but would also feel challenged by Woolf's religiously taken vow. Readers like Massingham would likely respond with shocked disdain at Woolf's apparent rejection of a worthy cause, but they might also feel a measure of uneasiness at the hints of subversive mockery in her tone. The feminist reader would sympathize with both the anger and the vow, but might well be puzzled, if not chagrined, by Woolf's seemingly childish response. But whatever their differences, all careful readers would perceive a wobble – a significant premonition that this article will not proceed in a straightforward way. It is precisely this wobble that enables Woolf to combine self-assertion – her angry gesture – with scripting a *negotiable* role for the other to play. By itself anger would polarize readers into those who share the anger and those who are affronted by it; the wobble makes it harder for readers to become entrenched in fixed positions, since Woolf's prose is itself destabilized by the element of performance in her angry stance.

As in "On Not Knowing Greek," the doubleness encoded in the first sentence of "The Plumage Bill" unfolds in the structure of the essay as a whole. Woolf proceeds to paint a harsh portrait of the unthinking, self-indulgent woman of fashion – the buyer of the feather – presenting her in a way that seems astonishingly to corroborate Massingham's critical view. But then in another twist, she renders a far more devastating portrait of men – the hunters and merchants who turn killing into a commodity, and the male parliament that fails to pass the Plumage Bill prohibiting the trade. Readers who follow Woolf's twists to this level, will see that *without denying Massingham's criticism of the women who purchase the feather* Woolf has asserted another perspective in which the actions of men are much more reprehensible.

But the next and more significant twist relates to the very ground of our inquiry, since Woolf prompts us to see the subject not as the violence done to birds but as Massingham's violence to women. Beyond the question of apportioning blame for the torture of egrets lies the question of our discriminatory assumptions about gender. And here Woolf's attack is as much on the readers who have read Massingham's words without protest as it is on Massingham for having written them. How can Woolf get her audience to see that the social code unconsciously condemns women's pleasures – their love of beauty for example – as sin, whereas men's pleasures – their lusts for hunting, women, and money – are accepted, even valorized? Again the twist becomes a crucial strategy: if she can get her readers to reverse the terms and imagine a similar attack on men's instincts, they will see how discriminatory the social encoding of gender is: the universal standard of justice leads a double life.

Rather than directly attacking Massingham's assumptions, Woolf echoes Massingham's final words, but enacts a twist by reversing his reference to gender. Massingham had tried to expose women's insensitivity to the birds by evoking the cultural association of women with children and the cultural designation of nurturing as a female quality: "They [the birds] have to be shot in parenthood for child-bearing women to flaunt the symbols of it... But what do women care? Look at Regent Street this morning!"[37] Having noted that the Regent Street shop windows contain guns and boots as well as flowers and dresses, Woolf writes, "But what do men care? Look wherever you like this morning! Still, one cannot imagine 'Wayfarer' putting it like that. 'They have to be shot for child-begetting men to flaunt the symbols of it... But what do men care? Look at Regent Street this morning!' Such an outburst about a fishing-rod would be deemed sentimental in the extreme. Yet I suppose that salmon have their feelings" (*E* III:243, ellipsis in Woolf).

The ironies both indict men for violence and, at the same time, prob-lematize this indictment. For, on one level, Woolf's statement is *more* valid than Massingham's but, on another level, it is – just like Massingham's – not valid at all. Woolf prompts her readers to reexamine "male" behavior – to question, for example, whether "child-begetting" should make one any less nurturing than "child-bearing" – but then, scripting a reciprocal as opposed to adversarial role for Massingham to play, she implies the ridicu-lousness, the reductiveness, of any wholesale condemnation of men. The repetition of "But what do men care?" enacts this further twist, shifting from a reasonable question to an unjust categorization. The second mean-ing allows Massingham to share Woolf's mockery of her "outburst" – but only at the cost of similarly repudiating his own words. Woolf thus asserts her own views while creating a space for her disputant to join her in a critique of all gender assumptions, no matter which sex's characteristics are at stake.

Woolf's conversational turns therefore have the potential of functioning as effective conflict strategies, chastising her adversaries while turning them into allies. But the first possible stumbling block is that readers must have the ability to grasp rhetorical complexity. The greater challenge is that they must be able to see what they are not prepared to look for, and to understand what their conditioning has predisposed them not to see. Unfortunately, readers who would have had no difficulty with Swift's "A Modest Proposal" nevertheless failed to detect satire from a woman's pen. In the sequel, Massingham (and not only Massingham and not only men, as a similar letter from a female correspondent in the *Women's Leader* indicates) is totally oblivious to Woolf's irony. He sees the wobble, but does not get much further in reading it than his own confusion, which he then attributes to Woolf: she has written an "ambiguous article" and "should have made herself clearer." He understands that she is raising the question of the difference between the sexes, but mistakenly concludes that her object is to blame the killing of birds on men. He notices the twist, but thinks it works detrimentally to "obscure the issue," failing to see that the twist redefines the issue itself.[38]

In answering Massingham a second time, Woolf rewrites her first re-sponse with little alteration in content, but with a radical change in style. Since she now addresses her remarks to readers who failed to follow her twists, she adopts their monolinear style: as she says of Massingham, "his meaning is plain enough" (*E* iii:244). She proceeds to "clear up some at least of [her] ambiguities" (244), meaning that she rewrites her previously rich, layered, ironic sentences as unproblematized statements of unequivocal

intent: "To torture birds is one thing, and to be unjust to women is another, and it was, I hope, plain to some of my readers that I was attacking
the second of these crimes and not the first...it seems to me more necessary to resent such an insult to women as Wayfarer casually lets fall
than to protect egrets from extinction" (245). But Woolf's response also
leaves no doubt that in thus clarifying her meaning she has failed in her
goal. Merely to condemn Massingham's remark is to deal with a symp-
tom; Woolf can address the root of the problem only if she can get him to
reexamine the things he takes for granted, to *experience* the effects of unconscious discrimination by trying life out the other way around. But there
is little possibility for reciprocity in the discourse of direct combat. Massingham is now entrenched in an oppositional position: either his words
will be "forced down [his throat]" or he must "justif[y them] up to the hilt"
(245).

The Plumage Bill exchange reveals what can happen when Woolf's negotiations break down. Because the strategies depend on a flexible reader
who can both detect and experience the twists, the effect can be merely
confusing for an uncomprehending or resisting reader who adheres to the
single-voice mode. To understand Woolf's rhetoric is therefore not always
to see it as successful; however, by analyzing it in the context of its reception,
we can grasp both how it works and why it sometimes fails. Pedagogically,
it is a fitting approach to employ if the goal is to teach a flexible and dynamic form of thinking. If her essays fail, the failure resides in the reader's
withholding participation in the thinking process. If the essays succeed,
the reader gains insight into both the subject and the interpretative models
used to address it. The remarkable potential for getting us self-reflexively
to examine our critical thinking is the great strength of Woolf's approach,
and it is equally powerful in the critical frames that I turn to next: how
we understand literature historically and how we evaluate what is a good
book.

READING HISTORICALLY

Woolf and modernist historicism

The further we are from the first constructions of modernism, the more
we realize that the early myths about its identity elided and obscured many
of its crucial elements. The early view that modernist writers detached
themselves from the public sphere – a view I am obviously disputing –
has been challenged from a variety of angles, not only in feminist and

gender studies, but in studies of imperialism and colonialism, nation and race, popular culture, and the publishing industry. But another entrenched preconception – modernism's ahistoricity, which is sometimes figured as a rupture from historical process – is only currently undergoing revision. The origins of this latter metanarrative are undoubtedly numerous: to name just a few, Frank Kermode's crisis-oriented theory of modernism as defined by an expulsion from an Edenically imagined past; Georg Lukács's Marxist critique of modernism's rejection of historical process in favor of a static aesthetic; and Paul de Man's attack on the modernists' desire to construct their own era as a new point of origin, a true present, to be fatally condemned as "organicist neofascism."[39] The difficulty with each view is its selective filter and its reduction of modernism to a single metanarrative. With the current turn both to historical studies of modernist literature and to the modernists' own historical writings, we are learning to distinguish not only among modernists but also among the multiple historical strands in modernist thought.

Not all modernists, it is true, were equally historical; there is an extreme difference between Forster's assertion, in *Aspects of the Novel*, that "Time, all the way through, is to be our enemy" and Woolf's continuing fascination with time's passage. Yet Forster's approach to the novel through genre rather than history is conditioned by what he feels qualified to do; his is "an imperfect vision," he explains, but one "suited to [his] powers." But whereas Forster could then comfortably say, "we cannot go [to the regions of history] because we have not read enough," for Woolf, it is impossible to read well without thinking historically.[40] Historical – and indeed historicist – thinking underlies the two *Common Readers* and most of her critical work.

Woolf's historical reading was informed by two primary concepts, both of which were at the cutting edge of the "new historicist" thinking of her time: the importance of everyday life and the provisionality of historical metanarratives. Although these approaches tend to be identified with late twentieth-century historicism and the work of theorists like Michel de Certeau and Hayden White, it is instructive to note that both elements were already emerging as radical transformations in the modernist period.[41] As inherited from the nineteenth century, the dominant forms of historiography continued to be political and national, but a quintessential (and somewhat Hemingwayesque) conversation in Woolf's 1921 diary records the incipient seismographic shifts. Lytton Strachey announces, "History must be written all over again. Its all morality –"; "& battles," adds Virginia Woolf (*D* II:115). Then a further comment of Woolf's – perhaps *seemingly* self-deprecatory – suggests the greater modernity of Woolf's approach over Strachey's. Placing Strachey in relation to Edward Gibbon, Woolf says, "He has a point of view & sticks to it... And so do you"; but about herself, she says, "I wobble" (115). The wobble is Woolf's engagement of the dialogic, her "turn & turn about"; applied to historical consciousness, it signals her awareness of the provisional effect of historical positioning on our reading of texts. Woolf goes beyond the historical critics, like her father, who conceived of the relative nature of different historical eras, to a conception of the relativity of historical narratives to the location – social, geographical, temporal, ideological – of the historian. Shifting the subject from morality and battle to the everyday, and writing a self-conscious, self-reflexive historical criticism are the two striking innovations that inform Woolf's historical approach.

Simply in what she chooses to tell, Woolf's writings subvert traditional history – a history she described as early as 1910 as invented by "gentlemen in tall hats in the Forties who wished to dignify mankind" (*E* 1:331). Her own version of history gives priority instead to women's lives and the lives of the obscure, to life-writing and literary writing, and to the history of the everyday. Although there were certainly some nineteenth-century precedents – such as Macaulay's famous chapter on the condition of England in 1685[42] – the new subject at the beginning of the twentieth century was the history of everyday life and history as perceived by ordinary people. In *Medieval People*, for example, Eileen Power imaginatively reconstructed the lives of six historical figures, five of whom were chosen to represent "the obscure lives and activities of the great mass of humanity."[43] In his 1927 essay "The Pageant of History," Leonard Woolf cited Power's book as part of the new history of the common man, although Leonard argued even more strongly for Virginia's approach, by suggesting that, instead of the daily detail of how people lived, history should seek out what went on in their heads, and should turn for this purpose to "contemporary accounts of events, old letters, and ancient diaries."[44] The turn to historical accounts written by ordinary people emerges most strikingly in the Mass Observation project, founded by Tom Harrison and others in 1937, to "study the everyday lives of people in Britain."[45] The project used two distinct methods: "A team of paid investigators recorded people's behavior and conversation in a variety of public situations" and "a panel of volunteer observers around the country kept diaries and responded to monthly questionnaires." Fittingly, Virginia Woolf was invited to review a Mass Observation survey (*L* VI:172) and her essay "Lives of the Obscure" appeared in January of the year in which Power's book was published.[46]

The second and even more radical strain in Woolf's approach to history discloses her remarkable similarity to the historian R. G. Collingwood. Collingwood, educated at Oxford and St. Andrew's, returned to Oxford as a professor of history after the First World War; there seem to have been no direct links between him and the Woolfs, other than T. S. Eliot's having studied with him for a brief period. The issue is therefore not one of influence but of consanguinity: Woolf and Collingwood were both on the cutting edge of their time. Collingwood designated his work as the first "philosophy of history," and he was the first systematically to challenge the reigning positivist historiography with a pluralistic constructivist argument. In an image prefiguring by just a few years the "fifty pairs of eyes" needed to see Mrs. Ramsay (*TTL* 303), or the "seven-sided carnation" which is at the same time "a whole flower to which every eye brings its own contribution" (*W* 137), Collingwood compared history to "a hundred people looking at the same tree all see[ing] different aspects of it."[47] History, Collingwood argued, can never be universal, can never be final: "No one historian ... can see more than one aspect of the truth; and even an infinity of historians must always leave an infinity of aspects unseen." Since every historian approaches history "from the point of view which is characteristic of himself and his generation," the past is always "a function of the present" and history must be rewritten in every age. History is thus "a world of perspectives" that "has no centre; its centre is everywhere and its circumference is nowhere."[48] Like Collingwood, Woolf alters the construction of history from fixed to kinetic, from absolute to provisional, from the truth of the past to the narrative of the present.[49] Like Collingwood, she understands history as a present construction, shaped by the present historian's interests and needs. In Woolf's essays, the result is a double focus, highlighting the historical context of the text that is being read and the historical location of the reader who is constructing the history. Both aspects of Woolf's historiography are fully formulated in a sketch written in the summer of 1906, predating both Collingwood and Power by many years.

"The Journal of Mistress Joan Martyn" (1906)

An early narrative sketch, written soon after her teaching of English history at Morley College, shows that Woolf was already thinking of history as a dialogic interaction between the historical text and the historian's understanding. "The Journal of Mistress Joan Martyn" presents a fictional account of a twentieth-century historian, Miss Merridew, who stops at a manor house owned by Mr. John Martyn, a descendant of generations who have inhabited the house since medieval times. In the first section, Miss Merridew discovers a manuscript; the second section presents the supposed document itself. The narrative of the present, by dramatizing historical research, conveys the excitement of following a trail but, at roughly two-thirds the length of the second, this opening section does much more. It stages a conversation – in fact, a debate – between two competing definitions of history: the one privileging objective facts and focused on issues of genealogy, property, and ownership, the other valuing human experience and a diary recording the details of daily life. Mr. Martyn defends the first approach, an approach that has, after all, informed the considerable reputation of the historian, Miss Merridew: she is an expert in the "system of land tenure in mediaeval England" (*CSF* 33). Yet Miss Merridew has complicated the issue – and engaged in many professional battles because of these complications – by her method of presenting land tenure material in relation to the life of the time. The historical document in Woolf's story is a fifteenth-century journal kept by a female Martyn ancestor and, as alternative history, it typifies the narratives of women's experience excluded in most histories of Woolf's time. The journal itself therefore becomes a focal point for the contested question of what constitutes history: the manuscript is dismissed as inconsequential by the family heir but valued as a treasure by a female historian.

The sketch thus suggests one response to the pedagogical question that plagued Woolf at Morley: "how is it *possible* to make them feel the flesh & blood in these shadows?"[50] Part of her answer is to make the past come alive through the immediacy of narrative, to "hook" her readers with details of the everyday, and to convey the excitement of the research process itself. But we also see the characteristic Woolfian gesture of drawing the reader into a discussion about fundamental theoretical issues by posing the question, what do we mean by "history"? Were it not for Miss Merridew's persistence, this particular manuscript would have been neglected and cast aside; it is Merridew's interest that transforms the journal from a meaningless bit of old paper into a meaningful document. But while Miss Merridew's new definition of history interrogates the old, it does not replace it; the manuscript is framed by a balanced debate. Mr. Martyn is equally dramatized and he presents an equally reasonable and emotional case: his passion for old family names is such that he says them over in his mind at night as his way of falling asleep. Woolf is not replacing one authoritative version with another but marking historical narrative with contextuality and provisionality. The implications are that not only the *meaning* of history but also what we consider to be historically *meaningful* is a product of the historian's understanding, even a product of historical desire. For all its non-theoretical prose, the sketch highlights the intensely theoretical subject that we would now call the textuality of history. By presenting two different but understandable views, Woolf shows how different readings produce different historical experiences – experiences, indeed, of different histories. In doing so, she alerts her readers to the impact of positionality on interpretation and prompts them to reflect on their own positionalities in relation to her text. Sharing Collingwood's historicist philosophy, Woolf does not, however, share his authoritative monologic prose; instead, she situates her reader in a dialogic fiction as another way of bringing the "shadows" alive.

Woolf's foregrounding of the constructed nature of history does not, however, erase the historical object. The fragmentary nature of the diary reminds us that we are not recovering the past but merely one of its traces; at the same time, there is much to be learned from that trace. The tension between material and human values in the frame narrative features equally in the narrative of the medieval past. Mistress Joan is glimpsed at the point of an arranged marriage based on estate interests rather than love, and initially the material world, filled as it is with robberies, murders, and war, poses a brutal opposition to the world that captures Joan's imagination – poetry and troubadour songs of romance. Again, however, the tensions are not simplistically polarized. Joan's mother has a humanistic dream of future material prosperity for England – not a world riven by competition and bloodshed, but a world of safe highways, sufficient food, and democratic sharing. The moats would be filled, the towers pulled down, and "there would be cheer for guest or serving man at the same table with the Lord" (*CSF* 60). While Joan can not accept her mother's vision as fully satisfying, and is concerned about the effect of broad straight highways on the winding corridors of the mind, the compelling nature of *each* vision suggests negotiation between different desires rather than exclusive choice.

In yet a further complexity, Woolf's historical narrative also offers an insight into narrative's function. Joan Martyn reads John Lydgate's poem about Helen and the battle of Troy out loud to the gathered family, hears the stories of the Round Table from a traveling singer, and listens with rapt attention to the tales and songs of the old women sitting round the fire. These tales of the past give her the sense of a living connection to it; in one of her favorite places, among the tombs of her ancestors, she is so moved by the forgotten names that she "would fain do some small act that would give them pleasure. It must be something secret, and unthought of – a kiss or a stroke, such as you would give a living person" (62). As the sense of the living past is passed on to Joan by the stories she reads and hears, so she in turn transmits her history to Miss Merridew, her twentieth-century reader, who in turn transmits her history to us. Historical narrative is both a site of ideological difference and a mode of human continuity; the dialogic and the phatic dimensions of history are joined.

Historical dialogism

The fundamental questions posed about the historical reading in "The Journal of Mistress Joan Martyn" become the basis for Woolf's historical essays and reviews. Woolf exposes the way historical narratives are determined by the biases of historians; at the same time, she does not conclude that the inevitable partiality of view diminishes the task of focusing on the historical object. She historically situates both the actual text under discussion and herself as a specifically located reader, with the object of learning more about both. Reading for Woolf is always a relational, interactive activity – a dynamic that applies to historical reading as well. Even when Woolf focuses on recreating a historical context, her underlying goal is comparative. She seeks out differences and commonalities between past and present to stimulate a contextual understanding of the past and to heighten her readers' awareness of their present positionalities. Paradoxically perhaps, she also suggests a transhistorical world that can be grasped as a collective whole.

Just as Collingwood saw history acquiring a different narrative in each generation, so Woolf saw literature as continually recreated through different historical readings. As a pioneer in reception theory, Woolf moved beyond I. A. Richards's analysis of the contaminating importation of subjective, personal associations to explore the broader issues later theorized by Hans Jacob Jauss: the way the reader's cultural, social, and material location informs her reading response. Aligned more with reception theories than with practical criticism, Woolf's purpose is not to expose historically conditioned interpretations as false or problematic; her interest lies in understanding why historical readers responded the way that they did. The thrust of Woolf's reading practice is always expansive: our own readings are supplemented by readings of the past; we read alongside and through other readers. In the opening paragraph of "The Countess of Pembroke's Arcadia," for example, Woolf draws attention both to historical differences and to the chain of continuity forged by multiple readings of the same work:

Each has read differently, with the insight and the blindness of his own generation. Our reading will be equally partial. In 1930 we shall miss a great deal that was obvious to 1655; we shall see some things that the eighteenth century ignored. But let us keep up the long succession of readers; let us in our turn bring the insight and the blindness of our own generation to bear upon the "Countess of Pembroke's Arcadia," and so pass it on to our successors. (*CR* 2:40)

Reading, for Woolf, is thus always historical, although it is not merely a product of historical environment. To transpose her words in *Orlando*, "the transaction between a [reader] and the spirit of the age is one of infinite delicacy": the balance is to "neither fight [the] age, nor submit to it; [to be] of it, yet [remain oneself]" (*O* 239–40). Similarly, in the chain of historical readings, the reader must resist the authority often attributed to the "great" critics, for if there is one strong message running through Woolf's essays, it is that we must think for ourselves. For a projected book on reading, she wrote. "It is all very well, when the impression [of reading Shakespeare] has spent itself, to take down Coleridge and Coleridge will delight... and instruct, but only in the margin of the mind. It is I who have read the play... No third person can explain or alter or even throw much light upon [our] relationship" (*E* III:478). Yet while each generation must read anew in its own terms, the tradition of cumulative reading is crucial for our broader understanding of the larger frames of literary meaning. The comparative crudity of our understanding of the novel when placed against the sophistication of dramatic criticism, for example, has much to do with the former's markedly fewer generations of readership: "The collective reading of generations which has set us at the right angle for reading plays has not yet shaped our attitude to fiction" (*E* III:338). For Woolf, our own readings are shadowed by those of historical readers and the more awareness we have of previous readings (including those of the "great" critics), the broader and deeper our own readings will be. Historical accretion becomes an avenue of access into the larger common mind.

To understand this "long succession of readers," we must constantly examine our own responses and reflect upon the way responses change. Where do we cry? Where do we laugh? What do we find offensive? What provokes our fear? Woolf constantly raises such questions to bring out the historical nature of emotional response. "But where the Victorians cried in 1854 what do we do in 1920?" she asks of "An Old Novel" (*E* III:216). Or she probes the effect of recent events. A collection of stories published in 1920 makes her feel that she is reading about a world that is now remote. Life has not changed but what matters in it has: "If there had not been a war we should not have felt this with anything like the same force" (*E* III:228).

In another essay, she notes that the modern sensitivity to physical suffering alienates the contemporary reader from John Evelyn's descriptions of human torture. Although Evelyn found the scenes unpleasant, he managed both to observe and describe them, leading Woolf to remark, "Allowing for his discomfort, there is enough discrepancy between his view of pain and ours to make us wonder whether we see any fact with the same eyes, marry any woman from the same motives, or judge any conduct by the same standards" (*CR* 1:81). But then, in a characteristic turn, the focus on historical difference twists around to reveal continuity. While Woolf acknowledges that the modern reader may have become sensitized to certain overt brutalities, a quick barb about the present state of the "humane instincts" dispels any sense of the superiority of modern civilization. Woolf evokes a similar relational twist when it comes to fear. Writing, in quick succession, "Gothic Romance" and "Henry James's Ghost Stories," she points to the gap between eighteenth- and twentieth-century sensibilities. The modern audience, she suggests, is too skeptical, too sophisticated, for the transparent horrors of corpses and ghosts. But then she shows how the same emotion is produced in *The Turn of the Screw* by its chilling psychological mixture of beauty and the obscene: "We are afraid of something, unnamed, of something, perhaps, in ourselves" (*E* III:325). As with the Evelyn essay, focusing on the distinctive qualities of the past yields a sense of historical separation, but reading through the lens of cultural translation exposes the continuing human being underneath.

In the area of morality, however, Woolf often seems to imply an absolute break with the Victorians, arguing that "an anxious inquiry into the state of the writer's morals" is no longer the reader's central concern (*E* 1:85). Similarly, she contrasts the nineteenth-century's disapproval of Sterne's immorality in his life with the twentieth-century reader's more likely objection to Sterne's excessive dwelling, in his writing, on the goodness of the "human heart" (*CR* 2:83). "[I]t is significant of the change of taste that has come over us," Woolf writes, "that it is Sterne's sentimentality that offends us and not his immorality" (84). The intentional affront to the Victorian sense of decencies, of course, lies in naming the difference in outlook a matter of "taste." As part of the revolution against conventional sexual mores, Woolf is less flexible than usual in her own position. Nevertheless, she still poses difficult questions about the relation between moral values and interpretation, beginning "Eliza and Sterne," for example, with one of the less resolvable problems confronting the biographer: "By what standard ... is he to judge the morals of the dead? By that of their day, of that of his own?" (*E* III:346). The twist here, however, is that admitting to different standards is part of the morality that Woolf endorses. The biographer's problem would be easily resolved by authorizing one's own morality, as the Victorians did "by taking it for granted that the truth was revealed about the year 1850 to the fortunate natives of the British Isles" (347). But Woolf's assertion that "times are changed" (347) demonstrates the fundamental principle that times *do* change and the presumption of *one* country in *one* era to a window on moral "truth" is exposed as an imperialist project. Woolf's provisionality and questioning, in this light, reveal that the modernist too has her morality but it is to be found not in more enlightened values but in a pluralistic, contextual understanding of value.

Historical reading, as Woolf pursues it, thus raises complex questions about difference and sameness. When we compare past and present, can we compare them on equal terms? Do we need to modernize the text, translate it into the present, in order to perceive its enduring appeal? These questions become explicit in the debates surrounding the performance of historical drama, since, in one sense, staging a play in modern terms foregrounds contemporary relevance but, in another sense, this act of translation may be necessary to produce the same effect it would have had for its historical audience. In the early twentieth century, these controversies surfaced around the staging of Shakespeare, where, in a number of pre-war productions, Harley Granville-Barker shocked London audiences by rejecting the customary use of lavish, realistic sets and reintroducing the non-scenic stage. In 1924, Woolf reviewed Granville-Barker's "Preface to a Midsommer Night's Dreame," not to take sides with Granville-Barker's shift to a more authentically Elizabethan stage but to pick up the implications of his arguments for understanding the cultural meaning of form. The successful performances of Shakespeare's time, she explains, if replicated for a modern audience, might well have lesser effect: "To us, whose eyes and ears have grown used to a far more elaborate setting, simplicity may seem bareness, reticence may appear starvation" (*E* III:439). But, picking up Granville-Barker's point that theatrical effects must not obscure the poetry, she concludes that producing Shakespeare has become a "highly ticklish undertaking" (439). Elsewhere in reviewing contemporary performances, she notes how the contemporary filter sometimes distorts the historical text – the line played for a gratuitous modern laugh in *The Cherry Orchard* (*E* III:247), for example, or the mumbled mangling of the naturally flowing repartee in *Love for Love* (*E* III:296). But she can also use modern "inauthenticity" to jolt the reader into a sudden defamiliarization of the historical text: by stating that Lydia Lopokova's Russian accent, when performing Shakespeare's "A Lover's Complaint," was "no more foreign than that of the Elizabethans would have been" (*E* IV:564), Woolf reminds her contemporary audience how distant from the original Shakespeare they always are. There are no rules for Woolf, and every performance must be judged on its own. Characteristically, in the review of Granville-Barker, her approach is that understanding the choices confronting a director enlivens the viewer's role, and the effect mirrors her own goal in these essays: "exciting our curiosity and stimulating our intelligence" (*E* III:439).

More broadly, Woolf's theoretical questions force us to negotiate the opposite polarities of alterity and identity. Her historical comparisons sometimes direct attention to difference, sometimes to similarity, but most often to both elements as competing tensions in our constantly shifting reading experience. She makes us aware that "this reading sixteenth-century writing as currently and certainly as we read our own is an illusion" (*CR* 2:9) while, at the same time, she inculcates the ability to "recognise the same man in different disguises" (*CR* 1:55) so that we may "hear the sound of his voice speaking across the ages so distinctly" (*CR* 2:39). Her historical critical praxis therefore involves three separate but interweaving activities: locating the text in a discrete historical period known by its unlikeness to the present, reflecting on the way the present is interrogated through this comparison, and translating both past and present (always problematically and provisionally) into the continuous now. Difference implies periodization, the discrete character of each era, the distinctive characteristics in the way people lived, the way they used language, the forms to which their emotions were attached. Continuities imply an ahistorical mode, a strand of anti-periodization that focuses on the persistence of the same. Woolf's essays advocate both the periodizing and the ahistorical consciousness. Recognizing difference is disruptive of the self; it prevents us from subjecting others to our own limiting views; it is a way of resisting false universalisms and appropriation and/or subjection of the other. But perceiving the difference of the other is also disruptive of the self in a formative, expansive way: as the different voices sink into our unconscious, they help us to recover abandoned or latent parts of ourselves. Continuities then give us a hold onto permanence in a world of flux and change. Recognizing sameness, we come to feel part of the larger human community, to feel the bonds of both love and responsibility that constitute our human ties. To negotiate between difference and sameness is to understand the nature of human community as composed of contrasting but continuous selves.

Orlando – the narrative of radically different selves who are nevertheless the same self – types the history uncovered in Woolf's essays.[51] Orlando lives through the cataclysmic effects of periodization – the changing clothes, customs, roles, assumptions that constitute the character of each age. But Orlando also sees through translucent time; in a vision of superimposed images in which "everything [is] partly something else," she gazes through three hundred years of history held in the reservoir of her unconscious – "this pool or sea in which everything is reflected" (*O* 290). Change or continuity, progress or stasis, loss or plenitude – which we see, Woolf suggests, depends not on the objective fact but on the way we look at it; or rather, the objective fact contains the multiple potentials of our relation to history. Since the text can mean different things at different times, to different readers, historical reading means not getting at the authoritative original meaning but finding a way, through the multiplicities of the text, to discover the meanings of most value for the present. It is this quality of excess in the relation between the written work and the reader that gives to literature its perpetual life. Justifying, on the centenary of Charlotte Brontë's birth, the addition of yet one more reader's impression to the wealth of established testimony, Woolf explains, "a book, in order to live, must have the power of changing as we change" (*E* ii:27). Since the past is in dialogic relation with the present, since we not only take up the book to read it but it also takes us and "reads us" (*CR* 1:48), the reflection in the glass, or in the pool, is always changing. Thus, "[t]o write down one's impressions of *Hamlet* as one reads it year after year, would be virtually to record one's own autobiography," and Brontë's works will similarly go on to "serve a generation yet unborn with a glass in which to measure its varying stature" (*E* ii:27). Much like her approach to the human subject, Woolf proposes that the changing, multiple meanings of the text are not inconsistent with the text's continuing identity. It is indeed the paradox of continuance and diversity that characterizes life in time.

From historicism to historicist reading

Orlando and the essays share a common historicism; Woolf's focus in the essays, however, is on the processes by which we come to such historical thinking and the ways in which we apply such historicism to our reading. As I have suggested, Woolf models a dynamic and pluralistic practice of reading through her discussions of individual works and, in these discussions, foregrounds her own thinking as a historicized fallible reader in a way that disrupts any implication of authoritative closure. However, reading the text through the filter of the present does not merely signify the provisionality of the critic's views; the relation between subject and object is crucial to Woolf's relational construct of reading. The fundamental dynamic in

Woolf's approach to historical reading is a dialectic between continuance
and diversity which she enacts by alternatively uniting her readers with, and
distancing them from, the text. Such shifts yield fluctuating revelations of
the historical text's familiarity and strangeness, and the reader's experiences
of identity and alterity, with individual essays often beginning with one of
these polarities and, in the course of discussion, shifting to the other. The
first *Common Reader*, for example, begins with human commonalities and
moves to an increasing perception of the difference and otherness of the
historical text, whereas the second *Common Reader* opens with an initial
perception of historical difference and moves to a recovery of the universal
and shared.

Each *Common Reader* begins with an essay – respectively, "The Pastons
and Chaucer" and "The Strange Elizabethans" – that directs our attention
not to the great literary masterpieces, but to such everyday writings as
letters and marginalia. In part, Woolf is establishing the embeddedness of
the literary work in the language of the people; in part, she is forging a
link to the life of the reader. The literary work is not a sacred object to be
elevated and admired; it is to be understood through its vital connection
to the common life that both enables its creation and provides the context
in which it has meaning. To understand that everyday historical life as well
as the literary text – for the two are inseparable – the reader must bring his
or her everyday experience into the hermeneutic sphere.

"The Pastons and Chaucer" proposes that Chaucer's writing of *The
Canterbury Tales* was made possible because contemporaneous families like
the Pastons wrote letters; phrased more theoretically, it argues that the kind
of poetry an age produces arises from the nature of the discourse that its
people have developed in their common speech. But – perhaps with her
students at Morley College in mind – Woolf opens her discussion by first
addressing the gap created by her reader's historical alienation from the medieval world. Situating us first in present time, Woolf points to the lonely
ruins of Caister Castle and John Paston's unmarked grave, but then quickly
animates the scene with voices from the past whispering about the fall of
such a powerful family and the plight of the neglected dead. Gossip – the
voice of the people – becomes the bridge to the past, for the voices are represented as if in a narrative present, even shifting briefly into the present tense:
"Tom Topcroft, the mad bricklayer, has broken loose again and ranges the
country half-naked" (*CR* 1:4). Next, the specificity of objects resurrects the
living Caister before our eyes, moving from a presentist description of "a
raw, new-built house, without telephone, bathroom or drains, arm-chairs
or newspapers" to a historically recreated scene of "wardrobes stuffed with

gowns of velvet and satin and cloth of gold, with hoods and tippets and beaver hats and leather jackets and velvet doublets; and... the very pillow-cases on the beds... of green and purple silk" (4, 5). Holding us in the past, Woolf then follows a narrative path from the practicalities and simple faith dominating the lives of the first John Paston and his wife Margaret to the gradual emergence of new sensibilities, refinements, and pleasures in the lives of their sons – a change in consciousness that finds its animating center in the advent of "books" and the birth of the reader (11). The young Sir John foregoes his practical duties for the "strange intoxication" of reading the poems of Lydgate and Chaucer, or curtails his work in order to "hasten home to sit in his chair and learn the end of the story" (11).

The technique Woolf has used – if successful – has done precisely that: drawn us into the Paston world through the power of narrative, the hold upon us of the story. But just at this point, Woolf's text signals a rupture, reiterating a phrase that, in its repetition – like Keats's "forlorn" – tolls us back to present reality. The words *"learn the end of the story"* (emphasis added) end one paragraph and then begin, in a different register, the next. Suddenly the spell is broken and narrative is supplanted by literary criticism: "To learn the end of the story – Chaucer can still make us wish to do that" (11). And from here Woolf launches into a comparative historical analysis in which the quality of medieval writing is understood – in its unselfconscious narrative, its straightforward, non-exoticized description of nature, its direct references to the body, its immediate observations of everyday life – as radically different from the writing of her own time. *The Canterbury Tales* is what modern writing is *not*, for Chaucer's text conveys a writer's easy, straightforward belief in his reality. And now the readers' distance from the text can be positively evoked for both a clearer apprehension of the historical object and a self-reflexive assessment of the present. In a point often overlooked, Woolf suggests that the limitation of *Ulysses* lies not in its explicit sexual references but to the absence, in Joyce, of Chaucer's ability "to speak without self-consciousness of the parts and functions of the body" (15). For its part, the medieval text lacks the suppleness and intimacy that later ages develop in "writing for writing's sake" (21). Yet the placing of Chaucer's writing is not unnuanced; straddling the novel and poetry, *The Canterbury Tales* mixes the "morality of ordinary intercourse" of the former with the heightened intensity and shaped wholeness of the latter (18). The present critic must neither simplify the past nor see it as simple, and the historical view here is neither nostalgic nor evolutionary. What one era has the other does not and vice versa; this whole middle section is an exercise in the twists of relational thinking.

The final section of Woolf's essay returns to the Paston letters, not, however, to narrativize and thus make the past come alive, but to develop further relational thinking about text and context. Now the solidity and stolidity of the Paston letters can be seen as the raw material of Chaucer's language, and as the conditions of his thought:

> But when Chaucer lived he must have heard this very language, matter of fact, unmetaphorical, far better fitted for narrative than for analysis, capable of religious solemnity or of broad humour, but very stiff material to put on the lips of men and women accosting each other face to face. In short, it is easy to see, from the Paston letters, why Chaucer wrote not *Lear* or *Romeo and Juliet*, but the *Canterbury Tales*. (22)

Ordinary life-writing makes possible the writing of the poet and in fact defines poetry's possibilities; or, as Woolf was soon famously to write, "masterpieces are not single and solitary births; they are the outcome of many years of thinking in common, of thinking by the body of the people" (*R* 98). If the middle of this essay establishes the way that historical reading depends on a comparative grasp of the relations between past and present, the ending asserts that historical reading also requires a holistic sense of the imbrication of literature with the social, economic, and linguistic life of its time.

"The Pastons and Chaucer" thus advances a theory of historical reading, while pedagogically, it makes use of narrative to lead the reader from historical alienation to identification, and finally to analytic understanding. In "The Strange Elizabethans," however, rather than trying to close the gap of historical alienation, Woolf dwells in it. Here the Elizabethans are explored as the historical other, and the past is represented as a strange and foreign land. The opening to the second *Common Reader* is thus to some extent the obverse of the first. Woolf now allows historical reading to be saturated with a sense of otherness so that reading the past – even for the English reader, the English past – must be approached as a task in transposition and translation.

Perhaps relying on the unquestioned canonical status accorded to Shakespeare, Woolf begins her second volume of essays by invoking the English assumption of familiarity with Elizabethan drama: "There are few greater delights than to go back three or four hundred years and become in fancy at least an Elizabethan" (*CR* 2:9). But possibly because of the profound impact of her early reading of Hakluyt's voyages, Woolf's writings about the Elizabethans are also strongly informed by her perception of historical reading as an encounter, like travel, with cultural difference.

An earlier essay, "Notes on the Elizabethan Play," for example, suggests that these dramas are now "for the ordinary reader an ordeal, an upsetting experience which plys him with questions, harries him with doubts, alternately delights and vexes him with pleasure and pains" (*CR* 1:48). Once we leave the beaten path of Shakespeare, the essay continues, the reader "fed on modern English literature" flounders in the fields of the fantastic (49). And so, in "The Strange Elizabethans," Woolf rapidly routs as illusory any comforting notions of familiarity, enacting a twist to imagine the Elizabethan laughter at the modern reader's clumsy attempts at pronunciation and bizarrely fantastic conceptions of Elizabethan life. And then, while she turns – much in the manner of "The Pastons and Chaucer" – to Elizabethan life-writing in search of a contextual entry into the Elizabethan mind, what she elucidates is the constant frustration of the modern desire for everyday detail, and the estranging effects of the Elizabethan preference for lofty eloquence and generalized sentiment. Reading Gilbert Harvey's letters and essays pushes her "almost beyond the limits of human patience," for the repetitious pomposities and inflated rhetoric make her "cry out in anguish for the boon of some meaning to set its stamp on them" (*CR* 2:16). What Woolf is doing with her *own* reader, however, is a complex mixture of push and pull; Woolf's castigation of Harvey's inflated style distances the reader from the Elizabethans, but the glimpses of human narrative – the frustrations of Harvey's innumerable failures and the adumbrated story of a nobleman's attempts to seduce Harvey's sister – keep drawing the reader in. Finally, turning to Harvey's commonplace book and his marginalia, Woolf brings the writing and the man together; in these smaller, more fragmentary forms, Harvey "wrote only for his own eye," and so a new voice emerges in which "he seems to write as if he were talking to himself" (20). These glimpses into his inner conflicts, his attempts to counsel and console himself, reverse the alienation created by his public prose, so that the essay ultimately turns upon its title and discovers the familiar in the heart of the strange: "when we say that Harvey lived we mean that he quarrelled and was tiresome and ridiculous and struggled and failed and had a face like ours – a changing, a variable, a human face" (23). Woolf has given her reader a greater understanding of the hyperbolic and generalizing character of Elizabethan rhetoric at the same time as she has connected the passions and desires of her historical figure with those of the readers of her day.

In the course of these two essays, Woolf thus moves back and forth between strangeness and familiarity, using narrative and everyday details to overcome the alienating effects of strangeness, yet analyzing language and discourse to underscore and highlight the distinctiveness of cultures in the past. Historical reading means constant negotiation between identity and alterity, and, in other essays, Woolf tells the story of her own reading as she herself negotiates – sometimes with difficulty – between these two poles. At such times, Woolf asks more from her reader than merely experiencing closeness and distance from the literary text. She asks that the methodology and practice of reading become a subject of scrutiny as well.

In her essay on *Robinson Crusoe*, for example, Woolf begins by getting her reader to think about the negative effects of reading literature through the lens of rigid a priori constructs. Beginning with the question of how to read Defoe, Woolf outlines the kinds of historical criticism commonly employed in her time: the genre approach through "the development of the novel" and the biographical approach through "the life of the author" (*CR* 2:51). The problem with these approaches for Woolf is in part the irrelevancy of much of their information, and she is mockingly biting about the biographer's obsession with such details as the shape of novelists' chins. More significantly, she raises concerns about the reductiveness of general constructs. Challenging the concept of periodization, Woolf highlights the differences among authors living at the same time. While "text-books" may group writers into historical periods, what chronological container, she asks, can fit the diverse shapes of Sir Walter Scott, Jane Austen, and Thomas Peacock? (53). But Woolf's main concern is the way such prefatory materials produce passive rather than responsive readings. "There is a piece of business to be transacted between writer and reader," she argues, and a preconceived theory is only too likely to become the obnoxious middleman, complicating and muddying the exchange (52).

Having foregrounded questions of how we read – and specifically how we read a historical text – Woolf proceeds to discuss her own reading in a way that recognizes both the historicity of the text and the historicity of the reader. While her discussion resembles formalist criticism in its analysis of Defoe's perspective, the historicist nature of her criticism is evident in her on-going commentary on the difference between the text's perspective and her own. Her reading produces a Defoe that much resembles the Defoe of generic or biographical criticism (in his emphasis on fact and his middle-class values), but the consideration she gives to her own positioning shows how the critic's present is an inextricable part of the interpretation and judgment of the past.

Woolf's initial impression of *Robinson Crusoe* is that it fails to give her the kind of pleasure that, as a modern reader, she expects from a perilous adventure on a lonely island, but instead of pointing out Defoe's failures, she analyzes the influence of her own biases in shaping her response: her resistance to Defoe derives from her post-Romantic preference for more poetic and imaginative treatments of solitude and isolation and her modernist expectation of a psychological treatment of this theme. Avoiding the stance of the objective historian even in representing this difference, however, she charts the kinetic process of her reading: how Defoe puzzles and annoys her and how she must struggle to close the gap between his perspective and her own. In the end, her struggle leads to theoretical speculation, but for Woolf this is the right dynamic: the text is not read through the theory; rather, theory arises out of the reading. Thus, on the one hand, she gives full ironic expression to her own distaste for national and class complacency: "There is no greater good fortune we are assured than to be born of the British middle class" (*CR* 2:55); on the other hand, her attempt to see through Defoe's eyes leads her to see and to appreciate the way he illuminates the value of everyday life: "he comes in the end to make common actions dignified and common objects beautiful" (57). Although Defoe takes "the opposite way from the psychologist's" and "describes the effect of emotion on the body, not on the mind," she discovers that, because his "fact is the right fact," he manages to convey the effects of desolation and solitude as powerfully as any modern psychological writer (57). By so exploring her varying responses to the text, Woolf both articulates difference and speculates about the lack of difference. At the end, the critical stance is inconclusive. Woolf remains a divided reader, unable totally to drop her ironic amusement at Defoe's prosaic faith in facts, yet unable to assert that her modernist way is, in the final tally, superior. The historicist experience is various, recording not merely the dialectic of difference and similarity, but the complex experience of the difficulty of coping with difference. Woolf exposes the way a reader can use amusement and explanation to contain and control the threat of difference, but then demonstrates the power of the text to unsettle that comfort – in effect, the power of the past to *disturb* the present. Her historical self-positioning thus works in two directions: to limit the present reading to the relativity of its moment and to expand present consciousness through the incorporation of historically "other" views.

Dialogic versus linear historical narratives

The dialogic historical narratives that I have been discussing are pervasive throughout Woolf's work, but they are not the only kind of history that Woolf tells. When the subject is reading, Woolf's focus is on understanding relationship as parallels and contrasts; there is no master plot of progression, no privileging of nostalgic or evolutionary plots. Yet there are times when Woolf does tell linear historical narratives involving patterns that are variously progressive, regressive, or recuperative. *A Room of One's Own*, as a striking case in point, constructs a double linear narrative: first, the increasing restriction and limitation of women's lives since the sixteenth century, caused by the hardening of gender roles, and second, the emancipatory counter-narrative of the emergence of women's writing. Of course, a problem with such metanarratives is that they inevitably argue their case through selection of evidence, and some feminist critics have criticized Woolf for imitating and reinscribing the same kind of exclusionary history that characterized the patriarchal model. In *Writing Women's Literary History*, for example, Margaret Ezell argues that, in constructing a continuous women's tradition, Woolf privileges fiction and writing for publication, obscuring both the significance of other genres and the circulation of manuscripts by early women writers. Ezell further objects to Woolf's claiming Aphra Behn as the first women writer, as if women's history began in the middle of the seventeenth century.[52] But the contrasting historicism of Woolf's essays suggests that *A Room of One's Own* is a strategic rather than representative historical model for her. To adopt Woolf's own reading practice, we need to approach this work as a historically located text, written at a particular time for a specific audience – an audience that, even in the published version, is encoded from the second, if not the first word: "But, you may say" (*R* 5). The teleological narrative of *A Room of One's Own* is best understood as "a piece of business" being "transacted between writer and reader" – the business, in this case, being to encourage and empower the women in the audience by inscribing them as the culminating point in a progressive narrative. The historical success of Woolf's project can be seen in the way it has supplied an effective model – until perhaps very recently – for the task of constructing an empowering past and enabling a progressive future. As essentialist history, Woolf's text may well be limiting; but contextualized in history, its rhetorical power is very clear.

Woolf's last project, "Anon" and "The Reader," functions as alternative history in a similar way – a more conventionally written history meant to expose the absences in the dominant models. Unfinished at the time of her death, Woolf's historical narrative (of what we might today call the changing methods of production and consumption of the literary text) shaped itself in her mind as a counter-discourse: "Try to write lit the other way round," Woolf noted to herself, while she considered the possibility – years before Borges – of casting her version of literary history as a review of a fictitious conventional history, detailing "[w]hat it omits." Woolf, it seems, wanted to attach her literature to life, to emotion, to both the "surrounding" and the "inner, current [*sic*]," and above all to writers and readers bound together in a rich dynamic relation – all things "left out in text books."[53] But ordering and structuring this work was a task that plagued Woolf with endless difficulty, as Brenda Silver has shown. Silver relates Woolf's difficulties to the context of the Second World War, but a further, more textual problem may have been the work's conflicting goals. It is evident from Woolf's notes and her drafts of the first two chapters that she wanted both to delineate a linear path from anonymous oral recitation to signed printed publication and also to range freely and widely, following variously the hints and signs of diversity and continuity between past and present. The work may have foundered on the tension between linear, consecutive narrative and "Reading at Random" (Woolf's original title). Perhaps, as Silver also speculates, if Woolf had been able to finish it, the final product would have been the third volume of *Common Reader* essays that Woolf was planning to write. In the essay collection, a chronological arrangement of the individual "case studies" allows some latitude for themes of change and development, while the individual character of each essay offers space for contradictory and pluralistic impulses.

There is, however, no reason why we should assume that this final work would or should have been like Woolf's earlier essays. If we remember to situate "Anon" and "The Reader" as Woolf's antiphonal response to rigidly author- or period-centered studies, then we will see the advantage of linear, objective narrative for her alternative history of the reader and of the book. Woolf's more traditionally linear histories need to be read as contextually situated, not essentialist, narratives. They represent yet another of the varieties of history that Woolf tells.

Historicist metanarratives of reading

What then is Woolf's metanarrative, not of history, but of historical reading? The final historicist dynamic that Woolf's essays engage is the accumulative layering of different historical readings. Given Woolf's adamant resistance to the authority of external critics – encapsulated, in *A Room of One's Own*, in the admonishing figure of the beadle – it is not surprising that she stresses the importance of individual reading and the necessity of working out opinions for ourselves. Yet, in the opening paragraph of "The Countess of Pembroke's Arcadia," as we have seen, Woolf positions herself at the end of a long succession of readers, acknowledging a historical tradition of which she forms a part. The essay then proceeds to tell the story of Woolf's reading, from her initial identification with the Elizabethan readers to a progressively modernist separation, but it is a simultaneous double or even multiple vision of Sydney's work that the narrative of reading upholds. Woolf shares with her imagined Elizabethan audience, and Sydney's privileged reader, the Countess of Pembroke, a delight in the *Arcadia* as escape; Sydney is "absenting himself from the present and its strife" (*CR* 2:41). In such transhistorical reading, Woolf posits both an atemporal understanding of genre and an equivalency in historical eras. But as Woolf traces her journey through Sydney's work, after she celebrates its "wild beauty" (41), its "energy" (41), its "elasticity" (44), its revelation of the heart's secret desires, she begins to succumb to boredom and eventually exasperation with the lack of control and direction, and the absence of any character complexity or "psychological subtlety" (49). Alert now to her own contrary modernist preferences, Woolf nevertheless can still appreciate Sidney's appeal for a more luxurious, languorous age, and ultimately the varied reception of the *Arcadia* over time accords with her sense of its multiple riches. Within it "all the seeds of English fiction lie latent" (49), all equally capable of stimulating the further writing of fiction. Each age can choose its own "legacy" from this treasure house (50), and Woolf neither privileges nor deprecates either past or present readings. What makes her approach broader than that of previous readers, however, is her ability to read through multiple historical lenses – through historically past, as well as historically present, eyes.

It is Woolf's modernist perspectivism, her ability to entertain different points of view, that allows her both to see the mix of incongruities within each era and the contextual value of all historical formations, including her own. For it is the paradox of modernism that its very endorsement of perspectivism prevents it from inscribing itself as the culminating point of a teleological narrative. As numerous critics have observed,[54] Woolf found in the Elizabethan playhouse the ideal model for her participatory literary community, but she did not ignore the comparative barbarism of the age, the pomposity and extravagance of its prose, its restriction of women's lives, or its imperialist plunderings.[55] Similarly, avoiding the nostalgic historical metanarrative, she also avoids the evolutionary one. In "Notes on an Elizabethan Play," for example, when Woolf asks her readers to reconstruct the Elizabethan audience in their minds, she urges them to "make the necessary alterations in perspective" and to enter "a different *but not more elementary* stage of your reading development" (*CR* 1:55, emphasis added). Whereas, she acknowledges, the moderns may have developed more "filaments of sensibility," the Elizabethans have, on their side, the ability to use "the ear and the eye," to relish new-coined words, to laugh with broad humor, and to believe in the Gods (55). And, in her late broadcast, "Craftsmanship," she mocks the self-comforting evolutionary mentality:

For though at this moment at least a hundred professors are lecturing upon the literature of the past, at least a thousand critics are reviewing the literature of the present, and hundreds upon hundreds of young men and women are passing examinations in English literature with the utmost credit, still – do we write better, do we read better than we read and wrote four hundred years ago when we were unlectured, uncriticized, untaught? Is our Georgian literature a patch on the Elizabethan? (*CE* 11:249).

At the same time, Woolf essays, particularly those on the development of individual writers, assume the possibility of contextual improvement – an improvement, we might say, within each reigning paradigm, whether that be within a cultural era or an individual's career. Every age develops its own cultural formation, every writer and reader develops a distinctive style, and the inculcation of the best reading and writing practices is necessary for the desired perfection of each form. But, cross-historically, there is no absolute improvement; the improvement Woolf seeks lies in the evolution of more inclusive practices. To have *all* people writing and reading would make for fully democratic participation, for a more flexible and hybrid art, and – I think she believed or at least hoped – for a more peaceful world. But the progressive project here is one of social, not literary, improvement. The new masterpieces would be the best forms for a democratic age, but in evaluative terms she does not suggest that they will surpass – though they might equal – the masterpieces of the past. But the very word "masterpieces" evokes standards and the idea of standards encodes an implicit narrative of possible improvement. Even if masterpieces themselves are not evolving into better and better works, how does an individual or an age evolve toward the creation of its own masterpieces? And how does the critic evolve toward the ability to recognize them? To address these questions, we must turn to the last aspect in Woolf's pedagogy that I will discuss: "reading evaluatively."

READING EVALUATIVELY

Evaluative acts

Virginia Woolf launched the feminist critique of literary value. In *A Room of One's Own* and *Three Guineas*, she vehemently claimed that expectations of scope, of subject matter, of style, even of literary structure and form, while usually applied as universal standards, are the products of contingent and localized ideological systems. In *A Room*, she condemned the hierarchical rankings of the academic establishment, stating, "I do not believe that gifts, whether of mind or character, can be weighed like sugar and butter, not even in Cambridge, where they are so adept at putting people into classes and fixing caps on their heads and letters after their names" (*R* 159). She connected the belief in ranked achievement with a male and upper-class system formed by the mentality that valorizes competitive sports among boys: "All this pitting of sex against sex, of quality against quality; all this claiming of superiority and imputing of inferiority, belong to the private-school stage of human existence where there are 'sides,' and it is necessary for one side to beat another side, and of the utmost importance to walk up to a platform and receive from the hands of the Headmaster himself a highly ornamental pot" (159). "As people mature," she continued, "they cease to believe in sides or in Headmasters or in highly ornamental pots" (159–60). In *Three Guineas*, she invited her readers to "pile mild scorn . . . upon degrees, and upon the value of examinations," to refrain from joining the ordered processions, and to refuse decorations and honors (*TG* 43, 71–72). The same protest against rankings of people carried over to judgments about books. In *A Room*, she wrote, "At any rate, where books are concerned, it is notoriously difficult to fix labels of merit in such a way that they do not come off. Are not reviews of current literature a perpetual illustration of the difficulty of judgement? 'This great book,' 'this worthless book,' the same book is called by both names. Praise and blame alike mean nothing" (*R* 160). In the pamphlet *Reviewing*, she pungently attacked what she named the "Gutter and Stamp" system – the approvals and disapprovals meted out by literary journalists, in such contradiction that they canceled each other out. In all these remarks, Woolf highlights the unreliability and arbitrariness of judgments and the ideological investments that they encode.

What, then, do we make of the places in Woolf's writing where she asserts that "a critic must be exacting" (*E* III:126), where she notes that she has "exactly appraised K[atherine Mansfield]'s story" (*D* II:49), where – in the same *A Room of One's Own* – she criticizes Charlotte Brontë's awkward narrative transition in *Jane Eyre* and suggests that the fiction of the hypothetical Mary Carmichael leaves considerable room for improvement? These are not aberrant slips of practice, for Woolf consistently claims the importance of evaluative acts. In "How Should One Read a Book?" she locates the "true complexity of reading" in the difficult but necessary transition from the first stage of receiving impressions to the second stage of passing judgment (*CR* 2:266), adding that readers must judge "with great sympathy and yet with great severity" (270). And, as she writes in "Phases of Fiction," making judgments is not only good reading practice; it is unavoidable: "nobody reads simply by chance or without a definite scale of values" (*CE* II:56).

How is it that Woolf, as a feminist, can make judgments of literary merit? That Woolf, the contextual historicist, can speak of a "definite scale of values"? Or that Woolf, as a modernist, can object to contradictory points of view? Are there discrepancies here between the understanding and the act, between her ideological critique of value and the way that value judgments enter directly and immediately into her work? As an editor at the Hogarth Press, she had to select some manuscripts for publication and reject others. As a reviewer, she was expected to express opinions about books. As a writer, she constantly revised her own writing to improve the language, the sound, and the flow. And as a reader, she was subject to sometimes violent reactions to books. William Plomer, for example, recounts a story of her heaving a novel by Charles Morgan out the window; whether "defenestration," as Plomer calls it, was a frequent evaluative act, it is worth noting that this incident accords with the fictionalized act of judgment depicted in "Middlebrow" in 1932.[56] Finally and most relevantly for my present concerns, the pedagogical aim in her essays depends on at least some concept of what "better" reading practices would be. Value judgments were both inevitable in her life and unavoidable for her goals.

The issue is therefore not evaluative as opposed to non-evaluative practices – since the latter are both impossible and unfeasible – but the signification of the valuing act. Woolf could be especially vituperative about evaluations made by reviewers, and quite possibly some of her antagonism was in response to the harsh reviews her own works had received. But the trenchant point behind her critique is that the conditions of the reviewer's task legislate against considered thought.[57] She had glimpsed the worst side of reviewing through Miss Williams, her student at Morley, whose job was merely to cull a few quotations to support a literary verdict that the editor pre-assigned. Not all reviewers were so low on the scale as poor Miss Williams, but in general Woolf thought the task of reviewing was severely limited by having to read too many books too quickly and having to make definitive pronouncements in a meager few lines of print. The emphasis consequently fell on the end judgment and not on the process of getting there. A literally graphic example – which Woolf may well have known – was the *Book Review Digest,* which, from

1906 to 1963, accompanied its excerpted reviews with a "+" or a "−" or, for divided opinions, with one of each. Presumably Woolf intended her gutter and stamp system as a satiric modest proposal but it was, in at least one actual publication, more or less in effect. And the reviewers wielded substantial power. As Leonard argued in *Books and the Public*, the reviewer's judgment determined whether a bookseller would stock a book and whether a library would buy it. But most important, the summary nature of the review placed the reviewer's opinion, and not the reader's, in the dominant role. Contradictions between reviewers thus differ radically from Woolf's positional twists. The first merely assert opposite views; the second ask readers to consider issues from different angles. The first present snap judgments for the reader to accept; the second pose questions and invite the reader to think. In sum, ornamental pots and fixed stamps stress what is concluded after the evaluating act; Woolf's essays stress the evaluating act itself. Her conclusions are characteristically provisional, contextual, and individual; and her stress falls on each reader's evaluating for her or himself.

"What is a Good Novel?" (1924)

In 1924, Woolf contributed to a symposium in *The Highway*, the journal of the Worker's Educational Association, on the question, "What is a Good Novel?"[58] Eleven prominent novelists[59] were asked to contribute a few paragraphs each, with Woolf as the only woman in the group.[60] While most contributors tried to specify the textual features that constitute good novel writing, Woolf characteristically emphasized the reader's activity and the ceaseless, ever-changing process of devising "a standard of one's own."[61] Woolf's two-paragraph contribution lacks the playfulness and irony often found in her longer essays but it captures both her belief in the impossibility of definitive standards and her desire, at the same time, to engage her readers in the evaluating act.

Of the eleven contributors, only four (Bennett, Fyfe, Oxenham, and Walpole) offer simple, dogmatic statements; most offer several criteria for judging a novel and two (Galsworthy and Phillpotts) describe the form of the novel with one of Woolf's favorite terms: "elasticity" or "elastic." Most of the cited authors of exemplary good novels were or became recognized names, although Mark Rutherford (William Hale White), W. H. Hudson, and Frank Swinnerton are less known today. Many of the contributors write about the difficulty of arriving at prescriptive definitions, although memorable characters and a true picture of life are frequently mentioned qualities. And there are several references to the novel's effect: it should be interesting or arresting, it should uplift and not depress the reader, it should "enlarge our interest in human nature."[62]

Woolf, then, is not unique in defining a good novel through affect, although she is the only one who includes discomfort as a component of the reader's response: "A good novel is any novel that makes one think or feel. It must get its knife in between the joints of the hide with which most of us are covered."[63] Also, while Bennett specifies the role that affect should play – a good novel "ought... to help to reconcile [the reader] to human nature and the cruelties of fate" – Woolf leaves the definition of the desired emotional satisfaction up to the reader: a good novel leaves "a lasting feeling, about matters which are of importance *to us* in one way or another" (emphasis added).[64] Then, whereas most other contributors avoid narrow prescription by suggesting the variety of aspects a good novel might display, Woolf disrupts the very assumption of prescription by listing what a good novel can do *without*: "A good novel need not have a plot; need not have a happy ending; need not be about nice or respectable people; need not be in the least like life as we know it." Also, although she endorses a good novel's unsettling effect, she uncouples disturbance from difficulty: "some of the best novels have been immediately popular and perfectly easy to understand."[65] She does, however, offer that contemporary novels may *appear* difficult, if what they offer is new and strange.

It would seem that one of Woolf's aims is to urge receptivity to the non-traditional; the other is to encourage readers to trust their own responses. Whereas all other contributors took the assignment as asking for *their* opinions, Woolf is singular for telling her readers how to go about forming their own: "The only safe way of deciding whether a novel is good or bad is simply to observe one's own sensations on reaching the last page." Woolf's recourse here is not to mere impressionism, however, since she does outline a critical practice: "The best way is to read the old and the new side by side, to compare them, and so gradually make out a standard of one's own."[66] Evaluating requires extensive reading, careful comparisons, and the slow development of understanding over time. Appropriately for the pages of *The Highway*, Woolf emerges as a teacher whose concern is to teach the students how to think. Furthermore, her model is democratically empowering: culture becomes the student's own possession when she relies not on critics and authorities but on herself.[67]

Woolf's contribution ends characteristically with a focus on the reader's activity. The problem remains, however, that making value totally subject to individual standards begs the question of the value of literature; the text becomes merely a function of the reader or merely the means to the reader's activity. In writing for this symposium, however, Woolf necessarily compresses her views and adapts them to the occasion; with her WEA audience in mind, she focuses on freeing their minds from preconceptions and empowering their own critical judgments. But the contours of her thinking go beyond what she could outline in two paragraphs. An extensive critical practice lies behind the one line, "to read the old and the new side by side, to compare them," but we must range widely throughout Woolf's essays to grasp its scope. Comparison is, for Woolf, the basis of the evaluative act but the answers to what we compare and how we compare are not amenable to a simple summing up.

The good reading of bad books

Woolf's emphasis on comparison means, in effect, that while there may be bad books, there are no books that are bad to read. Here we confront one of the major differences between her approach and that of most other critics who became, like her, enlisted in the cause of reading. In their different ways, Leavis, Pound, Eliot, and the various anthologies and home guides all took the approach of constructing canons – trying, amidst the proliferation of print, to direct the readers' choice of books. In contrast, Woolf advocated reading anything and everything one wants. In the broadcast "Are Too Many Books Written and Published?" she took, as we have seen, the part of excess. On the production side, she wanted books by a greater range of writers, by "tramps and du[ch]esses; by plumbers and Prime Ministers." On the consumer's side, she wanted any book that would stimulate appetites. Reminding Leonard that "the majority of readers today are reading for the first time," she admitted they would consume "sweets and cakes first": "the easy books and the flashy books and the books that ask no trouble in reading."[68] Since any book could perform a good function by drawing people to a love of reading, the range of reading she accepted went well beyond her reviews, even beyond what would be available in public libraries given their restriction by censorship and controlled selection. In an essay on Gothic romance, Woolf argued, "as literary critics are too little aware, a love of literature is often roused and for the first years nourished not by the good books, but by the bad. It will be an ill day when all the reading is done in libraries and none of it in tubes" (*E* III:305). In "Hours in a Library," she included reading "bad books" among continuing pleasures, quite apart from their initiating role for beginners:

And we soon develop another taste, unsatisfied by the great – not a valuable taste, perhaps, but certainly a very pleasant possession – the taste for bad books. Without committing the indiscretion of naming names we know which authors can be trusted to produce yearly (for happily they are prolific) a novel, a book of poems or essays, which affords us indescribable pleasure. We owe a great deal to bad books; indeed, we come to count their authors and their heroes among those figures who play so large a part in our silent life. (*E* II:58)

In "How Should One Read a Book?" she again argued for the simultaneous reading of the lesser along with the great, earning the compliment from *Punch* that the second *Common Reader*'s "remarks on the delights of rubbish-reading – an intelligent pig-holing among the refuse-heaps of time – are both sound and entertaining."[69]

In the earliest days of Woolf's reviewing, she maintained a rather steady diet of now mainly forgotten novels; "ordinary" novels, in fact, accounted for eighteen of the thirty-five essays she published in 1905. Sometimes she wrote a mere notice; often she expressed exasperation with implausible, contrived, and awkward plots; yet she often expressed genuine interest in the handling, not perhaps of hero and heroine, but of the minor characters in the book. In the novels of Jane Barlow, A. J. Dawson, Eleanor G. Hayden, A. Cunnick Inchbold, Margaret Booth, and H. A. Vachell, Woolf singled out for praise "the peasants in far-away Irish villages" (*E* I:38), "the life of the country people" (*E* I:39; 49), "the minor characters" (*E* I:65), "the atmosphere of family life" (*E* I:74), and the "rustic barbarity of the peasant life" (*E* I:96). She sensed that these writers – not so in control of plot convention to be able to handle it easily and unpretentiously – became true artists when they wrote what they themselves heard in the community's speech. In "ordinary" fiction, Woolf's ear picks up the same quality that she admires in Shakespeare and Scott and George Eliot, and especially in Hardy – an ability to access the common voice and tap "a pool of common wisdom, of common humour, a fund of perpetual life" (*CR* 2:249).

"Ordinary" reading also played a large role in her editorial life. In the course of her work, for example, she recommended publication of two novels by the working-class writer John Hampson (Simpson) – at the time of his first publication, a Cardiff waiter with a prison record; she supported the publication of an epic-length novel written by a salesman (Derrick Leon), which J. H. Willis describes as a "good read about the fortunes of a furniture store."[70] She approved "a good MS by a man called Graham," and the Press published his novel *The Good Merchant* the following year (*D* IV:195). And she detected some "real merit" in the poems of sixteen-year-old Joan Easdale (*L* IV:311), publishing *A Collection of Poems: Written between the Ages of 14 and 17* (1931), *Clemence and Clare (1932)*, and *Amber Innocent* (1939).[71] Shortly after Woolf's death, John Lehmann wrote, "For years nearly all the manuscripts that were submitted to the Hogarth Press passed through her hands, and she was always anxious to encourage even the slightest signs of talent among newcomers, and to urge publication whenever it was possible."[72] There is a range of interest here that clearly goes beyond classic or modernist texts.

I am not, in making the claim that Woolf encouraged all reading, arguing that she herself read everything, or read everything with pleasure. How far Woolf's knowledge of trashy books and rubbish extended is a question we might well ask. In the above quotations, by "bad books," she seems to have in mind popular novels, and by "rubbish-heaps" (*CR* 2:264), the numerous volumes of letters, diaries, biographies, and autobiographies that struggle into print and then quickly recede to a forgotten corner of some dusty shelf. Woolf wrote at various times for women's magazines such as *Vogue, Cosmopolitan*, and *Good Housekeeping*, and she read a fair number of newspapers, from the Labour *Daily Herald* to the conservative *Morning Post*, but there was undoubtedly a "trashy" that was beyond her ken. But it was not necessary for her to know the full range of the popular to grasp the way that any reading can spur an appetite for books. And her openness regarding reading pleasures did not interfere with her often ruthless judgment of the badness of some books. There is no contradiction between her encouraging all reading and her statement that "people who write books do not necessarily add anything to the history of literature" (*E* II:25) or her even more damning comment about "books which . . . no more deserve description than the dandelions of the year before last" (*E* II:304). Reading widely does not mean judging everything positively.

Nor did Woolf shy away from the judgment that there can be a *bad* reading of bad books. The subject of the last quoted essay, "Caution and Criticism," is a survey of over three hundred and sixty writers by a man who, while both a divine and a Cambridge graduate, was also a "devoted university extension lecturer" (*E* II:305, n. 2). That someone involved in adult education should introduce a wide democratic range of writing is something we might anticipate Woolf would approve. However, in her view, excessive caution makes for bad criticism; the book is marked by a "certain formal remoteness of manner" and an apparent lack of enthusiasm for, or even interest in, many of the books (304). How could she have resisted a satiric barb, when reading that one writer is "rarely wholly commonplace" or another, "not frequently disconcertingly empty of matter" (304)? While Woolf credits the author's fairness in finding "a good word not only for

Mr. Bennett and Mr. Wells, but for Mr. Tirebuck [a working-class writer] and Miss Milligan [an Irish poet]" (305), her objection to such criticism is that it neither increases the reader's pleasure nor prompts her to think. All books – whether good or bad – require good reading; Woolf always goes beyond *what* we read to the question of what we do with it.

How, then, should we use our broad reading? Perhaps Woolf's first response would be "for pleasure," since the joy of reading depends on variety. About herself, she noted, "It looks to me as if there were a regular cycle of (at any rate) *my* taste. About 6 weeks one taste lasts; the first 2 or 3 are the keenest in sensation."[73] Immersion in one kind of writing often sent her, for relief, to a different form, in what she referred to as "the natural swing of the pendulum" (*D* IV:283). Then, since Woolf conceived all writing as a whole, she needed to know more than an isolated part of it. By 1908, she had already articulated the opinion – so central to *A Room of One's Own* – that masterpieces are not "isolated births" (*E* 1:159). In "The Pastons and Chaucer," she used the "ordinary" writing of a period not to fill in context and background but to discover the ideas, the customs, the language, even the practices of writing that form the substance out of which great works are made. Ordinary writing, for Woolf, relates to masterpieces not as ephemeral to permanent, or as period interest to universal significance, nor even as life-writing to imaginative forms. All writing is part of the fabric of human thought, and the lesser work is contributory to, and therefore continuous with, the great. But the evaluative question is, how does the masterpiece differ? And that brings us to the third reason to read widely and omnivorously: in order to compare, and through comparison, to judge.

Masterpieces without canons

Evaluation depends on comparison; comparison depends on comprehensive reading. But how such comparison proceeds is a process Woolf modeled but did not define. Nevertheless, just as she asserts that reading occurs on two levels (unconscious immersion in the text and conscious reflection), so the act of evaluating for her involves both conscious and unconscious processes which, for simplicity's sake, she tended to describe as distinct stages. As I indicated earlier, in "How Should One Read a Book?" she ascribes the activity of the unconscious – receiving impressions and merging them into a whole – to the first stage of reading; the conscious act of judgment, to the second. We must allow the work to sink into our unconscious, let it settle, and then "float to the top of the mind as a whole" (*CR* 2:267); but then we must be prepared to state, "'here it fails; here it succeeds; this is bad; that is good'" (268). The phrasing here makes it sound as if falling in love must necessarily be followed by critical disillusionment, but it is closer to Woolf's overall argument to say that the initial, creative experience of reading needs to be supplemented by critical reflection. I say "supplemented" rather than "followed," since in practice, Woolf's critical reflection is not so discrete a process, nor so secondary a stage, and certainly not so aloof.

In some passages – notably, as I have shown, in her comments on Dostoevsky – Woolf suggests that in thinking, conscious and unconscious processes are not sequential but intertwined. A further and perhaps unexpected link between the two levels in reading is that each is informed by what we have read in the past. The importance of previous knowledge is obvious for conscious thought but the idea of unconscious textual activity is distinctive to Woolf. Like Immanuel Kant, Woolf develops an evaluative model that goes beyond logical rational analysis, but in her system, intuitive judgments derive not from a supersensual imagination but from a Woolfian "undermind," a level of unconscious or preconscious activity that engages our entire textual memory – ideally, the collective, textual unconscious of the human race. This concept is crucial for understanding how her evaluative model escapes both the endless relativity of subjective judgments and the assumption of a universal aesthetic ideal.

We might recall that, as early as 1903, Woolf sensed that "our minds are all threaded together" in one "common mind" *(PA* 178). In the typescript, "Byron & Mr. Briggs," she suggests further that intuitive judgments, by drawing not on personal emotion but on the "general emotions... which we have in common with others," reach toward a "universal validity" (*E* III:489). Consensual agreement may be only a distant goal; the significant implication is that the more we read, the more our intuitive responses are informed by collective experience. She shared, we may remember, Whitman's hope that "every man shall be his own priest," but what, for her, keeps individual judgment from being random and arbitrary is our unconscious immersion in the collective mind. A wide and catholic reading is thus a pedagogical imperative for unconscious and conscious alike. To be a good judge, Woolf asserts, it is necessary "to have read widely enough and with enough understanding"(*CR* 2:267–68), so that "as time goes on perhaps we can train our taste" (268).

On the conscious, analytic level, broad comparative reading exposes the relativizing effects of social and historical conditions. Once again, Woolf anticipates contemporary theory, here in particular the "contingencies of value" posited by Barbara Herrnstein Smith. Smith proposes a way out of the dilemma facing axiological criticism: "the [unsupportable] claim of certain norms, standards, and judgments to objective validity," on the one hand, and subjective, "personally whimsical" criticism on the other; value, she argues, should be conceived as "a changing function of multiple variables" – variables determined by such factors as history, culture, and situation.[74] The advantage of Smith's model is that it takes us beyond confrontations of differing values to an analysis of the way value operates, by alerting us both to the institutional production of value and to the "*counter*mechanisms" within the community for challenging, contradicting, and subverting normative claims. Furthermore, without inscribing a canon, she suggests criteria for literary permanence: works will survive in time if they can continue to relate in different ways to different questions readers bring to them; if they can be "amenable to multiple reconfiguration."[75]

Much of Woolf's practice doubles Smith's model: a contextual placement of texts and reception in relation to the assumptions and attitudes, social configurations, and material conditions of each time; a feminist development of "countermechanisms" to challenge normative claims; and a belief that works will survive in time if they are infinitely open to different questions and different readings, if they are "amenable to multiple reconfiguration."[76] In the drafts that Woolf left for her last planned work "The Reader," for example, she explains Shakespeare's lasting inexhaustible appeal: readers can recreate him endlessly in different ways.[77] Where Woolf goes further than Leavis's or Eliot's reevaluations, and even further than Smith's contingencies, is the unique combination of "universal validity" and contextual pluralism. Woolf contextualizes value in relation to the needs of the historical moment and the ideologies of individual readers; at the same time, her model of contingency is complemented by the legitimacy of intuitive preconscious judgments, informed by a collective human mind. Holding these two ideas together in dynamic tension, Woolf proleptically answers Smith's call for "a non-canonical theory of value and evaluation."[78] But Woolf's ability to negotiate these complexities rests on an apparent paradox at the heart of her evaluative practice: she celebrates masterpieces while she denounces canons.

Touchstones of value: unconventionality, conviction, unity

The experience of reading for Woolf is always subject to modifications prompted by further reading and analysis, but determining value for her is fundamentally a matter of intuitive response. If we look for consistencies and repeated motifs over the entire span of her essays, at least three primary touchstones of value emerge: unconventionality, conviction, and unity. While the first two might appear to be attributes of the writer and the third, of the work, their location is nonetheless in the reader's response. They become, in fact, different ways of saying that great literature will be capable of holding us under its spell.

Unconventionality, as Woolf uses it, does not necessarily imply that the ideas will be radical or iconoclastic; her touchstone here refers to seeing for oneself or, more literally, not allowing convention to control one's eyes. Woolf praises the poet Edward Thomas because he is "[n]ever perfunctory or conventional" (*E* II:163); Horace Walpole because "he saw truly, he judged independently" (*E* III:71) and Lady Ritchie because "[s]he had "the gift of an entirely personal vision of life," and "her own sense of character, of conduct, of what amused her, of what delighted her eye" (*E* III:14). "In other words," Woolf concludes, "she was a true artist" (14). Given Woolf's stress on the importance of thinking for oneself in reading, it is not surprising that she would seek this quality as a primary value to be sought in writing too.

Conviction is achieved when a writer is dedicated wholly to the communicative process, when the intensity is such that a writer's total complex of conscious and unconscious belief is communicated without fakery, without loss of courage, without repression.[79] We as readers *sense* a writer's conviction in turn when the text sinks into the depths of our minds, when "we seem not to read so much as to recollect what we have heard in some other life" (*E* II:115). In her contribution to *The Highway*, Woolf states that a good novel "must represent some conviction on the writer's part,"[80] and elsewhere she writes that "[t]he great novelist feels, sees, believes with such intensity of conviction that he hurls his belief outside himself and it flies off and lives an independent life of its own, becomes Natasha, Pierre, Levin, and is no longer Tolstoy" (*E* IV:261). In "A Modern Essay," she suggests that "the art of writing has for backbone some fierce attachment to an idea... something believed in with conviction or seen with precision and thus compelling words to its shape" (*CR* I:221). Communication of conviction depends on a chain of experiential connection: the writer must see for herself, yet fuse that vision into her art, which is then recreated in the mind and feelings of the reader. If the chain is successful, the reader absorbs the writer's apprehended vision in the final, reverberating impact of the book. There is an undeniable relation to T. S. Eliot's concept of the objective correlative, yet in Woolf's writing, the process involves a more holistic and subconscious transaction.

As concepts, unconventionality and conviction stress the value that Woolf places on the agency of the writer in the creation of art – perhaps her way of asserting that, while writers will inevitably be of their time, they should not be merely produced by it. But nowhere does she suggest that authenticity should be tested through the writer's intentionality; the litmus test is whether, in our reading, we have experienced life intensely from another point of view. The centrality of the reader's experience is absolutely clear in the touchstone Woolf refers to variously as unity, fusion, or cohesion, but consistently depicts as an emotional rather than textual pattern. It is "that central idea which, gathering the multiplicity of incidents together, produces upon our minds a final *effect* of unity" (*E* III:232); it is "a single *impression* of an overwhelming kind" (247); or it means that, "since all our *feelings* are in keeping, they form a whole which remains in our minds as the book itself" (340, emphasis added). Woolf's desire for unity has to do with emotional impact, not with the marks on the page. Given, too, her assertion that heterogeneous, hybrid forms are crucial to the expression of the "tumultuous and contradictory" experience of modern life (*E* IV:438),[81] her unity is not incompatible with multiplicity. She posits value in proliferating voices – at the individual level, the voices of the subconscious and, at the societal level, the voices of the communal chorus – but she seeks from masterpieces the concentrated emotional impact of original vision. These are tensions incorporated into Woolf's approach, but the tensions are interrelated and cross-generated: each side both prompts the need for, and poses the conditions for, the other side. Reacting against the restrictive, coercive effects of nineteenth-century convention, Woolf values unconventional perceptions and heterogeneous voices, but opening the floodgates of pluralism and multiplicity means that a fusion in momentary cohesion – a unified emotional impact – becomes all the more crucial a need.

Form and emotion: "On Re-reading Novels" (1922);
"The Art of Fiction" (1927)

Unity, of course, raises the issue of form – possibly the most vexed question pertaining to Virginia Woolf's literary values. Early criticism of her work seized upon Roger Fry's concept of significant form as an approach to her novels and, in the decades that followed, formalist critics sought to show how the elements in her fiction integrate into holistic patterns or visions. Yet matters of formal pattern and textual unity do not factor in Woolf's own criticism; instead, on matters of form, her attitude is skeptical and highly suspicious. Clayton Hamilton's *Materials and Methods of Fiction* receives from her a strongly negative review: his analytical approach, she considers, destroys the life of the book through dissection, as it seeks to regulate, standardize, and prescribe what is a highly individual art. His book, she devastatingly concludes, is a perfect work for academic specialists.

Woolf is less harsh on W. D. Howells's comments on form, perhaps because he prefaces his remarks with the disclaimer that form is "'one of those elusive things which you can feel much better than you can say'" (quoted by Woolf *E* II:324). Woolf herself follows with comments almost as intangible and vague: form may have something to do with the "power to omit," with the consequent use of language as "suggestion" rather than "repetition or explanation," and with "the magical power of the right words to do more" (324–25). But this very vagueness alerts her to possibilities of projection. Just as she images the modern view of ancient Greece as "a summer's day imagined in the heart of a northern winter" (*CR* 1:35), so she speculates that the moderns exalt the shapeliness of eighteenth-century literature because distance endows the past with the substance the present lacks: "Perhaps we feel the form of the eighteenth century so sharply because it is not merely beyond our reach but utterly opposed to our temper" (*E* II:325). And, because the reader's role is crucial to the apprehension of form, Woolf is extremely wary of any attempt to define the form of the present. She argues the difficulty of judging new work in the terms of the old critical language, and the near impossibility of devising a new language before the works have been truly absorbed into our minds. Again urging unconscious immersion in, and assimilation of, a book before judgment, she balks at precipitous conclusions about the absence of form in contemporary works: "Whether this particular quality is ever visible to the generation that is engaged in creating it seems very doubtful"(325).[82] In part, Woolf seems anxious to block negative assessments; in part, she is urging that we must fully absorb the work before we can fairly judge it. But there is an underlying fundamental principle here as well: when Woolf broaches the discussion of form, it is as an emotional rather than a textual pattern.

The distinction emerges most strongly when Woolf confronts the work that led critical discussions of fiction away from the material content of the story to the way that material is rendered: Percy Lubbock's *The Craft of Fiction*. Ostensibly reviewing several new editions of classic works, Woolf uses the topic "On Re-reading Novels" to present her own reflections on form. Taking Lubbock as her point of departure, Woolf both approves the greater rigor that he brings to discussions of fiction and, at the same time, disagrees with his method. This essay, however, is particularly tricky to interpret, since Woolf in effect conducts an imaginary conversation with Lubbock – moving in to his view to see things from his angle and then withdrawing to her own readings of fiction to put his view to the test. To further complicate matters, this essay has a mirror-image relation to a slightly later essay, "The Art of Fiction," on E. M. Forster's *Aspects of the Novel*. Reading the two reviews together reveals the way Woolf takes up positions in relation to the author she is discussing, never passively absorbing but always talking back. Also, rather than staying fixed in position, she shifts her own views between these essays, exposing what Lubbock and Forster in turn have left out.

Lubbock, for Woolf, loses touch with the novel as life; Forster overlooks its nature as art. Woolf's own position negotiates between them, shifting in each case to the side that raises objections as a way of letting the reader experience debate.[83] Her approach inevitably generates seeming contradictions so that, in the Forster review, she seems to be asking for "rules," even though they would be rules to be broken (*E* IV:460), whereas in response to Lubbock, she objects that his analysis of form introduces "an alien substance" between the reader and the book (*E* III:340). Yet, overall, her position aligns more with Lubbock's interest in "the method of story-telling" (343), since she finds even more problematic Forster's "unaesthetic attitude" that results in a book about fiction in which "nothing is said about words" (*E* IV:462). It would be wrong, however, to place Woolf on the side of technique as opposed to life; these are ultimately for her inseparable categories. But she respects, and demands respect for, the work of writing; she values, as evaluative acts, Flaubert's search for the right phrase, and Tolstoy's obsessive revisions (463).

The consistent view in both essays, however, is that the critical approach to fiction must differ from the critical approach to painting. In the Forster review, she asks, "How are we to take a stick and point to that tone, that relation, in the vanishing pages, as Mr. Roger Fry points with his wand at a line or a colour in the picture displayed before him?" (*E* IV:462). With regard to Lubbock, she states, "[t]his word 'form,' of course, comes from the visual arts, and for our part we wish that he could have seen his way to do without it"(*E* III:339).[84] It is not simply that we do not "see" the novel in the bound volume of a book in the way that we "see" a painting; it is that the ordering principle of fiction is entirely different. Emphasizing the experiential time of the reading process, Woolf argues, "the 'book itself' is not form which you see, but emotion which you feel" (340). The novel is motion, but not, as Forster seems to suggest, the mere forward movement of plot, the changing succession of incident that Woolf equates with the "movie novel" (*E* II:288–91; *E* IV:459). As her "test" reading of Flaubert's "Un Coeur Simple" reveals, the art of the novel depends on pacing, suspension, accumulation, and sudden cohesion to give us the experience of emotions in "their right relations to each other" (*E* III:340).

In the process of discussing Flaubert's emotional form, Woolf depends on both immediate submersion in the work and withdrawal for analysis, suggestive of the two-stage temporal process that the title "Re-reading Novels" implies. Yet in her criticism as a whole, intuitive and rational responses, affect and analysis, interpenetrate and connect. Response is inseparable from expectations, and Woolf frequently shows how consciously unraveling the encoded ideology in our expectations can alter our emotional response or, conversely, how intuitive response can initiate the work of revising ideological expectation. A dialogic interaction between affect and analysis is crucial for perceptive, and not merely responsive, reading. Good criticism also involves a dialogic negotiation between the literary work and ourselves, as we learn to relate the expectations we bring to it to the expectations it creates – for, to evaluate fairly, we must be able to grasp the text's own value system, to understand, as it were, how the text thinks. Our evaluative responses thus depend on a complex interweaving of various strands, as is finely illustrated in three of Woolf's essays on female authors, where judgments about literature form the controversial core.

Feminist reevaluations: George Eliot, Jane Austen, Elizabeth Barrett Browning

In "George Eliot," "Jane Austen," and "'Aurora Leigh,'" Woolf reevaluates women writers by exposing existing criteria as inadequate to the texts. Each essay begins by seeming to accept a prevailing critical judgment: that George Eliot is pretentious and humorless, that Jane Austen is limited in scope, that the writings of Elizabeth Barrett Browning lack form. Whereas the argumentative essay would set up these opinions as erroneous views or "straw men" to be refuted, Woolf first positions herself as one who understands and even shares these attitudes, but then subjects them to a "turn."

Apart from its first two sentences, Woolf's essay on George Eliot begins by invoking the late-Victorian response of laughter, experienced as a welcome release from the mid-Victorian worship of a cultural icon who now appears excessively solemn and stiff. Lady Ritchie's cameo portrait of Eliot not as a person but as "'a good and benevolent impulse'" (quoted by Woolf, *CR* I:162) captures precisely the aspects of Eliot that Woolf suggests have become comic over time. But the introductory sentences have already inserted a wobble: such mockery is, after all, "not very creditable to one's insight" (162) and it rests on a rather poor basis of knowledge: "To read George Eliot attentively is to become aware how little one knows about her" (162). The implication is that we should both reread the novels and learn more about George Eliot herself. For although in "'Robinson Crusoe,'" Woolf protests against a weak use of the biographical method, she never detaches literature from life.

Woolf proceeds, then, to probe the narrowness of the reigning image of George Eliot: it is limited to the impression a superficial observer might have had in her later years: the exterior view of "an elderly celebrated woman" (*CR* 1:164). If the person of the writer is to influence our literary judgments, Woolf insists, we must be sure it is the whole person. The essay then exposes the expectations that the late Victorian (mainly male) public measured this writer against: that she should possess charm and femininity, that women's struggles should be beautiful and picturesque, that her works should either possess the intensity of romance or be enlivened by the comic spirit, and that they should lead us to a world of pleasant or at least satisfying resolutions. Woolf's approach is not to deny the absence of these qualities in Eliot's writing, but to shift us to a different view of them. Eliot, Woolf concedes, lacked romantic intensity, but Woolf reverses her searchlight and examines the expectations of intensity and the values they encode: "She has none of that romantic intensity which is connected with a sense of one's own individuality, unsated and unsubdued, cutting its shape sharply upon the background of the world" (166). Intensity of this sort, Woolf implies, depends on elevating the individual to primary importance and relegating communal life to the background. But in Eliot's novels, the "minor" characters are more than background; they are the substance of English life – in Woolf's words, "the whole fabric of ancient rural England" (166). If Eliot lacks intensity, it is because she rejects egoism; against the energy and warmth of communal life in Eliot's novels, the expectation for "romantic intensity" seems rather shallow and thin.

Having dispelled mockery, the essay leads us through a series of perspectival shifts, letting us see every possible weakness in Eliot as, alternatively, a confrontation with real life. In her treatment of her heroines, Woolf admits, Eliot could be "self-conscious, didactic, and occasionally vulgar" (168). Too strong an identification with her characters and too penetrating an intellectual grasp of the causes for their suffering led Eliot to offend against the novelistic virtues of compression and narrativized scene. But again, a knowledge of context at least challenges, if it does not overturn, the verdict. After Woolf has presented the personal difficulties of Eliot's life, the failure of the Victorian social system to provide any viable model for male/female relationships and, finally, the "facts of human existence" (171) so fundamentally incompatible with the deepest of spiritual longings, how can we, Woolf asks, expect the deft crisp wit of Jane Austen? The self-consciousness and extensive ruminations in an Eliot novel, the fumbling portraits of her heroes, become signs not of the novelist's failure, but the failure of a social system, a genre, and a gender to provide an adequate form for Eliot's "difference of view" and "difference of standard" (171). At the same time, Woolf's exacting gaze does not fail to remark where Charlotte Brontë or Jane Austen succeeded and Eliot apparently did not; yet the complex reasons for success and failure, and the relative merits of such success and failure, make it impossible to sum up Eliot's novels in a categorical assessment of the whole. Eliot achieved more by pushing against the limits of the novel – for this is the essay that claims *Middlemarch* as "one of the few English novels written for grown-up people" (168) – than if she had written in a manner more satisfying to her audience's expectations. Woolf's verdict is "failure, in so far as it was a failure" (169), suggesting that failure in one direction may be a success in another, but also making us aware that what we consider failure may be conditioned by the norms we accept.

We begin the essay invited to share, though somewhat guiltily, relief at being able to laugh at sacred icons; by the end of the essay, we have looked at Eliot's world from the inside. The exteriorized view and ironic tone shift to sympathetic identification. The more Eliot's style is critically and historically understood, the more the affective power of the novels can be felt, until paradoxically "[w]e scarcely wish to analyse what we feel to be so large and deeply human" (167). The reversal is crystallized in Woolf's final words, which echo the opening of Algernon Swinburne's elegy for his brother poet, Baudelaire. Strewing "whatever [she has] in [her] power to bestow of laurel and rose" (172) over George Eliot's memory, Woolf acknowledges the earlier author as her forebear and sister novelist. Whatever our final judgment, the interplay between analysis and feeling has made it now possible to think of Eliot's "greatness" (171) and the critical tone has changed from one of condescension to one of respect.

In the dialogic process of evaluating literature, Woolf keeps turning her object about, exposing it from different angles and reversing the critical lens. In her discussion of Jane Austen, for example, we might feel surprised and shocked to encounter Woolf's reiteration of the platitudinous judgment that Jane Austen – fine though she was in her own way – was nevertheless a restricted and limited writer who at least saw the wisdom of "never trespass[ing] beyond her boundaries" (*CR* 1:137). But again Woolf gives a characteristic twist to her statement, reminding us to scrutinize the values we bring to a text. Out of context, Woolf's words merely repeat the cliché: "There were impressions that lay outside her province; emotions that by no stretch or artifice could be properly coated and covered by her own resources" (142). However, Woolf next performs a one hundred and eighty degree turn: "For example, she could not make a girl talk enthusiastically of banners and chapels" (142).[85] For Woolf, war and religion are the source of false and dangerous loyalties; an absence of enthusiasm here, like the absence of romantic intensity in George Eliot, is a mark not of failure but of a "difference of view," a "difference of standard."

There are other aspects, nonetheless, where Woolf does admit that Austen's writing could, with integrity, be more fully developed. But just as she warns us not to base an assessment of Eliot on the portrait of an elderly woman, so she reminds us not to judge Austen's abilities on the basis of what she had accomplished by the age of forty-two. Imagining Jane Austen's future, Woolf predicts that Austen's unwritten novels would have been "deeper and more suggestive," more communal and less individual, more anticipatory, in effect, of modernist fiction (145). Pointing to emerging signs of complexity in Austen's writing, Woolf further complicates the verdict of "limitation," while she prevents the criticism of Austen's completed novels from hardening into conclusions about limited potential. Given that "Jane Austen at Sixty" – the first version of this essay – was written when Woolf was less than two months away from her own forty-second birthday, we might well suspect the additional significance for her of resisting definitive, totalizing judgments of a writer who might legitimately be considered as having arrived at the mid-point of her career.

If Woolf's discussions of George Eliot and Jane Austen unite historical and biographical material with the literary works, Woolf's approach to Elizabeth Barrett Browning does exactly the opposite. Readers, Woolf states, already know more than enough about the lives of the Brownings, with the damaging effect of being distracted from the actual writing. Again, however, Woolf inserts the conventional assessment – in this case, that Barrett Browning as a poet lacked form – but this time Woolf alters perspective by plunging into an intense reading of "Aurora Leigh." Like the Wedding Guest listening to the tale of the Ancient Mariner, Woolf finds herself held spellbound like a "three years' child" (*CR* 2:204). The challenge then lies in reconciling the deep emotional impact of reading with the prevailing criticism that Barrett Browning's work is disordered and lacks form. The twists and turns of Woolf's thought are more intricate than we need to consider here; but one crucial shift is that she leads us to abandon the expectations conventionally aroused by the genres of the novel and the poem to consider what new expectations might be appropriate to the radical new form of the "novel-poem" (208). In this light, the absence of representational novelistic detail in "Aurora Leigh" is a consequence of Barrett Browning's desire to create a form "which is independent of... private lives and demands to be considered apart from personalities" (209). Such distance from individual life is not a weakness but a strength of the novel-poem – the form that, like the novel, chooses domestic life as its topos but, like the poem, imparts to us a sense of "life in general," the "time," and the "age," with "a heightened and symbolical significance" (212). Negative and positive valuations of "Aurora Leigh" thus exist side by side; the difference lies not in the text but in the reader's expectations. Looking for one thing we find absence; looking for another we find presence. The twist comes about with the crucial word "if":

Thus, *if* Mrs. Browning meant by the novel-poem a book in which character is closely and subtly revealed, the relations of many hearts laid bare, and a story unfalteringly unfolded, she failed completely. But *if* she meant rather to give us a sense of life in general, of people who are unmistakably Victorian, wrestling with the problems of their own time, all brightened, intensified and compacted by the fire of poetry, she succeeded. (212, emphasis added)

Woolf asserts the importance of reading according to the expectations determined by genre, but the possibility of new and hybrid genres necessitates an on-going scrutiny and adjustment of value.

In these three essays, Woolf combines historical and biographical knowledge, and textual observations, with intuitive, affective response. Analytical rational thinking can, as in the case of George Eliot, alter affective response; conversely, as in the case of Elizabeth Barrett Browning, intuitive response while reading can generate new understandings of form. And always there is the work of comparison – author against another, genre against genre, one era's reception juxtaposed to and scrutinized against another's. But additionally, the layers of the evaluative act are doubled by a meta-evaluative reflection that examines critical expectations and norms. Because evaluation will always depend, to some extent, on subjective views, and since responding subjectively is indeed what Woolf encourages us to do, then the evaluative critic must also be self-reflexive, both advancing critical judgments and interrogating the values underlying these judgments at the same time.

The self-reflexive evaluative critic: "An Essay on Criticism" (1927)

"An Essay on Criticism" uses the occasion of reviewing Hemingway both to evaluate him as a writer and to write a metacritical commentary on the evaluative process itself. From the beginning, however, Woolf sets her criticism in a skeptical frame. Placing her common readers in the right relation to "authority," she makes humorously clear the fallibility of critical judgment and the crucial necessity of refusing to "bow our submissive heads" (*E* IV:450). Then, taking Hemingway as a test case, she proposes self-reflexively to model the critical process, to expose "what prejudices affect it; what influences tell upon it" (450).

The task, Woolf writes, is "the old familiar business of ringing impressions on the counter" (454). When pennies were made of silver, and a pound sterling literally meant a pound's weight of pennies, the custom was to drop coins on a counter and use the sound to determine if the silver were pure – to test one's metal, so to speak, or to listen for the ring of truth. Sounding Hemingway, Woolf admits there is much in the coin that rings true: he displays an "admirable frankness" and "an equal bareness of style," a "purity of line" and the ability to deliver "a real emotion" – all indicative of "somebody of substance" and not "some ephemeral shape largely stuffed with straw" (451–52). But much of Hemingway's metal also proves counterfeit, revealing a fatal reticence that means his vision is ultimately held in check. And here the comparative nature of Woolf's criticism helps her to articulate the missing effects. Hemingway, Woolf decides, writes not in the Russian, but in the French manner: compact and contracted in style. When successful, he produces "good trenchant stories, quick, terse and strong" (454). But Woolf identifies problems – particularly in *Men Without Women* – in Hemingway's self-conscious virility, his excessive reliance on dialogue, and his tendency to blur his effects. Placing de Maupassant characters in Chekhovian situations, he sadly misses both the former's "sharp, unmistakable points by which we can take hold of the story" (455) and the latter's evocative halo of suggestion. Unlike Barrett Browning's innovative crossing of genres, Hemingway slips between two generic poles.

Woolf's sharp criticism of Hemingway might well be suspected of bias; indeed the mediating role of her own value system is an aspect that she makes us confront. At the outset, she remarks: "A prejudice of which the reader would do well to take into account is here exposed; the critic is a modernist" (451). And she concludes, "So we reveal some of the prejudices, the instincts and the fallacies out of which what it pleases us to call criticism is made" (455). But Woolf's acknowledgment of her specific expectations allows her to proceed with evaluation while, at the same time – rather in the way she handles Defoe – she displays an uncanny ability to shift to Hemingway's ground. As "a modernist" Woolf confesses a preference for writing that "make[s] us aware of what we feel subconsciously" (451); yet the limitation she detects in Hemingway's dialogue is not that he fails to satisfy her own desires but that he fails to live up to his own. The dialogue in *The Sun Also Rises* is limited to the "rapid, high-pitched slang" of a crowd in "some café" (453), and the overly tight control marks a repression of speech that Woolf attributes to fear: not only are Hemingway's characters "terribly afraid of being themselves"; she detects that Hemingway is too. Well before Hemingway used the toreador/writer equation in *Death in the Afternoon,* Woolf understands that, for him, "story writing has much in common with bull-fighting" (455), and she judges Hemingway on his own terms. The "true writer," she asserts "stands close up to the bull and lets the horns – call them life, truth, reality, whatever you like, – pass him close each time"(455).[86] But in Hemingway's work, "the thing that is faked is character; "Mr. Hemingway leans against the flank of that particular bull after the horns have passed" (453).

The critical strands of this essay are complex and interwoven: Woolf's intuited impression of Hemingway's work, her conscious comparative analysis of it in relation to French and Russian writers, her reflections on her modernist predilections, her sympathetic ability to grasp Hemingway's own narrative standard, and – just possibly – her uncanny insight into his work. At the time Woolf was writing, practically no one knew the extent of what Hemingway was hiding about himself. The true details about his war injuries, and his buried anxieties about gender, were matters for later biographers to reveal. Woolf's self-reflexive mode leads her readers to discover a good deal about the nature of criticism, but she may have perceptively intuited something about the nature of Hemingway too.

"An Essay on Criticism" is thus a practical application of the advice Woolf presents in "How Should One Read a Book?" We must begin with sympathetic identification and read the work according to "the laws of [the writer's] own perspective" (*CR* 2:260): "Do not dictate to your author; try to become him" (259). But we must be prepared to "pass judgment upon these multitudinous impressions" (266). We must objectively compare each book with "whatever is the best or seems to us to be the best in its own kind" (267). Yet "we cannot suppress our own idiosyncrasy without impoverishing it" (268). Good reading acknowledges the reader's expectations and desires so that they too become part of the objective and evaluative analysis that is crucial to the reader's active role. Overall, reading is a pluralist, self-reflexive practice comprising conscious and unconscious processes; and part of the conscious process is being conscious of ourselves.

The modernist democratic critic: "Modern Fiction" (1919; 1925)

Woolf's criticism is evaluative while it admits its bias; it admits its bias while it is at the same time openly responsive to different forms. It should therefore entail, for example, not privileging modernist practices over traditional realism but assessing the strengths and weaknesses of each mode. Yet an assumption exists, based largely on the essay "Modern Fiction," that Woolf was categorically opposed to "materialist" writers. But again if we resist taking her sentences out of context, we discover her evaluation of traditional realist writing depends on her judgment of how well it is done.

In her discussion of *Robinson Crusoe*, as we have seen, Woolf puts aside her "preconceptions" as a post-Romantic and modernist to accept the appropriateness of Defoe's focus on exterior reality in the context of his time. When prosaic facts are used tellingly, she finds, "the effect is as deep as pages of analysis could have made it" (*CR* 2:57). In "Four Figures," Woolf's respect for factual writing appears in her admiration for Dorothy Wordsworth's calm and exacting recordings of nature and the superiority of these self-effacing journals over Mary Wollstonecraft's more passionate, but excessively self-indulgent, prose. "Whatever Mary saw," Woolf writes, "served to start her mind upon some theory, upon the effect of government, upon the state of the people, upon the mystery of her own soul" (*CR* 2:164); Dorothy, on the other hand, "never confused her own soul with the sky" (164) and so received nature's supreme gift of "consolation and quiet" (172).

But Woolf could also be devastatingly critical of realist work, as in her reviews of *Mary Russell Mitford and her Surroundings* by Constance Hill. Yet while at first glance it might seem that Woolf is attacking the use of biographical fact, her ire is directed at Hill's inadequate conceptions of what constitutes fact, and poor judgments about which facts are important. Most of Hill's biography, Woolf objects, is pure invention and fantasy, while important facts have been staring her in the face unobserved. Miss Mitford was a daughter whose career was sacrificed to the demands of a selfish and domineering father – a story of obvious import for Woolf. Dr. Mitford took the money Mary won in a lottery to buy an expensive dinner set (*E* III:218), and the remainder of Mary's life was spent prostituting her creative talents to pay for her father's ever-increasing debts. Noting that "some pieces of Dr. Mitford's Wedgwood dinner service are still in existence," as is "a copy of Adam's Geography, which Mary won as a prize at school," Woolf ingenuously asks, "might not the next book be devoted entirely to them?" (*CR* 1:189). The irony is tellingly sharp on poor Miss Hill, who had the misfortune of being reviewed by Woolf in three places. At the same time, Woolf does propose which facts in Miss Mitford's life would serve the biographer well. Woolf advocates not a rejection of material circumstances, but the right selection and use of them.

An openness to divergent kinds of writing is also – although perhaps surprisingly – at the core of "Modern Fiction," the essay most invariably cited in discussions of Woolf and anthologized in collections on modernism or literary criticism. Together with "Mr. Bennett and Mrs. Brown," "Modern Fiction" has been taken as Woolf's modernist manifesto, leading critics to define her theme as the subjective inner world and her approach as impressionistic, poetic, and lyrical. But again, the twists and turns of Woolf's writing destabilize the grounds on which such conclusions depend.

On the most basic level, "Modern Fiction" explains the modernist break from the traditional novel and, in doing so, it offers useful material for relating Woolf's fictional practice to her theoretical ideas. Characteristically employing figurative language as a medium for literary analysis, Woolf casts modernism's new subject in a series of metaphors: "an incessant shower of innumerable atoms," "a luminous halo," and "a semi-transparent envelope" (*CR* 1:150). By representing experience as atomistic and pluralistic, and as continuous but non-sequential, her images imply a continuity of thought with Walter Pater's "quickened, multiplied consciousness," William James's "stream of thought" or "stream of consciousness," and Henri Bergson's concept of duration as continuous flux.[87] A link can also be made to the aesthetic theories of Roger Fry and Clive Bell, whose defense of post-impressionism rejected naturalistic representation in favor of expressionist art. Woolf thus fits within the general paradigm of modernism's shift from the rational and representational to the alogical and associative; however, her treatment of such binary opposition is neither so simple nor so neat. "Modern Fiction" does begin by setting up a dichotomy between the conventional novel, as epitomized in the works of Wells, Bennett, and Galsworthy and the alternative narrative possibilities presented by the works of Chekhov and Joyce. And this dichotomy is crystallized in the opposition between the term "materialists," which Woolf uses to sum up the traditional writers, and the term "spiritual," which she uses to describe Joyce. But in setting out her materialist/spiritual opposition, Woolf significantly qualifies and redefines both terms.

Woolf first introduces materialists in the conventional popular sense as those "concerned not with the spirit but with the body" (*CR* 1:147). The subsequent imagery, however, identifies the Edwardian materialist novelists with specific social traits. The particular "body" that is their subject ushers forth from the "well-built villa," settles into "some softly padded first-class railway carriage" and ensconces itself in the "very best hotel in Brighton" (148). Troping this type of novel as sewing on a button, Woolf delimits that image as well. In Woolf's fiction, sewing is usually a harmonious domestic image, linking Mrs. Dalloway and Rezia, for example, across boundaries of race and class. It is the activity of "Bond street tailors" (150) that Woolf specifically targets here. These qualifications gloss Woolf's reference to the "body," making it clear it is the classed body that she has in mind. Her objection is to the material self-satisfaction and privilege of the comfortable middle class, just as it is to narrative resolutions that, in a patriarchal manner, refer human problems to the care of the legislators and government officials.

The word "spiritual" is subjected to even greater redefinition and revision. References to "that innermost flame" and "the quick of the mind" seem first to imply the transcendent and rarefied consciousness with which Woolf is often aligned (151). But when she offers James Joyce as a representative "spiritual" writer, her example of his supposedly "spiritual" writing is the cemetery scene in *Ulysses*. This scene, we might remember, is characteristically physical and earthy in style, redolent with thoughts about "corpse manure, bones, flesh, nails," and the "tallowy kind of cheesy" of decomposing bodies.[88] That Woolf did not miss or ignore such passages is evident in the way she praises the scene not just for its "brilliancy" but also for its "sordidity" (151) – a word she added in the essay's second version. Then, in further twists on conventional meaning, Woolf locates the "spiritual" of the moderns in "the dark places of psychology" (152) and identifies the true character of Englishness with a delight not just in "the activities of the intellect" but in "the splendour of the body" as well (154). By suggesting that spirituality inheres in the mud and the rotting corpse, and by invoking "the dark places of psychology" and the body, Woolf embraces not only a physical subject matter but a metaphysics that locates the spiritual in the physical self. If the spiritual is what matters, what is eternal, what endures, then we know this through the body, through the unconscious, and that is the modernists' theme. Although Woolf opposes "spiritual" to "materialist," she disavows its conventional opposition to "matter" and its traditional religious sense. She shifts from an epistemology in which faith is the means by which we perceive God to one in which the unconscious is the means by which we perceive the living world.

Although the essay is thus constructed around a simple binary, qualifications and complexities reconfigure the binary's meaning. And by semantically altering cultural keywords, Woolf foregrounds historical change and shows how meaning is never simple, stabile, or fixed. She wrote that "words survive the chops and changes of time longer than any other substance" (*CE* II:247), but she also noted that "words are more impalpable than bricks" (*CR* 2:259). Writing her talk for the girls at Hayes Court School, Woolf explained, "words are more like fire than they are like clay... [T]hey change from generation to generation."[89] Like Raymond Williams many years later, Woolf recognized the continual need to scrutinize, to reconsider, and to revise our language as we participate in the evolution of cultural thought.

In a similar dynamic, the essay justifies one specific narrative form (i.e. serves as a modernist manifesto) but uses continual shifts in perspective to urge us not to enshrine that form as definitive. Rejecting, at the outset, the notion that there is an evolution in writing comparable to the evolution in technology (the motor car), Woolf posits the one significant change in the history of the novel as the increasing difficulty of knowing how to write. First elevating Joyce and Chekhov over Wells, Bennett and Galsworthy, Woolf later twists around to reveal the modernist writers as limited too. Joyce's treatment of indecency is too didactic; the Russians lack the English "instinct to enjoy and fight rather than to suffer and understand" (*CR* I:154). Woolf endorses modernist "spiritual" writers as historically alert to the new perceptions of her age but, in her larger view, the constraints of modernist form will in turn inspire new developments in the future. By representing the course of the novel as a series of endless substitutions, with each new form attempting to address previous lack, Woolf implies that there will never be a final resolution to the question how to write: "Any method is right, every method is right, that expresses what we wish to express" (152).

Woolf's dialogic evaluative criticism, then, works not to fix rigid judgments but to open up possibilities for further change and development. The modernist democratic critic casts writing as an ever-developing, *necessarily* on-going, changing process: "Every moment is the centre and meeting place of an extraordinary number of perceptions which have not yet been expressed. Life is always and inevitably much richer than we who try to express it" (*E* IV:439). Similarly, one of Woolf's last sentences affirms that, with the advent of the reader, "[w]e are in a world where nothing is concluded."[90]

Every reader will read differently; every reader will continue to speculate where the present writing leaves off; and Woolf's pedagogical project is to stimulate that on-going speculation. Woolf's encompassing, pluralistic vision inscribes an open participatory place for the voices of the future; her inclusive sense of community needs, for its realization, other voices to join. Fittingly, the essays of the democratic highbrow – and, I should now add, the books of her critics – achieve their aim when they "reach not their end, but their suspension in full career" (*CR* 1:66). The next words must be written by you.

Postscript: intellectual work today

The success of Woolf's criticism in her time can be measured by the wide-ranging press coverage of *The Common Readers*,[1] their successful sales records,[2] and the appreciative letters Woolf received from unknown readers.[3] Nevertheless, as English became a professional subject of university study in the West, the general literate reader was gradually replaced by the "student," and the academic study of English became the dominant mode of informed literary exchange. By the end of Woolf's lifetime, the approaches of critics like Lubbock, Richards, and Eliot were regarded more highly than Woolf's, as authority, objectivity, and a codifiable methodology were invoked to defend the study of English against the prestige increasingly accorded to science and technology. By mid-century, the New Critics and Formalists assumed what was to be an increasingly important role by countering the previous excesses of subjective impressionism with the rigors of close textual readings and by providing a vocabulary and methodology for the analysis of form. Woolf's essays were thus understandably overshadowed by the impersonal, objective analysis that came to dominate English studies in the West, but which was itself overshadowed in turn by the heavily theoretical writings that arose in resistance to the truth-oriented assumptions of New Critical and Formalist modes. Nevertheless, in the endless dynamics of change, the new theory, although it usefully introduced the concepts of provisionality and constructivism into our interpretative models, was becoming, by the end of the century, subject in turn to its own excess. Strangely, the concern with exposing and interrogating underlying ideologies produced some of the most ideologically determined criticism, as previously suppressed politics were gradually freed first to be expressed, and finally to assume a dominant role.[4] In addition, two consequences of high theory served further to separate specialist from non-specialist readings: a highly technical language emerged for each sub-group within theoretical discourse and an exclusive concentration on the constructed nature of all discourse threatened the loss of any common text.

More recently, we see in the West a new concern with the role of the university in general society and a more socially oriented project of cultural work. Without losing the crucial insights of the last few decades of theoretical writing, we may be returning – although in transformed and transformative ways – to close textual readings and to historical study, and perhaps to a broader audience of readers. It is becoming both more necessary and less fraught with pejorative implications to cultivate commonly accessible modes of academic writing and to acknowledge the complexities and diversities that disrupt our clear-cut theoretical models. We are perhaps on the verge of a new era that reassimilates our collective past in ways that respond to new current needs.

One effect is that a concern for the common reader and common reading is coming to be seen as integral to the university's mission, instead of being cast, as Woolf positioned it, in an oppositional role. And, in consequence, it is becoming increasingly appropriate for Woolf's literary criticism to be housed inside the academy rather than outside it. Also, as I have been indicating, the insights in Woolf's critical practice are highly compatible with many of the theoretical approaches that are relevant today: Mikhail Bakhtin's theories of the dialogic and heteroglossia, Isobel Armstrong's affective/cognitive model of reading, Louise Rosenblatt's transactional theories of reading, Hayden White's understanding of historical metanarratives, Mary Louise Pratt's speech-act theory, Barbara Herrnstein Smith's contingencies of value, to name but a few. The specific contribution Woolf brings to such theory, however, is that she handles it in ways that keep returning us to the literary text. Perhaps for this reason Woolf is no longer confined to courses on the modernist novel or feminist literary criticism; the essays are increasingly bringing her out into the general scholarly world.[5]

I do not imply, however, that Woolf models the ideal critical style. In the process of planning what was to be her third book on reading, Woolf hoped for a new critical style that would be "more colloquial" but also "more to the point" (*D* v:298). Possibly she worried that her imaginative suggestiveness might distract the reader from her serious radical critique. The geniality and urbanity of tone runs the risk of obscuring the sophisticated strategies, allowing us to forget that we must be constantly alert for ironies, braced for each view to be questioned and turned about, ready to respond to a subtext that questions the assumptions underlying every accepted approach. Nevertheless, the grace and plasticity of her prose allowed her to develop what was at the time a revolutionary style, not merely because it was suited to broad, common reading practices but because it offered a way to challenge established positions without putting a new authority in their place. The language itself may be tied to a cultural world we have left behind, but her fundamental insights have, if anything, even more relevance today.

Woolf's concept of reading combines far-ranging knowledge and fine discriminating judgments with a respect for cultural and historical difference and the free and open play of the mind. Her concept of community is based on the ideal of an inclusive, dialogic mix of voices, able to express their differences without violence because of the ways they have learned to negotiate different ideas, and able to affirm their common bonds because they have shared in both the preservation and the creation of culture. Finally, Woolf's intellectual activism obtains in her belief in the power of writing and reading, the power of literature, to help us achieve our broad intellectual and indeed social and ethical goals. "Thinking is my fighting" (*D* v:285), she proclaimed during the Second World War, or as Anna Snaith states, "Writing, far from locking her within some internal realm, is proof of her constant engagement with public debates."[6] Woolf affirms the work of the democratic highbrow in the public sphere, and affirms the validity of democratic highbrowism as a goal for all. And her goal is both individual and communal in scope. The moralist, she once stated (with characteristic humor), defends reading as "an innocent employment; and happiness, he will add, though derived from trivial sources, has probably done more to prevent human beings from changing their religions and killing their kings than either philosophy or the pulpit" (*CR* 1:79). If the cultural dynamics embodied in Woolf's dialogic model of reading can offer such a distinct alternative to the war-torn history of society, then her vision of democratic highbrowism might well mark, at the beginning of the twenty-first century, the most promising global pathway to a more peaceful, productive world.

Notes

INTRODUCTION: A WIDER SPHERE

1. For hostile denigrations of Woolf as "elitist," see Frank Swinnerton, *A London Bookman* (London, 1928), 111–18, 147–53 and Sean O'Faolain, "Virginia Woolf and James Joyce, or 'Narcissa and Lucifer,'" *The Vanishing Hero: Studies in Novelists of the Twenties* (London, 1956), 191–222. For the related but more positive view of her as a writer committed to the private realm, see Quentin Bell, *Virginia Woolf: A Biography*, 2 vols. (London, 1972), David Daiches, *The Novel and the Modern World* (Chicago, 1960), and generally the formalist studies of Woolf in the seventies. The more recent construction of Woolf as an aesthetic capitalist is argued in Lois Cucullu, "Retailing the Female Intellectual," *Differences* 9 (Summer 1997): 25–68 and, more positively, in Jennifer Wicke, "Coterie Consumption: Bloomsbury, Keynes, and Modernism as Marketing," *Marketing Modernisms: Self-Promotion, Canonization, Rereading*, ed. Kevin J. H. Dettmar and Stephen Watt (Ann Arbor, MI, 1996), 109–32. For a more complex and dialectic discussion of Woolf's relation to the market, see John Young, "Canonicity and Commercialization in Woolf's Uniform Edition," *Virginia Woolf: Turning the Centuries: Selected Papers from the Ninth Annual Conference on Virginia Woolf*, ed. Ann Ardis and Bonnie Kime Scott (New York, 2000), 236–43. Lawrence Rainey, *Institutions of Modernism: Literary Elites and Public Culture* (New Haven, 1998) also analyzes the complicity of "high" modernist writers in the operations of commodification and the creation of cultural capital, although it does not include Woolf.
2. Andrew McNeillie, Introduction, *E* III, xvii.
3. The list of terms is exceedingly long: intellectuals have also been categorized as traditional, hegemonic, universal, specific, critical, oppositional, radical, and most recently, diasporic.
4. For the distinction between intellectual and scholar, see John McGowan, *Democracy's Children: Intellectuals and the Rise of Cultural Politics* (Ithaca, NY, 2002), 1–4.
5. Andreas Huyssen, *After The Great Divide: Modernism, Mass Culture, Postmodernism* (Bloomington, IN, 1986).
6. John Carey, *The Intellectuals and the Masses: Pride and Prejudice among the Literary Intelligentsia, 1880–1939* (London, 1992), preface.

7. *Ibid.*, preface, and 24–25.
8. Since my book is devoted to advancing a view antithetical to Carey's, I have not attempted to answer him point by point. But as he proceeds, for example, to demonstrate Woolf's depiction of "that anonymous monster the Man in the Street" (*E* III:3), he fails to see that this reductive stereotype is precisely what Woolf is criticizing in the book under review. When he criticizes Woolf's unsympathetic treatment of Miss Kilman in *Mrs. Dalloway*, he does not consider the sympathetic views inside Miss Kilman's consciousness nor whether it is a person or a system that Woolf is showing to be at fault. For one of the reasons I think it is the latter, see pp. 92–93, chapter 2, in the present work.
9. Patrick Brantlinger, *The Reading Lesson: The Threat of Mass Literacy in Nineteenth-Century British Fiction* (Bloomington, IN, 1998), 206, 207.
10. Jonathan Rose, *The Intellectual Life of the British Working Classes* (New Haven, 2001), 10.
11. *Ibid.*, 431.
12. *Ibid.*, 402.
13. *Ibid.*, 425.
14. *Ibid.*, 7.
15. Anna Snaith, "'Stray Guineas': Virginia Woolf and the Fawcett Library," *Literature and History* (forthcoming). My thanks to the author for providing me with a copy of this essay.
16. See Beth Rigel Daugherty, "Morley College, Virginia Woolf and Us: How Should One Read Class?" *Virginia Woolf and Her Influences: Selected Papers from the Seventh Annual Conference on Virginia Woolf*, ed. Laura Davis and Jeanette McVicker (New York, 1998), 125–39; "Virginia Woolf Teaching/Virginia Woolf Learning: Morley College and the Common Reader," *New Essays on Virginia Woolf*, ed. Helen Wussow (Dallas, 1995), 61–77; and "Readin', Writin', and Revisin': Virginia Woolf's 'How Should One Read a Book?'" *Virginia Woolf and the Essay*, ed. Beth Carole Rosenberg and Jeanne Dubino (New York, 1997), 159–75.
17. Ann Banfield, *The Phantom Table: Woolf, Fry, Russell and the Epistemology of Modernism* (Cambridge, 2000), 17.
18. Anna Snaith, ed., "*Three Guineas* Letters," *Woolf Studies Annual* 6 (2000): 1–168.
19. Some of our findings were presented at the Twelfth Annual Virginia Woolf Conference at Sonoma State University in June 2002. See also Melba Cuddy-Keane, "Opening Historical Doors to the *Room*: An Approach to Teaching," *Re: Reading, Re: Writing, Re: Teaching Virginia Woolf: Selected Papers from the Fourth Annual Conference on Virginia Woolf*, ed. Eileen Barrett and Patricia Cramer (New York, 1995), 207–15.
20. These examples may be found in Correspondence of Various Persons re: Books, Articles in Letters III: Correspondence of Virginia Woolf, MHP.
21. Brenda Silver, *Virginia Woolf Icon* (Chicago, 1999), 5.
22. *Ibid.*, 5, 76, 72.

23. Anna Snaith, *Virginia Woolf: Private and Public Negotiations* (Basingstoke, 2000).
24. See Roman Jakobson, "Closing Statement: Linguistic and Poetics," *Style in Language*, ed. Thomas A. Sebeok (Cambridge, MA, 1960), 350–77.
25. Marc Angenot, "The Concept of Social Discourse," *English Studies in Canada* 21 (March 1995):1–19. Angenot's project analyzes all forms of printed materials produced in French in the year 1889.
26. John McGowan, *Democracy's Children*, 212.
27. Ibid., *226*.

I DEMOCRATIC HIGHBROW: WOOLF AND THE CLASSLESS INTELLECTUAL

1. Lewis Carroll, *Alice in Wonderland*, ed. Donald J. Gray, 2nd edn. (New York, 1992), 163; Raymond Williams, *Keywords: A Vocabulary of Culture and Society* (London, 1976), 21.
2. Richard Slotkin, quoted in Michael Kammen, *American Culture, American Taste: Social Change and the 20th Century* (New York, 1999), 5.
3. W. Russell Neuman, *The Future of the Mass Audience* (Cambridge, 1991).
4. In my use of these terms, mass culture means producing or exploiting a uniform taste in a large population; mass communication involves using technological means to distribute information widely; and popular culture, defined as created for and responding to the desires of the people, does not necessarily involve large numbers and incorporates a diversity of interests and needs. For further arguments distinguishing among mass culture, popular culture, and mass communication, see Raymond Williams, *Culture and Society, 1780–1950* (Harmondsworth, 1958), 287–94.
5. Williams, *Keywords*, 198–99.
6. *OED*, 2nd edn., s.v. "popular."
7. Thomas Bender, "Intellectual and Cultural History," *The New American History*, rev. edn., ed. Eric Foner (Philadelphia, 1997), 182.
8. *OED*, s.v. "highbrow high-brow."
9. J. B. Priestley, *To an Unnamed Listener*, "To a High-Brow," ts of broadcast October 17, 1932, BBC Written Archives Centre, reprinted in *John O'London's Weekly*, December 3, 1932, 712. The Nicolson talk has proved not possible to locate.
10. Williams, *Keywords*, 98.
11. *Ibid.*, 159–61.
12. See Eliot's letter of November 23, 1848: "We have brought you [Mother Nature] many gentle maidens and high-browed, brave men." *The George Eliot Letters*, ed. Gordon S. Haight, vol. 1 (New Haven, 1954), 273.
13. Laura Troubridge, *Life amongst the Troubridges*, ed. Jacqueline Hope-Nicholson (London, 1966), 169.
14. See the use of "high-browed" in H. G. Wells, *Ann Veronica* (1909; London, 1980) 111, 132; and of "high-brow" in Sinclair Lewis, *Our Mr. Wrenn* (New York,

1914), 61, 111. The *OED* indicates that "highbrow" originated as a colloquial term in the US; Graves and Hodge state that "'low-brow' and 'high-brow' were American terms first popularized in England by H. G. Wells." Robert Graves and Alan Hodge, *The Long Week-end: Social History of Great Britain 1918–1939* (London, 1940), 50.

15. *Punch*, April 22, 1925, 437.
16. *Punch*, December 23, 1925, 673.
17. Frank Swinnerton, "Mrs. Woolf on the Novel," *A London Bookman*, 113.
18. Arnold Bennett, "A Woman's High-Brow Lark," *Evening Standard*, November 8, 1928; extract reprinted in *Virginia Woolf: The Critical Heritage*, ed. Robin Madjumdar and Allen McLaurin (London, 1975), 232, 233.
19. "Queen of the High-Brows," *Evening Standard*, November 28, 1929; reprinted in *Virginia Woolf: The Critical Heritage*, 258, 259.
20. Aldous Huxley, "Foreheads Villainous Low," *Music at Night and other Essays* (London, 1957), 201, 209, 208.
21. Desmond MacCarthy, "Highbrows," *Experience* (Covent Garden, London, 1935), 307, 310.
22. Leonard Woolf, *Hunting the Highbrow* (London, 1927), 10, 11.
23. Q. D. Leavis, *Fiction and the Reading Public* (1932; London, 1965), 74, 67.
24. Warren Deeping, quoted by Q. D. Leavis, *ibid.*, 68.
25. Woolf's disclaimer of "waterish" is then supported by a jocular attempt to write in "a red-blood style" – an image echoing a previous reference to "the high-brow public and the red-blood public" (*CR* 1:206, 207).
26. "Middlebrow" is the title that Woolf indicated she would give to her planned revision; however, since the original version was eventually published under this title, I will for convenience use it here.
27. Many of the concerns in this chapter are raised in Deborah Anne Moreland, *Contexts and Connections: Virginia Woolf, Wyndham Lewis, and Low Culture*, (Ann Arbor, MI, 1998). In this admirably researched and detailed dissertation, Moreland also treats Woolf's relation to the brows as complex and similarly recognizes Woolf's classless ideal. In my view, however, Woolf is a little more aware and a little more in control of the complexities than Moreland allows.
28. The editorial note to Woolf's diary entry gives the date of Priestley's talk as October 10 (*D* IV:129); however, through a comical mishap, his talk was delayed until the following week. Priestley – at the time, an unseasoned broadcaster – arrived at the studio without his script and, somewhat unusually, no copy of it was at the BBC. While a hunt for the script proceeded, the audience was kept waiting and, according to *The Spectator*, for fifteen minutes all that was heard was the "punctual ticking of the studio clock." C. H. W., "A Radio Review," *Spectator*, October 15, 1932, 520. The talk was rescheduled for the following week.
29. Critic, "A London Diary," *New Statesman and Nation*, October 29, 1932, 506–07.
30. Priestley, "To a High-brow," ts 6.
31. *Ibid.*, [1].

32. *Ibid.*, 5.
33. Harold Nicolson, Diary 1932, *The Vita Sackville-West and Harold Nicolson Manuscripts, Letters and Diaries from Sissinghurst Castle, Kent*, The Huntington Library, California, and other libraries (Brighton, Sussex, 1988), ts 86, 88, 91.
34. I would like to thank James Codd, of the BBC Written Archives Centre, and the Research and Study Library at the Leeds Central Library for their helpful assistance in my search.
35. "The Intellectual Distrusted: Hon. Harold Nicolson and Anglo-Saxons: Talk to a 'Low-Brow,'" *Yorkshire Post*, October 25, 1932.
36. Woolf's Priestlian allusions might even extend back to her review of his essays in 1924, in which she stated that, while lucid and informative, they nevertheless fell short of the "true business of the critic, which is to make us reconsider our opinions, and test, if we do not accept, his values" (*E* III:442).
37. J. B. Priestley, "High, Low, Broad," *Saturday Review*, 20 Feb. 1926, 222, reprinted in *Open House: A Book of Essays* (London, 1929), 162, 165.
38. Later, by announcing her postal code as "Bloomsbury, W. C. I," Woolf undercuts Priestley's coterie implications of "Bloomsbury" by restoring its literal referent to geographical space.
39. Lawrence Lipking, "The Genius of the Shore: Lycidas, Adamastor, and the Poetics of Nationalism," *PMLA* III (March 1996):205–21.
40. See, for example, Rupert Brooke's likening a tour guide in Montreal to a pastor shepherding his flock: "I had never understood *Lycidas* before. We were sheepish enough, and fairly hungry. However, we were excellently fed." *Letters from America*, preface Henry James (London, 1916), 51.
41. "In the latest kind of novel – Virginia Woolf's, for example – events have become merely interruptions in a long wool-gathering process, a process, that is used chiefly to provide occasions for little prose poems." Desmond MacCarthy, "The Bubble Reputation," *Life and Letters*, ed. Desmond MacCarthy, vol. VII, no. 40 (September 1931), 182.
42. Woolf also mocks Priestley's insulting remarks, in his broadcast, about the physical signs of high-brow degenerateness by claiming, as her one sign of being invalid, a touch of gout inherited from centuries of drunken ancestors.
43. J. B. Priestley, "Men, Women and Books: Tell Us More About These Authors!" *Evening Standard*, October 13, 1932.
44. Concurrently with Raleigh's *Letters*, Woolf was reading the autobiography of Beatrice Webb, whose style Woolf vastly preferred. Always "rational & coherent," Webb differed significantly from Raleigh because her focus was not on self alone but on self in relation to the larger "history of the 19th Century"; in addition, Woolf wrote, "Unlike that self-conscious poseur Walter Raleigh she is much more interested in facts & truth than in what will shock people & what a professor ought not to say" (*D* III:74).
45. *The Letters of Sir Walter Raleigh, 1879–1922*, ed. Lady Raleigh, vol. I (London, 1926), 268. Woolf quotes only from the second sentence and she does not make the point about the date.

46. *Ibid.*, 137. Here too Woolf presents a shortened quotation and omits the last sentence.

47. Limits of space have led me to omit discussion of another of Woolf's unfinished drafts, posthumously published as "Three Characters." Although isolated phrases from these sketches are sometimes used to evidence Woolf's views, the errors and ambiguities in the numerous versions make these highly problematic texts. To take one of the clearer examples, the published version transcribes the typescript "woed" as "wed," but the manuscript shows this word as "owed." The reading is clearly crucial, occurring as it does in the statement that poets like Shakespeare and Keats have "owed" their life blood to the lowbrow. Other signs of hasty conception and execution in Woolf's versions raise even greater questions about intention. See "Three Characters," Holograph, M.1.4, Berg; "Three Characters," ts, B.9.i, MHP; and "Three Characters," *Adam International Review* 364–66 (1972): 24–26.

48. Vita Sackville-West, *Books and Authors*, "Books of the Week," *Listener*, October 26, 1932, 610.

49. The reference is certainly to Priestley's column in the *Evening Standard* three days before, but by "see," Woolf might also have been alluding to the possibility of Sackville-West's bumping into Priestley at the BBC, since, owing to the rescheduling of his talk, their broadcasts ended up within a few hours of each other. Harold Nicolson, trying to tune in, testifies to the juxtaposition: "Vita broadcasts on D. H. Lawrence but the machine goes wrong and I cannot hear her. Sam fetches his portable and I hear Priestley on a talk 'to a high-brow.'" Nicolson, Diary 1932, ts 86.

50. Writing to Sackville-West Woolf states that she has not read anything but *Sons and Lovers* (possibly meaning other than *Women in Love*), but she wrote to Ottoline Morrell a few days earlier, requesting Morrell's "D.H.L. memoir" because she had just finished reading Lawrence's letters (*L* v:122, 117).

51. Sackville-West, "Books."

52. While offended with Lawrence's demagoguery, at the same time, Woolf wrote to Ottoline Morrell, "he was so hounded by those brutes the army and the public that one's entire sympathy is with him" (*L* v:117). Most likely she turned down the review to avoid the harsh criticisms she knew she would have to make.

53. Woolf is presumably referring to G. E. Moore's ethical ideal of beauty.

54. Williams, *Keywords*, 83,

55. *Ibid.*, 86.

56. A similar conclusion is reached by James Tarrant, leading him to distinguish between market democracy and moral democracy, which, he argues, most writers in the field of education fail to differentiate. See James Tarrant, *Democracy and Education* (Aldershot, 1989), especially 16–21 and 74–186.

57. Leonard Woolf, *The Modern State: a six-part series, Listener*, October-November 1931: "Is Democracy Failing?" October 7, 1931, 571–72; "Have We the Right to Be Happy?" October 14, 1931, 615–16; "Democracy and Equality," October 21, 1931, 666, 669; "Should We Do What We Want?" October 28, 1931, 711, 712, 745; "Gods or Bees?" November 4, 1931, 766, 767; "Citizens of the World," November 11, 1931, 817.

58. *Ibid.*, October 14, 615.
59. *Ibid.*, October 21, 666.
60. *Ibid.*, October 28, 745.
61. *Ibid.*, October 21, 669.
62. *Ibid.*, November 11, 817.
63. *Ibid.*, October 28, 745.
64. Obviously, however, Leonard's assumption is that any rational human being would arrive at the same conclusions.
65. My assessment of the trend was corroborated by a scan on WorldCat of 304 titles with the keyword "democracy" from 1918–1932.
66. The Hogarth list, for example, includes *Financial Democracy* (1933) by Margaret Millar and Douglas Campbell and *Caste and Democracy* (1933) by K. M. Panikkar. Raymond Postgate's *What to Do with the BBC* (1935) implicates another cultural realm by attacking the undemocratic policies of the national broadcasting system.
67. John Dewey, *Democracy and Education: An Introduction to the Philosophy of Education* (New York, 1916), 101.
68. *Ibid.*, 26.
69. R. H. Tawney, "An Experiment in Democratic Education," *The Radical Tradition: Twelve Essays on Politics, Education and Literature*, ed. Rita Hinden (London, 1964), 79.
70. L. P. Carpenter, *G. D. H. Cole: An Intellectual Biography* (Cambridge, 1973), 50.
71. G. D. H. Cole, quoted in *ibid.*, 50.
72. G. D. H. Cole, "The Doubtful Value of Lectures in University Education," *New Statesman*, October 7, 1922, 8.
73. "Culture and Democracy," *Listener*, October 5, 1932, 472; "The Changing Audience," *Listener*, October 5, 1932, 484.
74. "Wireless Discussion Groups," *Listener*, October 28, 1931, 739; September 28, 1932, 437.
75. The foundational study demonstrating Woolf's involvement in these spheres is Naomi Black, "Virginia Woolf and the Women's Movement," *Virginia Woolf: A Feminist Slant*, ed. Jane Marcus (Lincoln, NE, 1983), 180–97. For two recent discussions, see Jane Goldman, *The Feminist Aesthetics of Virginia Woolf: Modernism, Post-Impressionism and the Politics of the Visual* (Cambridge, 1998) and Snaith, *Virginia Woolf*.
76. Not all readers were convinced by Dewey's model, however; one reviewer exclaimed angrily that Dewey ignored the pursuit of a quiet, reflective life in favor of being a "good mixer." "Dewey's Philosophy of Education," *Nation* (NY), May 4, 1916, 481.
77. An essay published the previous month, though not using the specific word "democracy," argues a similar democratic view. Here Woolf praises Arthur Symons's essays for their quiet assumption that "to care for art is the most natural thing in the world" and that "to write is the most normal occupation for man, or woman either" (*E* II:68). Conversely, Woolf argues, most criticism makes art seem "remote from the interests of ordinary people" (68).

78. Sadly, we might wonder what else she might have written about Whitman had she had time. In 1938, finally free from the prodigious effort of writing *Three Guineas*, she wrote, "I think of Walt Whitman: Walpole's Letters; & White's Selbourne. 3 Gs has won me the right to go back to that world: no doubt a more 'real' world: but debarred by brambles for 4 years" (*D* v:137).

79. Whitman's lines first appeared in *Leaves of Grass* in 1860; they were later relocated in *Passage to India* and finally in *By the Roadside*.

80. For my argument that the communal model in *Between the Acts* is based on collective participation rather than unified identity, see Melba Cuddy-Keane, "The Politics of Comic Modes in Virginia Woolf's *Between the Acts*," *PMLA* 105 (March 1990): 273–85.

81. J. Johnston and J. W. Wallace, *Visits to Walt Whitman in 1890–1891*, written by Two Lancashire Friends (London, 1917), 17, 18–19, 19. In the last quotation, we might almost hear Bernard speaking, in *The Waves*.

82. Bucke was a Canadian doctor who became one of Whitman's biographers, editors, and literary executors. Bucke's book *Cosmic Consciousness* was reprinted many times and widely read, receiving praise as well from William James in his *Varieties of Religious Experience*.

83. Johnston and Wallace, quoted by Woolf (*E* II:205).

84. Johnston and Wallace, quoted by Woolf (*E* II:207).

85. See also Woolf's essays "Rachel" (*E* 1:351–54) and "The Novels of George Gissing" (*E* 1:355–62) for the detrimental effects of poverty on artistic careers.

86. Natania Rosenfeld observes, however, that Leonard Woolf on the Webbs is pot calling kettle black. Natania Rosenfeld, *Outsiders Together: Virginia and Leonard Woolf* (Princeton, 2000), 117.

87. Mark Starr, *Lies and Hate in Education* (London, 1929), 10–11. The Duke of Devonshire, for example, welcomed the Exhibition in *The Times* by noting that "An immense number of children were being imbued with something of the Imperial spirit" (*E* III:414; n. 3).

88. "The King Opens the Exhibition," *Manchester Guardian*, April 24, 1924.

89. Williams coins the word "mass-democracy" to refer to the unforeseen problems created by the "immensely powerful media of mass communication" through which "public opinion has been moulded and directed, often by questionable means, often for questionable ends." Williams, *Culture and Society*, 288.

90. Discussing the first two essays, "The Docks of London" and "Oxford Street Tide," Pamela Caughie rejects Susan Squier's reading in terms of class contrasts and argues that the second essay displaces binary-oriented rhetorical conventions with a flexible model of signifying systems subject to constant change. Like Caughie in emphasizing Woolf's destabilizing rhetoric, I focus on the fourth and fifth essays to relate Woolf's problematizing of binaries to the problems posed by mass democracy. See Pamela Caughie, "Purpose and Play in Woolf's *London Scene* Essays," *Women's Studies: An International Journal* 16 (1989): 389–408.

91. Squier does see Woolf's age of architecture as promising a liberation from gender categories, although she reads the ambivalent ending of this essay as Woolf's uncertainty about values attached to class. The uncertainty, as I see it, is not about values but about the possibility of realizing them in the foreseeable future. See Susan M. Squier, *Virginia Woolf and London: The Sexual Politics of the City* (Chapel Hill, NC, 1985).
92. For a thoughtful presentation of different views, see Mary M. Childers, "Virginia Woolf on the Outside Looking Down: Reflections on the Class of Women," *Modern Fiction Studies* 38 (Spring 1992): 61–79; for a discussion of Childers, see Snaith, *Virginia Woolf*, 116.
93. For related forms, see my discussions of the pamphlet *Reviewing*, the broadcast "Are Too Many Books Written and Published?" and the collection, *The Hogarth Letters*.
94. In proposing this view, Rachel Bowlby, I think, devalues intellectual work. See *WE*, 200, n. 9.
95. See William Morris, *Three Works: A Dream of John Ball, The Pilgrims of Hope, News from Nowhere* (London, 1973), 330–40, for Morris's sense that the achievement of a socialist utopia would mean the end of the novel as the nineteenth century knows it.
96. The text to which Woolf refers is George Meredith's *The Case of General Ople and Lady Camper*.
97. For a working-class writer's corroboration of Woolf's point, see chapter 2.
98. Comparing *Between the Acts* with Leonard Woolf's *The War for Peace*, Natania Rosenfeld comments: "Both Woolfs are concerned with the autonomy of the reading/playgoing public; both books posit an open-endedness, a plot whose outcome is decided, democratically, by others." Rosenfeld, *Outsiders*, 13.
99. Northrop Frye, *The Educated Imagination* (Toronto, 1963), 65.

2 WOOLF, ENGLISH STUDIES, AND THE MAKING OF THE (NEW) COMMON READER

1. Richard Altick, *The English Common Reader: A Story of the Mass Reading Public, 1800–1900*, 2nd edn. (1957; Columbus, OH, 1998), 375–76.
2. Peter Keating, *The Haunted Study: A Social History of the English Novel 1875–1914* (1989; London, 1991), 400; J. L. Dobson, "English Studies and Popular Literacy in England: 1870–1970," *Further Studies in the History of Reading*, ed. Greg Brooks, A. K. Pugh, and Nigel Hall (Widnes, Cheshire, UK, 1993), 83; John A. Blyth, *English University Adult Education 1908–1958: The Unique Tradition* (Manchester, 1983), 23.
3. Raymond Williams, *The Long Revolution* (London, 1961), 19; Dobson "English Studies," 85–88.
4. Blyth, *English University Adult Education*, 46.
5. Richard Garnett, "The Use and Value of Anthologies," *The Universal Anthology*, ed. Richard Garnett et al., vol. 1 (London, New York, Paris, Berlin, 1899), xiii, xxii.

6. G. M. Trevelyan, *English Social History: A Survey of Six Centuries, Chaucer to Queen Victoria* (London, 1943), 582.

7. Covering Letter by A. L. Smith, Master of Balliol, quoted by Blyth, *English University Adult Education*, 27.

8. For an excellent survey of the state of adult education around the world, prepared in coordination with this conference, see *International Handbook of Adult Education* (London, 1929).

9. J. H. Willis, *Leonard and Virginia Woolf as Publishers* (Charlottesville, VA, 1992), 364; Q. D. Leavis, *Fiction and the Reading Public*, 22; Janice Radway, *A Feeling for Books: The Book-of-the-Month Club, Literary Taste, and Middle-Class Desire* (Chapel Hill, NC, 1997), 187.

10. W. E. Simnett, *Books and Reading* (London, 1926); Francis Henry Pritchard, *Books and Readers* (London, 1931); Hugh Walpole, *Reading* (London, 1926); Sir Arthur Quiller-Couch, *On The Art of Reading* (New York, 1920), 239; Ezra Pound, *How to Read* (1931; New York, 1971); F. R. Leavis, *How to Teach Reading: A Primer for Ezra Pound* (Cambridge, 1932); Lyman Abbot, *et al.*, eds., *The Guide to Reading* (New York, 1924).

11. "Wireless Discussion Groups," *Listener*, October 28, 1931, 739.

12. Molly Travis states that "[o]ne of the hallmarks of literary modernism was its preoccupation with teaching readers." But in larger terms – as she herself suggests – it was a preoccupation of the period, of modernists and non-modernists alike. Molly Abel Travis, *Reading Cultures: The Construction of Readers in the Twentieth Century* (Carbondale, IL, 1998), 19.

13. E. M. Forster, *Books and Authors*, "Not New Books," *Listener*, December 28, 1932, 651.

14. Trevelyan, *English Social History*, 582.

15. Foreword, the Readers' Library, quoted by Q. D. Leavis, *Fiction*, 14.

16. *Books and the Public*, ed. editor of the *Nation, et al.* (London, 1927): Editor of the *Nation* [Hubert Henderson], "Books and the Public," 14, 9; J. M. Keynes, "Are Books Too Dear?" 19; Basil Blackwell, "Mass-Suggestion and The Book Trade," 46, 47–48; Leonard Woolf, "On Advertising Books," 48–52; Jeffrey E. Jeffrey, "The Printed Word," 67.

17. W. Fox, *Printers, Press and Profits* (London, 1933), 27.

18. *Ibid.*, 20; Willis, *Leonard and Virginia Woolf*, Appendix B.

19. Willis, *Leonard and Virginia Woolf*, Appendix B; Leonard Woolf, *Downhill all the Way: An Autobiography of the Years 1919–1939* (London, 1967), 143.

20. Altick, *English Common Reader*, 316, 313–14.

21. Leonard and Virginia Woolf, "Are Too Many Books Written and Published?" ts of broadcast, July 15, 1927, BBC Written Archives Centre.

22. Kate Whitehead, "Broadcasting Bloomsbury," *Yearbook of English Studies* 20 (1990):125; see also Paddy Scannell and David Cardiff, *A Social History of British Broadcasting 1:1922–39, Serving the Nation* (Oxford, 1991).

23. For correspondence relating to this broadcast, see the Leonard Woolf Papers, Part I Work life, R. Broadcasting, i. Letters between broadcasting organizations and LW, University of Sussex Library.

24. Leonard and Virginia Woolf, "Are Too Many Books," 10.
25. *Ibid.*, 10–11. When, in 1935, seeing increased secondary school education as a potential new market, Penguin indeed began to publish paperbacks of "good literature at the price of a packet of cigarettes," it must have been gratifying for Woolf to have them select the first *Common Reader* as one of the early volumes in their series. Blyth, *English University Adult Education*, 118; John Mepham, *Virginia Woolf: A Literary Life* (New York, 1991), 193. Its price of 6d in 1938 would have been a significant boon for adult working-class buyers, since one reviewer had pointed out somewhat ironically that the original price of 12s 6d was too expensive for most common readers to buy. Gerald Gould, "The Common Reader," *Lansbury's Labour Weekly* (July 6, 1925), 12.
26. This broadcast preceded by several years Benjamin's now famous essay arguing that the authenticity of an original work of art endows it with an "aura" that its technical reproduction destroys. See Walter Benjamin, "The Work of Art in the Age of Mechanical Reproduction," *Illuminations*, ed. Hannah Arendt, trans. Harry Zolin (1936; New York, 1969), 217–51.
27. Leonard and Virginia Woolf, "Are Too Many Books," 11.
28. Pierre Bourdieu, *The Field of Cultural Production: Essays on Art and Literature*, ed. Randal Johnson (New York, 1993), 37.
29. Keating, *Haunted Study*, 456.
30. See my Introduction, page 9.
31. D. J. Palmer gives some indication of the heat that could be generated by literary debates in the 1870s; in a printed battle between F. J. Furnivall and Swinburne over the suitability of metrical analyses of Shakespeare, Furnivall referred to Swinburne as "Pigsbrook" and prompted "an acrimonious 'flyting'" which scarcely added to the dignity of either party." D. J. Palmer, *The Rise of English Studies* (London, 1965), 38.
32. The foundational study of the history of English studies in England is Palmer, *ibid.* For a concise overview, see Keating, *Haunted Study*, 446–56. Information specific to the development of Cambridge studies is provided in S. P. Rosenbaum, *Victorian Bloomsbury: The Early Literary History of the Bloomsbury Group* (New York, 1987), 109–22 and Anne Samson, *F. R. Leavis* (Toronto, 1992), 9–33. See also F. L. Lucas, "English Literature," *University Studies: Cambridge 1933* (London, 1933), 259–60.
33. Samson, *Leavis*, 9.
34. Franklin E. Court, "The Social and Historical Significance of the First English Literature Professor in England," *PMLA* 103 (1988): 796–807.
35. Samson, *Leavis*, 9.
36. Keating, *Haunted Study*, 455.
37. Woolf's "In a Library," however, positively reviews a non-academic book by a professor and extension lecturer, finding it supported by "a background of extremely wide and serious reading" that does not, however, draw attention to itself: "The learning is suppressed rather than obtruded" (*E* II:52).
38. Virginia Woolf, Holograph Reading Notes, XVIII.B.7, Berg.

39. The English Association, founded in 1906, launched *The Year's Work in English Studies* in 1919; *The Review of English Studies* began publication in 1925, and the journal *English* in 1936. In North America, *PMLA* commenced earlier, in 1884.
40. Rosenbaum, *Victorian Bloomsbury*, 119.
41. In 1921, Woolf had made a similarly damning comment about John Middleton Murry: "at this moment I incline to think him a damned swindler – only a swindler so plausible that he'll become Professor of English literature in the University of Oxford" (*D* II:123).
42. The published *Diary* transcribes this line as "so that talk about his writing palls[?]" (*D* IV:178). My own reading of the last word is "galls."
43. A few months before her conversation with Eliot, Woolf had refused an honorary Doctor of Letters from Manchester University, commenting "Nothing would induce me to connive at all that humbug" (*D* IV:148); just before Eliot's visit, she noted in her diary that she would refuse to accept the Leslie Stephen lectureship which, she wryly noted, had not been offered to her (*D* IV:177).
44. The Woolfs published a novel by Lucas in 1926, a study of tragedy in 1928, and a book of poems in 1929.
45. Lucas's other major attack on T. S. Eliot, in *The Decline and Fall of Romanticism* (1936), is noted by Woolf when it first appears: "Peter Lucas attacks Tom [Eliot] as usual, but he says for the last time" (*L* VI:85).
46. See F. L. Lucas, *Studies French and English* (London, 1934), 295, 303, 305, 320, 320, 308.
47. *Ibid.*, 295, 325.
48. *Ibid.*, 322.
49. *Ibid.*, 314, 319.
50. *Ibid.*, 310, 312, 313.
51. *Ibid.*, 295, 318.
52. *Scrutinies* II, by various writers, ed. Edgell Rickword (London, 1931), 2, 240.
53. *Ibid.*, 38, 136, 197, 242, v–vi.
54. *Ibid.*, 213, 216.
55. William Cole, *A Journal of My Journey to Paris in the Year 1765*, ed. Francis Griffin Stokes (London, 1931).
56. The title Woolf gives as "The Diary of a Somersetshire Parson" most likely refers to *The Journal of a Somerset Rector* (London, 1930) which Woolf wrote about in detail in her own diary in December 1930 and went on to discuss in *The Common Reader 2*. Woolf may have confused the title with another work she had reviewed, *The Diary of a Country Parson* (London, 1924). The third book is William Guy Carr, *By Guess and by God: The Story of the British Submarines in the War* (New York, 1930).
57. Woolf's "Swift's Journal to Stella," "Impassioned Prose," and "The Novels of George Meredith" are included in the bibliographies, but "The Weekend," "The Schoolroom Floor," "Joseph Conrad," "Notes on an Elizabethan Play," "Thomas Hardy's Novels," "An English Aristocrat," and "Geraldine and Jane" are not.

58. "Summary of Periodical Literature," *The Review of English Studies* 1 (1925): 254.
59. *Ibid.*, 5 (1929): 185, 276.
60. The fact that Woolf's essay – like all leading articles – did not carry a signature does not seem to have been a factor. The three essays of hers listed in the bibliography were unsigned leading articles as well, as were T. S. Eliot's listed essays, "Lancelot Andrewes" and "Thomas Middleton."
61. Lucas, *Studies French and English*, 269.
62. These are the four major movements in nineteenth-century working-class education identified in the historical background provided in the report *Oxford and Working-class Education*, 2nd and rev. edn. (Oxford, 1909).
63. P. N. Furbank, *E. M. Forster: A Life*, vol. 1 (London, 1978), 97, 174.
64. Thomas Kelley, *A History of Adult Education in Great Britain* (Liverpool, 1962), 193–94.
65. For details of Woolf's preparation for her classes, see Daugherty, "Morley College," 132.
66. Quoted in *Oxford and Working-class Education*, 6.
67. Furbank, *Forster: A Life*, 1:175–76.
68. Virginia Woolf, "Report on Teaching at Morley College," appendix B in *Virginia Woolf: A Biography* by Quentin Bell, 2 vols. (London, 1972), 1: 202, 203.
69. Daugherty provides an excellent summary of the kinds of educational backgrounds Morley College students would have had. Daugherty, "Morley College," 130–31.
70. Woolf, "Report on Teaching," 203.
71. Furbank, *Forster: A Life*, 1:147, 174.
72. E. M. Forster, *Howards End* (1910; London, 1973), 118.
73. Beth Daugherty, "Virginia Woolf Teaching/Virginia Woolf Learning: Morley College and the Common Reader," *New Essays on Virginia Woolf*, ed. Helen Wussow (Dallas, 1995), 70, 74, 74.
74. Furbank, *Forster: A Life*, 1:147. For George ("Dadie") Rylands, Forster's lectures "talked to the Common Reader"; for Leavis, they were characterized by "intellectual nullity." Oliver Stallybrass, introduction to *Aspects of the Novel* by E. M. Forster (Harmondsworth, 1976), 13–14.
75. See my discussion of "talking with" in chapter 3.
76. See *Oxford and Working-class Education*, 49–51. In a similar fashion, G. H. Thompson disagreed violently with R. B. Haldane, president of Birkbeck College, labeling Haldane's educational goal of enabling movement from one class to another as "rot": "We don't want our children to remove from one class to another. We want them to stay where they are" (quoted in Blyth, *English University Adult Education*, 45–46). Thompson's goal was an emancipated working class.
77. *Oxford and Working-class Education*, 51–52. Note the strong resemblance to Woolf's remark in *A Room* about the disadvantages in being locked in as well as locked out.

78. *Ibid.*, 57.
79. G. D. H. Cole, "Workers' Education: Achievements – Needs – Prospects, I and II," *The Highway: A Monthly Review of Adult Education and the Journal of the Workers' Educational Association*, 15 (April, May 1923):114.
80. Cole, "Doubtful Value," 8. See Tom Steele for the view that the move toward vocational goals was particularly noticeable in the new universities and that the adult education movement was regarded as the possible saviour of a general cultural education. *The Emergence of Cultural Studies: 1945–65: Cultural Politics, Adult Education and the English Question* (London, 1997).
81. G. D. H. Cole, "Crisis in Workers' Education," *The Highway: A Journal of Adult Education* 16 (Winter 1923): 19.
82. For further documentation of these views, see Rose, *Intellectual Life*, 282–85.
83. G. D. H. Cole, "The W. E. A. and the Future," *The Highway: A Quarterly Review of Adult Education* 17 (Summer 1925): 97–101.
84. A Member of the W. E. A., "The Place of Academic People in Workers' Educational Movements," *The Highway: A Monthly Journal of Education for the People* 13 (October 1920): 6.
85. Altick, *English Common Reader*, 194.
86. For many, however, the tutorial class still was not sufficiently effective in reaching the working class; in 1913–14, for example, 47.5 percent of the students were listed as manual workers; the rest fell into categories of clerks, telegraphists, teachers, housewives, shop keepers, and shop assistants (Blyth, *English University Adult Education*, 14). Members of the WEA, however, differed in their definitions of working class; Albert Mansbridge, for example, was willing to include clerks and artisans in the working-class group. See Roger Fieldhouse, *The Workers' Educational Association: Aims and Achievements 1903–1977* (Syracuse, NY: 1977), 4.
87. G. D. H. Cole, "The Tutors' Conference," *The Highway: A Monthly Review of Adult Education and the Journal of the Workers' Educational Association* 15 (October 1922): 4.
88. Cole, "Doubtful Value," 8, 9.
89. "Correspondence: The Doubtful Value of Lectures in University Education," *New Statesman*, October 14, 1922, 43, 44. The quotations are from letters from W. M. Bayliss, University College, London; G. C. Field, University Club, Liverpool; and J. L. Stocks, St. John's College, Oxford. The other two letters were from F. B. Kirkman and F. A. Bromley, Weston Vicarage, Bath.
90. Cole, "Workers' Education," 97, 98, 115.
91. Carpenter, *G. D. H. Cole*, 119–20.
92. Cole's own position straddled both sides. The son of a self-made man and estate agent, he worked for a time as an unpaid research assistant for the Amalgamated Society of Engineers, establishing a close connection with trade unionists. But he went on to become the first full-time tutorial class tutor at the University of London, and a Fellow at Oxford in 1925. By his own admission, his ideas were controversial within the WEA as they no doubt were within the university as well.

93. In 1929, the Hogarth Press published Cole's *Politics and Literature*, written at Leonard Woolf's express and rather rare invitation, as part of a new line on educational and cultural topics (Willis, *Leonard and Virginia Woolf*, 253). Between 1931 and 1941, Leonard published ten of Cole's articles in the *Political Quarterly*. Later Hogarth publications included Cole's *The Machinery of Socialist Planning* (1938) and *Books and People* (1938) by his wife Margaret Cole.

94. Leonard, too, though he greatly admired Cole's work, acknowledged that "there was no gentleness or consideration when Douglas and Margaret Cole knocked on any door." Leonard Woolf, *Downhill*, 220.

95. Although the published version places the talk in May of 1940, Woolf's diaries and letters suggest that the actual date was April 27.

96. Melba Cuddy-Keane, "The Rhetoric of Feminist Conversation: Virginia Woolf and the Trope of the Twist," *Ambiguous Discourse: Feminist Narratology and British Women Writers*, ed. Kathy Mezei (Chapel Hill, NC, 1996), 137–61.

97. Woolf wrote to Sackville-West, "I lectured for an hour yesterday" (*L* VI:394).

98. Recollecting his apprenticeship at the Hogarth Press, Richard Kennedy writes that Woolf "talked about working class writers being under a disadvantage, like women, as writers." *A Boy at the Hogarth Press*, introduction Bevis Hillier (London, 1972), 32.

99. See pp. 133–34 for a discussion of Woolf's critique of this central "I."

100. Woolf makes a covert reference to her father when she refers to "an eminent Victorian who was also an eminent pedestrian" and who urged walkers to disregard injunctions against trespassing (*CE* II:181); here Leslie Stephen makes an interesting counter to the beadle, in *A Room of One's Own*, who instructs non-fellows to keep off the grass.

101. I make this argument in "Virginia Woolf and the Varieties of Historicist Experience," *Virginia Woolf and the Essay*, ed. Beth Carole Rosenberg and Jeanne Dubino (New York, 1997), 59–77.

102. See my Introduction for my basic point about the need to read Woolf's sentences in their context.

103. Cole, "Crisis in Worker's Education," 19.

104. John Lehmann, foreword, *Folios of New Writing* 3 (Spring 1941): 6.

105. The names that Woolf cites, discussing academic rivalry in the time of Dr. Bentley (*CR* I:194).

106. Woolf's point about wholeness should not be taken to imply the humanist construct of the unified self; using all parts of the mind might indeed be more generative of multiplicity than integration.

107. "The Leaning Tower: Replies," *Folios of New Writing* 3 (Spring 1941): 25.

108. As Molly Travis comments, "This common reader – independent, possessed of cultural memory and a sense of history, and exercising a well-honed critical judgement – was for Woolf the last line of defense against fascisms both foreign and domestic." Travis, *Reading Cultures*, 40.

109. For extensive documentation that Leavis's pedagogical style did not enact the dialogics that his theory promoted, see Ian MacKillop and Richard Storer, eds., *F. R. Leavis: Essays and Documents* (Sheffield, 1995).
110. "It seems that every door is shut against him, that he has set himself a most hopeless task, and that writing must be in every pulse of his being if he can survive and express himself at last." "The Leaning Tower: Replies," 32. These sentiments would not have been unfamiliar to Woolf, since she received several such expressions from readers responding to *A Room*.
111. *Ibid.*, 33.
112. *Ibid.*, 34.
113. *Ibid.*, 35.
114. *Ibid.*, 42.
115. *Ibid.*, 44–45.
116. Woolf quoted by Lehmann, *ibid.*, 45.
117. Hermione Lee, *Virginia Woolf* (London, 1996), 414. Woolf herself relied upon Mudie's and the London Library; as well, *Three Guineas* might not have been written without the resources of the Women's Service Library.
118. Mepham, *Virginia Woolf*, 192.
119. Consider her treatment in both *Jacob's Room* and *A Room of One's Own* of the British Museum and her depiction of regulated admission to the Oxbridge library in the latter work.
120. Quoted by Keating, *Haunted*, 419.
121. *Oxford and Working-class Education, 10.*
122. Keating, however, argues that the public library, supported by local ratepayers, was less vulnerable to such censorship than the circulating libraries with their national organization and their middle-class boards. Keating, *Haunted Study*, 280–82.
123. Anna Snaith makes the point that this library was a hospitable place not only for professional women, but also for housewives and members of the WEA. Snaith, "'Stray Guineas.'"
124. Desmond MacCarthy, *The World of Books*, "Some Literary Reviews," *Sunday Times*, February 2, 1941. Given the high percentage of women in the WEA at this time, presumably MacCarthy means an audience *including* working men.
125. Alan Hibbe, personal communication, May 28, 1993.

3 WOOLF AND THE THEORY AND PEDAGOGY OF READING

1. Altick, *English Common Reader*, 1, 5–6.
2. Graham Good, *The Observing Self: Rediscovering the Essay* (London, 1988), 150–51.
3. David McWhirter, "Woolf, Eliot, and the Elizabethans: The Politics of Modernist Nostalgia," *Virginia Woolf: Reading the Renaissance*, ed. Sally Greene (Athens, OH, 1999), 246.

4. See Woolf's essay "Montaigne" (*CR* 1:58–68) and Leonard's *The Journey Not the Arrival Matters: An Autobiography of the Years 1939–1969* (London, 1969).

5. Susan Stanford Friedman, "Virginia Woolf's Pedagogical Scenes of Reading: *The Voyage Out, The Common Reader*, and her 'Common Readers,'" *Modern Fiction Studies* 38 (1992): 105, 109, 118.

6. Pamela Caughie, *Virginia Woolf and Postmodernism: Literature in Quest and Question of Itself* (Urbana, IL, 1991), 179.

7. Rosenblatt's undergraduate study was at Barnard College, Columbia University, where John Dewey played a prominent role.

8. Louise Rosenblatt, *Literature as Exploration*, 5th edn. (1938; New York, 1995) and *The Reader, the Text and the Poem; The Transactional Theory of The Literary Work*, rev. edn. (1978; Carbondale, IL, 1994).

9. Margery Sabin, "Starting from the Particular in Literary Reading," *ADE Bulletin* (MLA Publications) 117 (1997): 11, 12.

10. J. Hillis Miller, "Cultural Studies and Reading," *ADE Bulletin* (MLA Publications) 117 (1997): 18.

11. Kate Flint, "Reading Uncommonly: Virginia Woolf and the Practice of Reading," *The Yearbook in English Studies* 26 (1996): 187–98.

12. In 1925, recording her difficulties in weaving together the different elements in a scene in *The Years*, for example, Woolf wrote, "Who was it who said, through the unconscious one comes to the conscious, & then again to the unconscious? I rather think it was Miss West [Hogarth's manager] about childrens drawings last night at tea" (*D* IV 282–83).

13. Consider the well-known examples of Milton's Eve and Pope's Belinda.

14. Isobel Armstrong, "Textual Harassment: the Ideology of Close Reading, or How Close is Close?" *Textual Practice* 9 (1995): 403, 402. For a discussion of submersion and resistance as conflicting desires negotiated in Woolf's own reading, particularly in the ways (both colonizing and liberating) the self is constituted in language, see Pierre-Eric Villeneuve, "Communities of Desire: Woolf, Proust, and the Reading Process," *Virginia Woolf and Communities: Selected Papers from the Eighth Annual Conference on Virginia Woolf*, ed. Jeanette McVicker and Laura Davis (New York, 1999), 22–28.

15. Armstrong, "Textual Harassment," 403, 405, 418.

16. *Ibid.*, 417.

17. Perry Meisel, *The Absent Father: Virginia Woolf and Walter Pater* (New Haven, 1980), 222.

18. I. A. Richards, *Practical Criticism* (1929; New York, 1962), 13.

19. The book under discussion was Arthur and Dorothea Ponsonby, *Rebels and Reformers: Biographies for Young People* (London, 1917).

20. Virginia Woolf, "A Sketch of the Past," *Moments of Being*, ed. Jeanne Schulkind, 2nd edn. (London, 1985), 150.

21. For the relation of Woolf's rhetorical strategies to linguist Amy Sheldon's studies of contemporary gendered conflict strategies, see Cuddy-Keane, "Rhetoric of Feminist Conversation," 145–47.

22. In the event, the topics chosen by the writers were so varied that clashes between the views were rare. The only real opposition was posed by Peter Quennell's rebuttal to Woolf's own letter, and although she had invited rebuttal, she was less than pleased to get it from Quennell (*L* v:82).

23. The conversational twist also offers a useful approach to Woolf's use of shifting focalization in her fiction.

24. Mikhail Bakhtin, "Discourse Typology in Prose," trans. Richard Balthazar and I. R. Titunik, *Readings in Russian Poetics: Formalist and Structuralist Views*, ed. Ladislav Matejka and Krystyna Pomorska (Ann Arbor, MI, 1978), 176–96. Recognizing the close historical proximity of Woolf and Bakhtin is important for an understanding of modernist theory. Although Bakhtin continued to write well into the 1940s, since the English translations of his work appeared much later he tends to be treated as a contemporary theorist.

25. The significance of this essay has also been noted by Beth Rosenberg, who approaches the dialogic elements in Woolf's writing through an exploration of Woolf's (re)reading of the conversational element in Johnson's prose, and by Leila Brosnan, for whom the Otway conversation aptly figures the dual complexity of the text as a subject of discussion and the essayist as a speaking subject. My analysis, however, indicates that Woolf's purpose is not to avoid attacks from "disgruntled readers," as Brosnan suggests, but to get readers to consider questions from both sides. Beth Carole Rosenberg, *Virginia Woolf and Samuel Johnson: Common Readers* (New York, 1995); Leila Brosnan, *Reading Virginia Woolf's Essays and Journalism: Breaking the Surface of Silence* (Edinburgh, 1997), 135.

26. Although Woolf suffered acutely when her work was attacked, the setbacks were emotional. Once she shook off the depression she countered criticism with a greater belief in herself: "Now I think the thing to do is to note the pith of what is said ... then to use the little kick of energy which opposition supplies to be more vigorously oneself" (*D* iv:101). How well she succeeded can be judged by Leonard Woolf's comment that "the moment always came when she stiffened herself against the critics, against herself, and against the world." Leonard Woolf, *Downhill*, 57.

27. For a sensitive discussion of Woolf's varying responses to public pressure, see Patrick Collier, "Woolf, Privacy and the Press," *Virginia Woolf: Turning the Centuries: Selected Papers from the Ninth Annual Conference on Virginia Woolf*, ed. Ann Ardis and Bonnie Kime Scott (New York, 2000), 223–29. Elena Gualtieri contributes a crucial complexity to discussions of Woolf and the public by distinguishing the "idealized public" from the "mass audience." Elena Gualtieri, *Virginia Woolf's Essays: Sketching the Past* (Basingstoke, 2000), 59. Further investigation of the multiple "publics" that Woolf herself saw as definitive of the twentieth-century audience may help us to read Woolf's response to her "public" as always context specific.

28. For the significance of the classics in the education of Virginia Woolf's male contemporaries, see Rosenbaum, *Victorian Bloomsbury* and for the role of the classics versus the vernacular in producing two differently gendered educational

communities, see Juliet Dusinberre, "Virginia Woolf and Montaigne," *Textual Practice* 5 (1991): 219–41.

29. Most critics – even postmodernist critics like Pamela Caughie and Rachel Bowlby, both of whom comment insightfully on multiple discourse in Woolf's other works – have read "On Not Knowing Greek" as unproblematized and non-ironic. Caughie, *Virginia Woolf*, 187; Bowlby, introduction, *WE*, xxi. This reading, however, merely indicates how comfortable Woolf makes the traditional ideological chair. For other perceptions of the twists and turns in this essay, however, see Edward Bishop, "Metaphor and the Subversive Process of Virginia Woolf's Essays," *Virginia Woolf* (London, 1991), 67–78 and Good, *The Observing Self*, 116–17.

30. In a much later review of Stravinsky's "The Tale of a Soldier," Woolf comments that "Like all highly original work, it begins by destroying one's conceptions, and only by degrees builds them up again" (*E* IV:364).

31. Mary Louise Pratt, "Ideology and Speech-Act Theory," *Poetics Today* 7 (1986): 61, 68.

32. See note 21 above.

33. A similar deployment of the twist informs the structure of *A Room of One's Own* where, after a probing analysis of the polarization of men versus women, Woolf then overturns such binary thinking: "Perhaps," she suggests, "to think... of one sex as distinct from the other is an effort" (*R* 145), because to maintain any one state of consciousness for a long time means "unconsciously holding something back, and gradually the repression becomes an effort" (146–47). Woolf enacts deconstruction before Derrida.

34. In her study of the discourse of the "proper lady," Mary Poovey draws on Gilbert and Gubar's analysis of "feminine 'swerves'" – the use of double-voice discourse as a way of presenting a "surface design" of "conformity" that is then disrupted and subverted by deeper subtextual meanings; Poovey then focuses on the way such "strategies in art" are also "strategies for living" which enable the writer to accommodate her identity – as formed both by, and apart from, the hegemony – through "the articulation of simultaneous, if contradictory, self-images." Mary Poovey, *The Proper Lady and the Woman Writer: Ideology as Style in the Works of Mary Wollstonecraft, Mary Shelley, and Jane Austen* (Chicago, 1984), 44–46. The difference of Woolf's technique, however, is that she moves the subtext into the main text to expose the contesting discourses and to examine their ideological foundations.

35. H. W. Massingham ["Wayfarer"], "A London Diary," *Nation*, July 10, 1920, 464.

36. The policy of the journal states that it will "advocate a real equality of liberties, status, and opportunities between men and women. So far as space permits, however, it will offer an impartial platform for topics not directly included in the objects of the women's movement, but of special interest to women" (*E* III:526).

37. Massingham, "London Diary," 463–64.

38. H. W. Massingham, Letter, *Woman's Leader*, July 30, 1920, 588.

39. This is Ronald Bush's term for de Man's critique. Ronald Bush, "Paul de Man, Modernist," *Theoretical Issues in Literary History*, ed. David Perkins (Cambridge, MA, 1991), 56.
40. Forster, *Aspects of the Novel*, 27. S. P. Rosenbaum's assertion that "most of Bloomsbury would have agreed with [Forster's] formalistic dictum, 'History develops, Art stands still'" needs to be qualified, as Rosenbaum does, by excepting Virginia Woolf. See Rosenbaum, *Victorian Bloomsbury*, 14.
41. For a fuller discussion of Woolf's complex relation to contemporaneous historiography, see Cuddy-Keane, "Virginia Woolf and the Varieties of Historicist Experience," 59–77.
42. See chapter 3 of Thomas Babington Macaulay, *History of England from the Accession of James II*, vol. 1 (New York: Harper & Brothers, 1849).
43. Eileen Power, *Medieval People* (1924; London, 1963), 18.
44. Leonard Woolf, "The Pageant of History," *Essays on Literature, History, Politics, Etc.* (1927; Freeport, NY, 1970), 134.
45. "Mass Observation," leaflet, The Mass-Observation Archive, University of Sussex Library (*c.* 1992).
46. Woolf declined Kingsley Martin's invitation to review the Mass Observation book – a suitable request to a novelist who had just published *The Years* – because she was "completely submerged" in *Three Guineas*.
47. R. G. Collingwood, *Essays in the Philosophy of History*, ed. William Debbins (1921–30; Austin, TX, 1965), 54.
48. *Ibid.*, 54, 138–39, 56.
49. Woolf parts company with Collingwood, however, when it comes to his elevation of the specialist and his increasingly dogmatic and authoritarian tone.
50. Virginia Woolf, "Report on Teaching," 203.
51. For an excellent discussion of Woolf's historicism in *Orlando*, see Rachel Bowlby, *Virginia Woolf: Feminist Destinations* (Oxford, 1988), 128–45.
52. Margaret Ezell, *Writing Women's Literary History* (Baltimore, 1993).
53. Virginia Woolf, "'Anon' and 'The Reader': Virginia Woolf's Last Essays," ed. Brenda Silver, *Twentieth Century Literature* 25 (1979): 374.
54. For a recent discussion, see McWhirter, "Woolf, Eliot, and the Elizabethans."
55. See, for example, "Rambling Round Evelyn," "The Strange Elizabethans," "The Countess of Pembroke's Arcadia," *A Room of One's Own*, and "Traffics and Discoveries."
56. William Plomer, contributor to *Recollections of Virginia Woolf by her Contemporaries*, ed. Joan Russell Noble, intro. Michael Holroyd (Harmondsworth, 1973), 121.
57. Leila Brosnan draws heavily on a vitriolic unpublished prose poem to demonstrate Woolf's "animosity" toward journalists, yet Brosnan goes on to document the extensive amount of time Woolf devoted to revisions of her own journalism. My argument is that it was the nature of journalistic practice that Woolf objected to, not journalism itself. Brosnan, *Reading Virginia Woolf's Essays and Journalism*, 70–91.

58. "What is a Good Novel? A Symposium," *The Highway: A Journal of Adult Education* 16 (Summer 1924): 100–10.
59. The others were Henry Baerlein, Arnold Bennett, J. D. Beresford, Hamilton Fyfe, John Galsworthy, Compton Mackenzie, Alfred Ollivant, John Oxenham, Eden Phillpotts, and Hugh Walpole.
60. Authorship in *The Highway* was definitely male-dominated, with G. D. H. Cole as one of the most frequent contributors. Other regular writers included C. E. M. Joad – the husband of Marjorie Thomson Joad who was an assistant to the Woolfs at the Hogarth Press from January 1923 to February 1925 (*D* III:II, n. 15) – and R. H. Tawney, who worked closely with Leonard during the 1926 strike. Lee, *Virginia Woolf*, 533. Woolf's single contribution appears significantly in a brief period when *The Highway* had a woman editor – Barbara Wootton, Director of Studies for Tutorial Classes in London. Such gendered author-participation is in marked contrast to the fact that, during the war, although many adult education activities were curtailed, the WEA was strengthened by the influx of women students. By the end of the war, the number of women attending tutorial classes almost doubled (Blyth, *English University Adult Education*, 21).
61. "What is a Good Novel?" 110.
62. *Ibid.*, 103.
63. *Ibid.*, 109. In this, Woolf is closer to Kafka's statement: "I think we ought to read only the kind of books that wound and stab us . . . A book must be the axe for the frozen sea within us." Kafka to Oskar Pollak, January 27, 1904, *Letters to Friends, Family, and Editors*, trans. Richard and Clara Winston (New York, 1977), 16.
64. "What is a Good Novel?" 102, 109.
65. *Ibid.*, 109–10, 110.
66. *Ibid.*, 110. A very different article appeared in *The Highway* two years later, written by Leonard Woolf. Reviewing *How to Read Literature* by George E. Wilkinson, Leonard took the writer to task for what he saw as the writer's very limited argument in favour of each reader's "discover[ing] for himself the effect which each book, by its material or its words, has on him." In Leonard's view, reading literature requires a different angle of the mind from reading books, and to learn the literary angle, criticism is invaluable. Leonard Woolf, review of *How to Read Literature* by George E. Wilkinson, *The Highway and "Students' Bulletin"* 20 (December 1927), 38. The Woolfs often had differing views, but it would seem that not harmony but lively, intelligent exchange was what mattered to both of them.
67. Significantly, when *The Highway* ran a symposium, a few years later, on the case for and against the Book Society, J. B. Priestley argued strongly for the model of relying on a panel of jurors for the selection of books, indicating the added advantage of acquiring first editions that over time would increase in value. Allan Monkhouse, sounding like Woolf, argued that it was exceedingly bad training to be encouraged to rely on authorities, particularly when the authorities tended to be the same group of people. "Advice to Bookbuyers,"

The Highway 22 (February 1930): 9–12. Clemence Dane, "The Case for the Book Society I," 9–10; J. B. Priestley, "The Case for the Book Society II," 10–11; Allan Monkhouse, "The Case Against a Selection Committee," 11–12.

68. Leonard and Virginia Woolf, "Are Too Many Books?" 6, 10.

69. "Bloomsbury Unbends," *Punch*, October 26, 1932, 474.

70. Willis, *Leonard and Virginia Woolf*, 188, 266.

71. Woolf must have enjoyed the signs of a wonderfully bizarre talent, especially in the first poem in Joan Easdale's first collection; perhaps it is the still lingering notion of Woolf's elitism that makes her continuing interest in Easdale appear "very odd" to J. H. Willis (*ibid.*, 187) and "peculiar" to Hermione Lee (*Virginia Woolf*, 615).

72. John Lehmann, "A Postscript," *Folios of New Writing* 3 (1941): 45.

73. Virginia Woolf, Notebook, B.2.m, MHP; quoted by Lee, *Virginia Woolf*, 408.

74. Barbara Herrnstein Smith, *Contingencies of Value: Alternative Perspectives for Critical Theory* (Cambridge, MA., 1988), 54, 11, 15.

75. *Ibid.*, 40, 51.

76. For a fuller discussion of Woolf's relation to Smith, see Melba Cuddy-Keane, "'A Standard of One's Own'," *Virginia Woolf: Turning the Centuries: Selected Papers from the Ninth Annual Conference on Virginia Woolf*, ed. Ann Ardis and Bonnie Kime Scott (New York, 2000): 230–36.

77. See Virginia Woolf, "'Anon' and 'The Reader'," 425–26, 430–32.

78. Smith, *Contingencies*, 24.

79. Ellen Tremper similarly identifies "conviction" as an important evaluative word for Woolf, associating it as well with the unimpeded activity of the unconscious in the initial stages of both creation and reception. Ellen Tremper, *"Who Lived at Alfoxton?": Virginia Woolf and Romanticism* (Lewisburg, PA, 1998).

80. Woolf, "What is a Good Novel?" 110.

81. See my discussion of "Poetry, Fiction, and the Future" in chapter 1.

82. For a further development of this theme, see "How it Strikes a Contemporary" (*CR*1).

83. Her oppositional "talking back" to each critic is even more evident in her reading notes, which provide a running commentary on these works. See Holograph Reading Notes, xxv.B.30 and xxvi.B.33, Berg.

84. Woolf interestingly omits to mention that Lubbock's opening pages are replete with qualifiers that show him to be in fundamental agreement with her approach: just as a symphony is not to be equated with the score, he argues, so is a novel not the same as the words on the page; fiction is a "passage of experience" and one in which the reader – who acts as a novelist too – shares the responsibility for creation. For her dialectic purposes, Woolf locates Lubbock a little more oppositionally than his argument deserves. Percy Lubbock, *The Craft of Fiction* (1921; New York, 1957), 15.

85. Woolf refers here to the chapel scene in chapter 9 of *Mansfield Park* – a scene that may well be an allusive intertext in Woolf's more stringent critique of imperialism and church-going in chapter 17 of *The Voyage Out*. Woolf presumably has in mind Mary Crawford's lively puncturing of the hypocrisy

of religious observances. Woolf may have misremembered Fanny's longing for the poetry of banners – or she may be crediting Austen's light touch in adumbrating Fanny's possibly naïve attachment to a romantic past.

86. We know that Hemingway read this review, and that it made him angry (*E* IV:456, n. I). But it may also have sharpened his understanding of the relation between bullfighting and writing.

87. See Walter Pater, *Studies in the History of The Renaissance* (1873; New York, 1919), 213; William James, *The Principles of Psychology* (New York, 1890), 243, 245; and Henri Bergson, *An Introduction to Metaphysics*, trans. T. E. Hulme (1903; New York, 1912).

88. James Joyce, *Ulysses* (1922; New York, 1966), 108.

89. "Virginia Woolf's 'How Should One Read a Book?'" ed. Beth Rigel Daugherty, *Woolf Studies Annual* 4 (1998): 147.

90. Virginia Woolf, "'Anon' and 'The Reader'," 429.

POSTSCRIPT: INTELLECTUAL WORK TODAY

1. The *Critical Heritage* volume, by selecting reviews from the *TLS*, the *Calendar*, the *Manchester Guardian* and the *Criterion*, severely limits our sense of the attention Woolf's essays received. Reviews of the first *Common Reader*, for example, appeared in such diverse periodicals as, on the one hand, *The Queen*: (subtitled) *The Lady's Newspaper And Court Chronicle* (July 15, 1925) and, on the other, *Lansbury's Labour Weekly* (June 6, 1925; July 4, 1925); they ranged geographically from the *Aberdeen Press and Journal* (May 20, 1925), to the *Cape Times* (June 11, 1925), to the *Springfield Republican* (July 12, 1925).

2. Penguin, for example, issued *The Common Reader* in 1938 and *The Common Reader: Second Series* in 1944, in its popular Pelican series, in runs of 50,000 each. B. J. Kirkpatrick and Stuart N. Clarke, *A Bibliography of Virginia Woolf*, 4th edn. (Oxford, 1997), 36, 92.

3. See my comments on Woolf's fan-mail, p. 7. For further comment on the enthusiastic responses of unknown readers to Woolf's novels, see Leonard Woolf, foreword to Mitchell A. Leaska, *Virginia Woolf's Lighthouse: A Study in Critical Method* (London, 1970), 11–12.

4. For a comment on this process and its problematic in terms of new global thinking, see Douwe Fokkema, "Orientalism, Occidentalism, and the Notion of Discourse: Arguments for a New Cosmopolitanism," *Comparative Criticism* 18 (1996): 227–41.

5. Many instructors, teaching in different periods of English literature, regularly introduce discussion of a literary work through Virginia Woolf's essay on it. I have also been told that her essay "The Tale of the Genji" is widely respected and used in classrooms studying classical Japanese literature.

6. Snaith, *Virginia Woolf*, 3.

Bibliography

Abbot, Lyman, *et al. The Guide to Reading*. The Pocket University. New York: Nelson Doubleday, 1924.

"Advice to Bookbuyers." *The Highway* 22 (February 1930): 9–12. Clemence Dane, "The Case for the Book Society 1," 9–10; J. B. Priestley, "The Case for the Book Society 11," 10–11; Allan Monkhouse, "The Case Against a Selection Committee," 11–12.

Altick, Richard. *The English Common Reader: A Story of the Mass Reading Public, 1800–1900*. Foreword Jonathan Rose. 2nd edn. Columbus: Ohio State University Press, 1998.

Angenot, Marc. "The Concept of Social Discourse," *English Studies in Canada* 21 (March 1995): 1–19.

Armstrong, Isobel. "Textual Harassment: the Ideology of Close Reading, or How Close is Close?" *Textual Practice* 9 (1995): 401–20.

Bakhtin, Mikhail. "Discourse Typology in Prose." Trans. Richard Balthazar and I. R. Titunik. In *Readings in Russian Poetics: Formalist and Structuralist Views*, ed. Ladislav Matejka and Krystyna Pomorska, 176–96. Ann Arbor: Michigan Slavic Publications, 1978.

Banfield, Ann. *The Phantom Table: Woolf, Fry, Russell and the Epistemology of Modernism*. Cambridge: Cambridge University Press, 2000.

Bell, Quentin. *Virginia Woolf: A Biography*. 2 vols. London: Hogarth, 1972.

Bender, Thomas. "Intellectual and Cultural History." In *The New American History*, ed. Eric Foner, 181–202. Rev. edn. Philadelphia: Temple University Press, 1997.

Benjamin, Walter. "The Work of Art in the Age of Mechanical Reproduction." 1936. In *Illuminations*, ed. Hannah Arendt, trans. Harry Zolin, 217–51. New York: Schocken Books, 1969.

Bennett, Arnold. "Queen of the High-Brows." *Evening Standard*, November 28, 1929, 9. Reprinted in *Virginia Woolf: The Critical Heritage*, ed. Robin Madjumdar and Allen McLaurin, 258–60. London: Routledge & Kegan Paul, 1975.

"A Woman's High-Brow Lark," *Evening Standard*, November 8, 1928, 7. Extract reprinted in *Virginia Woolf: The Critical* Heritage, ed. Robin Madjumdar and Allen McLaurin, 232–33. London: Routledge & Kegan Paul, 1975.

Bergson, Henri. *An Introduction to Metaphysics.* 1903. Trans. T. E. Hulme. New York, Putnam, 1912.

Bishop, Edward. "Metaphor and the Subversive Process of Virginia Woolf's Essays." In *Virginia Woolf*, 67–78. London: Macmillan, 1991.

Black, Naomi. "Virginia Woolf and the Women's Movement." In *Virginia Woolf: A Feminist Slant*, ed. Jane Marcus, 180–197. Lincoln: University of Nebraska Press, 1983.

"Bloomsbury Unbends." *Punch, or the London Charivari*, October 26, 1932, 474.

Blyth, John A. *English University Adult Education 1908–1958: The Unique Tradition.* Manchester: Manchester University Press, 1983.

Bourdieu, Pierre. *The Field of Cultural Production: Essays on Art and Literature.* Ed. Randal Johnson. New York: Columbia University Press, 1993.

Bowlby, Rachel. "Introduction: A More Than Maternal Tie." *A Woman's Essays: Selected Essays* 1, by Virginia Woolf. London: Penguin, 1992.

Virginia Woolf: Feminist Destinations. Oxford: Basil Blackwell, 1988.

Brantlinger, Patrick. *The Reading Lesson: The Threat of Mass Literacy in Nineteenth-Century British Fiction.* Bloomington: Indiana University Press, 1998.

Brooke, Rupert. *Letters from America.* Preface Henry James. London: Sidgwick & Jackson, 1916.

Brosnan, Leila. *Reading Virginia Woolf's Essays and Journalism: Breaking the Surface of Silence.* Edinburgh: Edinburgh University Press, 1997.

Bush, Ronald. "Paul de Man, Modernist." In *Theoretical Issues in Literary History*, ed. David Perkins, 35–59. Cambridge, MA: Harvard University Press, 1991.

Carey, John. *The Intellectuals and the Masses: Pride and Prejudice among the Literary Intelligentsia, 1880–1939.* London: Faber & Faber, 1992.

Carpenter, L. P. *G. D. H. Cole: An Intellectual Biography.* Cambridge: Cambridge University Press, 1973.

Carroll, Lewis. *Alice in Wonderland*, ed. Donald J. Gray 2nd edn. New York: Norton, 1992.

Caughie, Pamela. "Purpose and Play in Woolf's *London Scene* Essays." *Women's Studies: An International Journal* 16 (1989): 389–408.

Virginia Woolf and Postmodernism: Literature in Quest and Question of Itself. Urbana: University of Illinois Press, 1991.

"The Changing Audience." *Listener*, October 5, 1932, 484.

Childers, Mary M. "Virginia Woolf on the Outside Looking Down: Reflections on the Class of Women." *Modern Fiction Studies* 38 (Spring 1992): 61–79.

C. H. W. "A Radio Review." *Spectator*, October 15, 1932, 520.

Cole, G. D. H. "Crisis in Workers' Education." *The Highway: A Journal of Adult Education* 16 (Winter 1923): 17–21.

"The Doubtful Value of Lectures in University Education." *New Statesman*, October 7, 1922, 8–9.

"The Tutors' Conference." *The Highway: A Monthly Review of Adult Education and the Journal of the Workers' Educational Association* 15 (October 1922): 4.

"The W. E. A. and the Future." *The Highway: A Quarterly Review of Adult Education* 17 (Summer 1925): 97–101.

"Workers' Education: Achievements – Needs – Prospects, I and II." *The High-way: A Monthly Review of Adult Education and the Journal of the Workers' Educational Association* 15 (April 1923): 97–98 and 15 (May 1923): 114–15.

Collier, Patrick. "Woolf, Privacy and the Press." In *Virginia Woolf: Turning the Centuries: Selected Papers from the Ninth Annual Conference on Virginia Woolf*, ed. Ann Ardis and Bonnie Kime Scott, 223–29. New York: Pace University Press, 2000.

Collingwood, R. G. *Essays in the Philosophy of History.* Ed. William Debbins. 1921–30. Austin: University of Texas Press, 1965.

"Correspondence: The Doubtful Value of Lectures in University Education." *New Statesman*, October 14, 1922, 42–44.

Court, Franklin E. "The Social and Historical Significance of the First English Literature Professor in England." *PMLA* 103 (1988): 796–807.

Critic. "A London Diary." *New Statesman and Nation*, October 29, 1932, 506–07.

Cucullu, Lois. "Retailing the Intellectual." *Differences* 9 (Summer 1997): 25–68.

Cuddy-Keane, Melba. "'A Standard of One's Own': Virginia Woolf and the Question of Literary Value." In *Virginia Woolf: Turning the Centuries: Selected Papers from the Ninth Annual Conference on Virginia Woolf*, ed. Ann Ardis and Bonnie Kime Scott, 230–36. New York: Pace University Press, 2000.

"Opening Historical Doors to the *Room*: An Approach to Teaching." In *Re: Reading, Re: Writing, Re: Teaching Virginia Woolf: Selected Papers from the Fourth Annual Conference on Virginia Woolf*, ed. Eileen Barrett and Patricia Cramer, 207–15. New York: Pace University Press, 1995.

"The Politics of Comic Modes in Virginia Woolf's *Between the Acts*." *PMLA* 105 (March 1990): 273–85.

"The Rhetoric of Feminist Conversation: Virginia Woolf and the Trope of the Twist." In *Ambiguous Discourse: Feminist Narratology and British Women Writers*, ed. Kathy Mezei, 137–61. Chapel Hill: University of North Carolina Press, 1996.

"Virginia Woolf and the Varieties of Historicist Experience." In *Virginia Woolf and the Essay*, ed. Beth Carole Rosenberg and Jeanne Dubino, 59–77. New York: St. Martin's, 1997.

"Culture and Democracy." *Listener*, October 5, 1932, 472.

Daiches, David. *The Novel and the Modern World.* Chicago: University of Chicago Press, 1960.

Dakyns, Arthur L. "Teaching v. Lecturing." *The Highway: A Monthly Review of Adult Education and the Journal of the Workers' Educational Association* 15 (November 1922): 23.

Daugherty, Beth Rigel. "Morley College, Virginia Woolf and Us: How Should One Read Class?" In *Virginia Woolf and Her Influences: Selected Papers from the Seventh Annual Conference on Virginia Woolf*, ed. Laura Davis and Jeanette McVicker, 125–39. New York: Pace University Press, 1998.

"Readin', Writin', and Revisin': Virginia Woolf's 'How Should One Read a Book?'" In *Virginia Woolf and the Essay*, ed. Beth Carole Rosenberg and Jeanne Dubino, 159–75. New York: St. Martin's, 1997.

"Virginia Woolf Teaching/Virginia Woolf Learning: Morley College and the Common Reader." In *New Essays on Virginia Woolf*, ed. Helen Wussow, 61–77. Dallas: Contemporary Research, 1995.

Dewey, John. *Democracy and Education: An Introduction to the Philosophy of Education*. New York: Macmillan, 1916.

"Dewey's Philosophy of Education." Review of *Democracy and Education*. *Nation* (NY), May 4, 1916, 480–81.

Dobson, J. L. "English Studies and Popular Literacy in England: 1870–1970." In *Further Studies in the History of Reading*, ed. Greg Brooks, A. K. Pugh, and Nigel Hall, 83–96. Widnes, Cheshire: United Kingdom Reading Association, 1993.

Dusinberre, Juliet "Virginia Woolf and Montaigne." *Textual Practice* 5 (Summer 1991): 219–41.

Editor of the *Nation, et al. Books and the Public*. London: Hogarth, 1927. [Hubert Henderson], "Books and the Public," 9–17; J. M. Keynes, "Are Books Too Dear?" 17–27; Stanley Unwin, "Are Books a Necessity?" 27–31; Michael Sadlier, "Ambiguities of The Book Trade," 31–44; Basil Blackwell, "Mass-Suggestion and The Book Trade," 44–48; Leonard Woolf, "On Advertising Books," 48–52; Henry B. Saxton, "The Condition of The Book Trade," 55–62; Jeffrey E. Jeffrey, "The Printed Word," 66–70.

Eliot, George. *The George Eliot Letters*. Ed. Gordon S. Haight. Vol. 1. New Haven: Yale University Press, 1954.

Ezell, Margaret. *Writing Women's Literary History*. Baltimore: Johns Hopkins University Press, 1993.

Fieldhouse, Roger. *The Workers' Educational Association: Aims and Achievements 1903–1977*. Syracuse, NY: Syracuse University Press, 1977.

Flint, Kate. "Reading Uncommonly: Virginia Woolf and the Practice of Reading." *The Yearbook in English Studies* 26 (1996): 187–98.

Fokkema, Douwe. "Orientalism, Occidentalism, and the Notion of Discourse: Arguments for a New Cosmopolitanism." *Comparative Criticism* 18 (1996): 227–41.

Forster, E. M. *Aspects of the Novel*. Ed. Oliver Stallybrass. 1927. Harmondsworth: Penguin, 1976.

Books and Authors, "Not New Books." *Listener*, December 28, 1932, 651.

Howards End. 1910. London: Edward Arnold, 1973.

Fox, W. *Printers, Press and Profits*. A Study of the Newspaper and General Printing Trades in London and the Provinces – their share bonuses, their profits, their dividends, their directors and their workers. London: The Labour Research Board, 1933.

Friedman, Susan Stanford. "Virginia Woolf's Pedagogical Scenes of Reading: *The Voyage Out, The Common Reader*, and Her 'Common Readers.'" *Modern Fiction Studies* 38 (1992): 101–25.

Frye, Northrop. *The Educated Imagination*. Toronto: CBC Publications, 1963.

Furbank, P. N. *E. M. Forster: A Life*. 2 vols. London: Secker & Warburg, 1978.

Garnett, Richard. "The Use and Value of Anthologies." In *The Universal Anthology*, ed. Richard Garnett *et al.*, 1:xiii–xxiii. 33 vols. London: Clark Company; New York: Merrill & Baker; Paris: Emile Terquem; Berlin: Bibliothek Verlag, 1899.

Goldman, Jane. *The Feminist Aesthetics of Virginia Woolf: Modernism, Post-Impressionism and the Politics of the Visual*. Cambridge: Cambridge University Press, 1998.

Good, Graham. *The Observing Self: Rediscovering the Essay*. London: Routledge, 1988.

Gould, Gerald. "The Common Reader." *Lansbury's Labour Weekly*, July 6, 1925, 12.

Graves, Robert and Alan Hodge. *The Long Week-end: Social History of Great Britain 1918–1939*. London: Faber & Faber, 1940.

Griggs, J. Brock. Letter. *Listener*, October 28, 1931, 744.

Gualtieri, Elena. *Virginia Woolf's Essays: Sketching the Past*. Basingstoke: St. Martin's, 2000.

Higham, John. "The Study of Intellectual American History." In *Writing American History: Essays on Modern Scholarship*. Bloomington: Indiana University Press, 1970.

Huxley, Aldous. "Foreheads Villainous Low." In *Music at Night and other Essays*. London: Chatto & Windus, 1957.

Huyssen, Andreas. *After The Great Divide: Modernism, Mass Culture, Postmodernism*. Bloomington: Indiana University Press, 1986.

"The Intellectual Distrusted: Hon. Harold Nicolson and Anglo-Saxons: Talk to a 'Low-Brow.'" *Yorkshire Post*, October 25, 1932, 4.

International Handbook of Adult Education. London: World Association for Adult Education, 1929.

Jakobson, Roman. "Closing Statement: Linguistic and Poetics." In *Style in Language*, ed. Thomas A. Sebeok, 350–77. Cambridge, MA: MIT Press, 1960.

James, William. *The Principles of Psychology*. Vol. 1. New York, Holt, 1890.

Johnston, J. and J. W. Wallace. *Visits to Walt Whitman in 1890–1891*. Written by Two Lancashire Friends. London: G. Allen & Unwin, 1917.

Joyce, James. *Ulysses*. New York: Random House, 1966.

Kafka, Franz. *Letters to Friends, Family, and Editors*. Trans. Richard and Clara Winston. New York: Schocken Books, 1977.

Kammen, Michael. *American Culture, American Taste: Social Change and the 20th Century*. New York: Knopf, 1999.

Keating, Peter. *The Haunted Study: A Social History of the English Novel 1875–1914*. 1989. London: HarperCollins, 1991.

Kelley, Thomas. *A History of Adult Education in Great Britain*. Liverpool: Liverpool University Press, 1962.

Kennedy, Richard. *A Boy at the Hogarth Press*. Illustrated by author. Intro. Bevis Hillier. London: The Whittington Press, 1972.

"The King Opens the Exhibition." *Manchester Guardian*, April 24, 1924.

Kirkpatrick, B. J. and Stuart N. Clarke. *A Bibliography of Virginia Woolf*. 4th edn. Oxford: Clarendon Press, 1997.

"The Leaning Tower: Replies." Edward Upward, "The Falling Tower"; B. L. Coombes, "Below the Tower"; Louis MacNeice, "The Tower That Once"; John Lehmann, "A Postscript." *Folios of New Writing* 3 (Spring 1941): 24–46.

Leavis, F. R. *How to Teach Reading: A Primer for Ezra Pound*. Cambridge: Gordon Fraser, Minority Press, 1932.

Leavis, Q. D. *Fiction and the Reading Public*. 1932. London: Chatto & Windus, 1965.

Lee, Hermione. *Virginia Woolf*. London: Chatto & Windus, 1996.

Lehmann, John. Foreword. *Folios of New Writing* 3 (Spring 1941): 5–6.

"A Postscript." *Folios of New Writing* 3 (Spring 1941): 24–46.

Lewis, Sinclair. *Our Mr. Wrenn*. New York: Harcourt Brace, 1914.

Lipking, Lawrence. "The Genius of the Shore: Lycidas, Adamastor, and the Poetics of Nationalism." *PMLA* III (March 1996): 205–21.

Lubbock, Percy. *The Craft of Fiction*. 1921. New York: Viking, 1957.

Lucas, F. L. *Studies French and English*. London: Cassell, 1934.

MacCarthy, Desmond. "The Bubble Reputation." In *Life and Letters*, ed. Desmond MacCarthy, vol. VII, no. 40 (September 1931), 174–92.

"Highbrows." In *Experience*. Covent Garden: Putnam, 1935.

The World of Books, "Some Literary Reviews." Review of *La France Libre, Horizon*, ed. Cyril Connolly, *Folios of New Writing*, ed. John Lehmann, *New Writing in the Penguin Series*, ed. John Lehmann. *Sunday Times*, February 2, 1941.

MacKillop, Ian and Richard Storer, eds. *F. R. Leavis: Essays and Documents*. Sheffield: Academic Press, 1995.

Madjumdar, Robin and Allen McLaurin, eds. *Virginia Woolf: The Critical Heritage*. London: Routledge & Kegan Paul, 1975.

"Mass Observation." Leaflet. The Mass Observation Archive, The Library, University of Sussex (*c.* 1992).

Massingham, H. W. Letter. *Woman's Leader*, July 30, 1920, 588.

Massingham, H. W. ["Wayfarer"]. "A London Diary." *Nation*, July 10, 1920, 462–64.

McGowan, John. *Democracy's Children: Intellectuals and the Rise of Cultural Politics*. Ithaca, NY: Cornell University Press, 2002.

McWhirter, David. "Woolf, Eliot, and the Elizabethans: The Politics of Modernist Nostalgia." In *Virginia Woolf: Reading the Renaissance*, ed. Sally Greene, 245–66. Athens: Ohio University Press, 1999.

Meisel, Perry. *The Absent Father: Virginia Woolf and Walter Pater*. New Haven: Yale University Press, 1980.

A Member of the W. E. A. "The Place of Academic People in Workers' Educational Movements." *The Highway: A Monthly Journal of Education for the People* 13 (October 1920): 5–6.

Mepham, John. *Virginia Woolf: A Literary Life*. New York: St. Martin's, 1991.

Miller, J. Hillis. "Cultural Studies and Reading." *ADE Bulletin* (MLA Publications) 117 (1997): 15–18.

Moreland, Deborah Anne. *Contexts and Connections: Virginia Woolf, Wyndham Lewis, and Low Culture.* Ann Arbor, MI: University Microfilms, 1998.

Morris, William. *Three Works: A Dream of John Ball, The Pilgrims of Hope, News from Nowhere.* London: Lawrence & Wishart, 1973.

Neuman, W. Russell. *The Future of the Mass Audience.* Cambridge: Cambridge University Press, 1991.

Nicolson, Harold. Diary 1932, ts. *The Vita Sackville-West and Harold Nicolson Manuscripts, Letters and Diaries from Sissinghurst Castle, Kent. The Huntington Library, California, and other libraries.* Brighton, Sussex: Harvester Microform, 1988.

Noble, Joan Russell, ed. *Recollections of Virginia Woolf by Her Contemporaries.* Intro. Michael Holroyd. Harmondsworth: Penguin, 1973.

O'Faolain, Sean "Virginia Woolf and James Joyce, or 'Narcissa and Lucifer.'" In *The Vanishing Hero: Studies in Novelists of the Twenties*, 191–222. London: Eyre & Spottiswoode, 1956.

Oxford and Working-class Education. Being the Report of a Joint Committee of University and Working-class Representatives on the Relation of the University to the Higher Education of Workpeople. 2nd and rev. edn. Oxford: Clarendon, 1909.

Palmer, D. J. *The Rise of English Studies.* London: Oxford University Press, 1965.

Pater, Walter. *Studies in the History of The Renaissance.* 1873. New York: Boni and Liveright, 1919.

Plomer, William. *Recollections of Virginia Woolf by Her Contemporaries.* Ed. Joan Russell Noble. Intro. Michael Holroyd. Harmondsworth: Penguin, 1973.

Poovey, Mary. *The Proper Lady and the Woman Writer: Ideology as Style in the Works of Mary Wollstonecraft, Mary Shelley, and Jane Austen.* Chicago: University of Chicago Press, 1984.

Pound, Ezra. *How to Read.* 1931. New York: Haskell House, 1971.

Power, Eileen. *Medieval People.* 1924. London: Methuen, 1963.

Pratt, Mary Louise. "Ideology and Speech-Act Theory." *Poetics Today* 7 (1986): 59–72.

Priestley, J. B. "High, Low, Broad." *Saturday Review*, 20 February 1926: 222. Reprinted in *Open House: A Book of Essays*, 162–67. London: Heinemann, 1929.

"Men, Women and Books: Tell Us More About These Authors!" *Evening Standard*, October 13, 1932, 11.

To an Unnamed Listener, "To a High-Brow." ts of broadcast October 17, 1932, at 9.20 pm: 1–6. BBC Written Archive Centre. Published in *John O'London's Weekly* December 3, 1932, 712.

Pritchard, Francis Henry. *Books and Readers.* London: George G. Harrap, 1931.

Punch April 22, 1925, 437.

Punch December 23, 1925, 673.

Quiller-Couch, Sir Arthur. *On The Art of Reading.* New York: G. P. Putnam's Sons, 1920.

Radway, Janice. *A Feeling for Books: The Book-of-the-Month Club, Literary Taste, and Middle-Class Desire.* Chapel Hill: University of North Carolina Press, 1997.

Rainey, Lawrence. *Institutions of Modernism: Literary Elites and Public Culture.* New Haven: Yale University Press, 1998.

Raleigh, Walter. *The Letters of Sir Walter Raleigh, 1879–1922.* Ed. Lady Raleigh. Preface D. Nichol Smith. 2 vols. London: Methuen, 1926.

Review of John Dewey, *Education and Democracy. Nation,* May 4, 1916, 480.

Richards, I. A. *Practical Criticism.* 1929. New York, Harcourt, Brace & World, 1962.

Rickword, Edgell, ed. *Scrutinies* II. By various writers. London: Wishart, 1931.

Rose, Jonathan. *The Intellectual Life of the British Working Classes.* New Haven: Yale University Press, 2001.

Rosenbaum, S. P. *Victorian Bloomsbury: The Early Literary History of the Bloomsbury Group.* New York: St. Martin's, 1987.

Rosenberg, Beth Carole. *Virginia Woolf and Samuel Johnson: Common Readers.* New York: St. Martin's, 1995.

Rosenfeld, Natania. *Outsiders Together: Virginia and Leonard Woolf.* Princeton: Princeton University Press, 2000.

Sabin, Margery. "Starting from the Particular in Literary Reading." *ADE Bulletin* (MLA Publications) 117 (1997): 10–14.

Sackville-West, Vita. *Books and Authors,* "Books of the Week." Review of *The Letters of D. H. Lawrence,* ed. Aldous Huxley; *Etruscan Places* by D. H. Lawrence; *The Common Reader: Second Series* by Virginia Woolf. *Listener,* October 26, 1932, 610.

Samson, Anne. *F. R. Leavis.* Toronto: University of Toronto Press, 1992.

Scannell, Paddy and David Cardiff. *A Social History of British Broadcasting I: 1922–39, Serving the Nation.* Oxford: Basil Blackwell, 1991.

Schröder, Leena Kore. "'The drag of the face on the other side of the page': Virginia Woolf, Bakhtin and Dialogue." *Durham University Journal* 87: 1 (January 1995): 111–20.

Silver, Brenda R. "Introduction: The Uncommon Reader." *Virginia Woolf's Reading Notebooks.* Princeton: Princeton University Press, 1983.

Virginia Woolf Icon. Chicago: University of Chicago Press, 1999.

Simnett, W. E. *Books and Reading.* London: G. Allen & Unwin, 1926.

Smith, Barbara Herrnstein. *Contingencies of Value: Alternative Perspectives for Critical Theory.* Cambridge, MA: Harvard University Press, 1988.

Snaith, Anna, ed. "*Three Guineas* Letters." Edited with an intro. and index. *Woolf Studies Annual* 6 (2000): 1–168.

"'Stray Guineas': Virginia Woolf and the Fawcett Library." *Literature and History.* Forthcoming.

Virginia Woolf: Public and Private Negotiations. Basingstoke: Macmillan, 2000.

Squier, Susan M. *Virginia Woolf and London: The Sexual Politics of the City.* Chapel Hill: University of North Carolina Press, 1985.

Stallybrass, Oliver. Introduction to E. M Forster, *Aspects of the Novel*. 1927. Harmondsworth: Penguin, 1976.
Starr, Mark. *Lies and Hate in Education*. London: Hogarth, 1929.
Steele, Tom. *The Emergence of Cultural Studies: 1945–65: Cultural Politics, Adult Education and the English Question*. London: Lawrence & Wishart, 1997.
"Summary of Periodical Literature." *The Review of English Studies* 1–5 (1924–29).
Swinnerton, Frank. *A London Bookman*. London: Martin Secker, 1928.
Tarrant, James. M. *Democracy and Education*. Aldershot: Avebury, 1989.
Tawney, R. H. "An Experiment in Democratic Education." In *The Radical Tradition: Twelve Essays on Politics, Education and Literature*, ed. Rita Hinden, 70–81. London: Allen, 1964.
Travis, Molly Abel. *Reading Cultures: The Construction of Readers in the Twentieth Century*. Carbondale: Southern Illinois University Press, 1998.
Tremper, Ellen. *"Who Lived at Alfoxton?": Virginia Woolf and Romanticism*. Lewisburg, PA: Bucknell University Press, 1998.
Trevelyan, G. M. *English Social History: A Survey of Six Centuries, Chaucer to Queen Victoria*. London: Longmans, Green & Co., 1943.
Troubridge, Laura. *Life Amongst the Troubridges*. Ed. Jacqueline Hope-Nicholson. London: J. Murray, 1966.
Villeneuve, Pierre-Eric. "Communities of Desire: Woolf, Proust, and the Reading Process." In *Virginia Woolf and Communities: Selected Papers from the Eighth Annual Conference on Virginia Woolf*, ed. Jeanette McVicker and Laura Davis, 22–28. New York: Pace University Press, 1999.
Walpole, Hugh. *Reading*. Being one of a series of essays edited by J. B. Priestley and entitled, *These Diversions*. London: Jarrolds, 1926.
Wells, H. G. *Ann Veronica*. 1909. London: Virago, 1980.
"What is a Good Novel? A Symposium." Henry Baerlein, Arnold Bennett, J. D. Beresford, Hamilton Fyfe, John Galsworthy, Compton Mackenzie, Alfred Ollivant, John Oxenham, Eden Phillpotts, Hugh Walpole, Virginia Woolf. *The Highway: A Journal of Adult Education* 16 (Summer 1924): 100–10.
Whitehead, Kate. "Broadcasting Bloomsbury." *Yearbook of English Studies* 20 (1990): 121–31.
Whitman, Walt. *The Correspondence* v: 1890–1892. *The Collected Writings of Walt Whitman*. Ed. Edwin Haviland Miller. 6 vols. New York: New York University Press, 1969.
Wicke, Jennifer. "Coterie Consumption: Bloomsbury, Keynes, and Modernism as Marketing." In *Marketing Modernisms: Self-Promotion, Canonization, Rereading*, ed. Kevin J. H. Dettmar and Stephen Watt, 109–32. Ann Arbor: University of Michigan Press, 1996.
Williams, Raymond. *Culture and Society, 1780–1950*. Harmondsworth: Penguin, 1958.
Keywords: A Vocabulary of Culture and Society. New York: Oxford University Press, 1976; London: Fontana, 1976.
The Long Revolution. London : Chatto & Windus, 1961.

Willis, J. H. *Leonard and Virginia Woolf as Publishers*. Charlottesville: University of Virginia Press, 1992.

"Wireless Discussion Groups." *Listener*, October 28, 1931, 739.

"Wireless Discussion Groups." *Listener*, September 28, 1932, 437.

Woolf, Leonard. *Downhill all the Way: An Autobiography of the Years 1919–1939*. London: Hogarth, 1967.

Foreword to Mitchell A. Leaska, *Virginia Woolf's Lighthouse: A Study in Critical Method*. London: Hogarth, 1970.

Hunting the Highbrow. London: Hogarth, 1927.

"Letters Between Broadcasting Organizations and LW," I.R.i, The Leonard Woolf Papers. University of Sussex Library.

The Modern State: a six-part series. Listener. October–November 1931. "Is Democracy Failing?" October 7, 1931, 571–72; "Have We the Right to Be Happy?" October 14, 1931, 615–16; "Democracy and Equality." October 21, 1931, 666, 669; "Should We Do What We Want?" October 28, 1931, 711, 712, 745; "Gods or Bees?" November 4, 1931, 766, 767; "Citizens of the World." November 11, 1931, 817.

"The Pageant of History." In *Essays on Literature, History, Politics, Etc.*, 125–48. 1927. Freeport, NY: Books for Libraries Press, 1970.

Review of *How to Read Literature*, by George E. Wilkinson. *The Highway and "Students' Bulletin"* 20 (December 1927): 38.

Woolf, Leonard and Virginia Woolf. "Are Too Many Books Written and Published?" Unpublished ts of broadcast. July 15, 1927. BBC Written Archives Centre.

Woolf, Virginia. "'Anon' and 'The Reader': Virginia Woolf's Last Essays." Ed. Brenda Silver. *Twentieth Century Literature* 25 (1979): 356–441.

Between the Acts. London: Hogarth, 1941.

Collected Essays. 4 vols. Ed. Leonard Woolf. London: Hogarth, 1966–67.

The Common Reader: First Series. 1925. Ed. Andrew McNeillie. London: Hogarth, 1984.

The Common Reader: Second Series. 1932. Ed. Andrew McNeillie. London: Hogarth, 1986.

The Complete Shorter Fiction of Virginia Woolf. Ed. Susan Dick. Expanded and rev. edn. London: Hogarth, 1989.

The Diary of Virginia Woolf. Ed. Anne Olivier Bell and Andrew McNeillie. 5 vols. London: Hogarth, 1977–84.

The Essays of Virginia Woolf. Ed. Andrew McNeillie. 4 vols. to date. London: Hogarth, 1986–.

Holograph Reading Notes. The Virginia Woolf Manuscripts. The Henry W. and Albert A. Berg Collection. The New York Public Library.

Letter. *Woman's Leader and the Common Cause*, August 6, 1920.

"Letter to a Young Poet." In *The Hogarth Letters* (first published 1933), intro. Hermione Lee, 211–36. Athens: University of Georgia Press, 1986.

The Letters of Virginia Woolf. Ed. Nigel Nicolson and Joanne Trautmann. 6 vols. London: Chatto and Windus, 1975–80.

The London Scene. New York: Random House, 1975.

Monk's House Papers. University of Sussex Library.

Mrs. Dalloway. London: Hogarth, 1925.

Night and Day. London: Duckworth, 1919.

Orlando. London: Hogarth, 1928.

A Passionate Apprentice: The Early Journals, 1897–1909. Ed. Mitchell Leaska. London: Hogarth, 1990.

"Report on Teaching at Morley College." Appendix B in *Virginia Woolf: A Biography* by Quentin Bell, vol. 1:202–04. London: Grafton, 1972.

Roger Fry: A Biography. London: Hogarth, 1940.

A Room of One's Own. London: Hogarth, 1929.

"A Sketch of the Past." In *Moments of Being*, ed. Jeanne Schulkind, 61–159. 2nd edn. London: Hogarth, 1985.

"Three Characters." *Adam International Review*, 364–66 (1972): 24–26.

"Three Characters." Holograph, M.1.4, The Virginia Woolf Manuscripts. The Henry W. and Albert A. Berg Collection. The New York Public Library.

"Three Characters." ts., B.9.i., Monk's House Papers. University of Sussex Library.

Three Guineas. 1938. London: Hogarth, 1986.

To the Lighthouse. London: Hogarth, 1927.

"Virginia Woolf's 'How Should One Read a Book?'" Ed. Beth Rigel Daugherty. *Woolf Studies Annual* 4 (1998): 123–85.

Virginia Woolf's Reading Notebooks. Ed. Brenda Silver. Princeton: Princeton University Press, 1983.

The Waves. London: Hogarth, 1931.

A Woman's Essays: Selected Essays 1. Ed. Rachel Bowlby. London: Penguin, 1992.

Young, John. "Canonicity and Commercialization in Woolf's Uniform Edition." In *Virginia Woolf: Turning the Centuries: Selected Papers from the Ninth Annual Conference on Virginia Woolf*, ed. Ann Ardis and Bonnie Kime Scott, 236–43. New York: Pace University Press, 2000.

Index

academic, 15: disciplinary boundaries, 70, 79; discourse, 72, 79; periodicals, 71, 80, 207–08
Ackerley, Joe, 24, 29
Adult School movement, 81
affect, feeling, 126, 171, 180, 181–82
Ainger, Canon Alfred, 92
Altick, Richard, 59, 64, 90, 117
American fiction, 120
androgyny, 132
Angenot, Marc, 9, 199
aristocracy. *See under* class
Armstrong, Isobel, 126–27, 195
art, 20, 29, 33, 54, 84, 112, 190
audience, 14, 51, 108, 143–45: "a far wider circle," 112; creation of new, 2, 17, 52; expectations of, 27–28, 155–56; participants of lectures, 98, 100–01, 107
Austen, Jane, 123, 162, 184–85, 218–19
authority, 79, 97–98, 109–10, 121, 133–34, 157, 187: of authorial voice, 141, 142; of critics, 153, 165, 194, 217; in lectures, 98, 103

Bakhtin, Mikhail, 136, 195
Banfield, Ann, 7
Baudelaire, Charles, 184
BBC, 18–19, 29, 37, 38–39, 61, 65–66: Leonard Woolf's series of six talks, 35–37, 51; "Are Too Many Books Written and Published?, 64–65; *Books and Authors*, 62; *Books of the Week, Bestsellers of Yesterday*, 62; "To an Unnamed Listener," 16, 23, 135; "Wireless Discussion Groups," 39
Behn, Aphra, 164
Bell, Clive, 190
Bell, Julian, 72
Bender, Thomas, 15
Benjamin, Walter, 66, 207
Bennett, Arnold, 19, 22, 29, 170–71, 175, 190, 192
Bergson, Henri, 190

binaries, 29, 118, 126, 141, 151, 190–92: falsity of, 17–18, 21–22, 25, 31, 34, 215
biography, use of, 162, 183, 189
Blackwell, Basil, 63
Book Guild, 61
Bookman (New York), 19
Book-of-the-Month Club, 61
Book Review Digest, 169
books, the book, 10, 60–61, 67, 110, 159, 165
Book Society, 61
Borges, Jorge Luis, 164
Bourdieu, Pierre, 9, 67–68, 72
Bowlby, Rachel, 205, 215
Brantlinger, Patrick, 3
British Empire Exhibition (Wembley), 45–47
British Institute of Adult Education, 38: *The Way Out*, 60
British Museum, 61, 109, 212
broadcasting. *See* BBC
Brontë, Charlotte, 123, 157, 168, 184
Brooke, Rupert, 201
Brosnan, Leila, 214, 216
"brow" controversy, 23, 25, 27, 28, 39: and Bloomsbury, 201; and lowbrowism, 19, 21, 22; and stereotypes, 24, 27
Brown, Alec, 76
Browning, Elizabeth Barrett, 185–86, 187
Bucke, Dr. Richard Maurice, 43, 204
Butler, Samuel, 61–62

Cambridge. *See under* university
canons, 61, 80, 160–61, 172, 177, 208, 209
Carey, John, 3, 198
Carlyle, Jane Welsh, 80
Carlyle, Thomas, 45
Carpenter, L. P., 38
Carroll, Lewis, 13
Caughie, Pamela, 119, 120, 204, 215
Cecil, David, 111
censorship, 110, 212
Certeau, Michel de, 147

DATE DUE

The Library Store   #47-0106